PRAISE FOR *STORIES OF IDENTITY AMONG BLACK, MIDDLE CLASS, SECOND GENERATION CARIBBEANS*

"Told mainly through vignettes, Yndia Lorick-Wilmot shows how her Black Caribbean middle class respondents filter (gender, sexual, ethnic) identity through specific geographies, and distinct front-and back-stage personas that guide how Afro-Caribbeans 'move through the world.' Avoiding the more common assimilationist to studying immigrants, she melds postcolonial, intersectional, and double consciousness frames as she checks still-resonant assumptions (á la Moynihan and his ilk) of what it means to be black in the USA."

—Vilna Bashi Treitler, PhD, University of California at Santa Barbara, USA

"Building on the work of W. E. B. Du Bois, Lorick-Wilmot formulates the notion of triple identity consciousness and mounts a compelling critique of the endurance of white supremacy and finds among respondents a palpable commitment to the advancement of 'positive human excellence for all.'"

—Steven J. Gold, PhD, Michigan State University, USA

"In an engaging, self-reflexive style of oral history, Lorick-Wilmot uses undervalued but necessary frameworks of class, post-colonial theory, transnationality, and the diaspora to show that the middle class Caribbean second generation is also the Black American experience."

—Nadia Y. Kim, PhD, Loyola Marymount University, USA

Yndia S. Lorick-Wilmot

Stories of Identity among Black, Middle Class, Second Generation Caribbeans

We, Too, Sing America

palgrave
macmillan

Yndia S. Lorick-Wilmot
Northeastern University
Boston, Massachusetts, USA

ISBN 978-3-319-62207-1   ISBN 978-3-319-62208-8   (eBook)
DOI 10.1007/978-3-319-62208-8

Library of Congress Control Number: 2017947767

Cover illustration: © Westend61 GmbH / Alamy Stock Photo
Cover design by Ran Shauli

Printed on acid-free paper

This Palgrave Macmillan imprint is published by Springer Nature
The registered company is Springer International Publishing AG
The registered company address is: Gewerbestrasse 11, 6330 Cham, Switzerland

Acknowledgments

Like the popular Igbo and Yoruba (Nigerian) proverb states, *it takes a village to raise a whole child*, for me, it took a village to write this book. This book would not have been possible without the continued support of those who believed in the project and my ability to bring it to fruition. As always, my family remains my anchor and salvation. My family—my husband Damian and children Justin and Sydney, my parents Taecha and Curives, and extended relatives and family friends located throughout the United States and the Caribbean islands of Grenada and Trinidad—too many to mention here, have given me their love, encouragement, and patience each day and throughout the writing process. I could not have done this without you all.

Over the course of this project, I have benefited from the informal and formal support of my special community of friends, writers, and colleagues, to name a few—Natasha Gordon-Chipembere, V.B.T, Alicia Anabel Santos, Anton Nimblett, Delida Sanchez, Michele Simms-Burton, Tawana Thompson, Summer Edward, Todne Thomas, Tiffany Manuel, Jaronda Miller-Bryant, Dolores Ortiz, Maureen Kelleher, and Gordana Rabrenovic. I am grateful to each of you for engaging me in endless discussions and debates, and providing insightful comments that helped me contend with the sociological framing of the stories told and issues raised throughout the book. I also thank Alexis Nelson, my editor at Palgrave Macmillan for her encouragement and patience, and her editorial support staff for their preparation of the manuscript.

Finally, I want to especially thank the women and men whom I interviewed. Their beautiful, heart-wrenching, and ever complex stories reflect the lived experiences of so many children of Caribbean immigrants living in the United States, including my own. During our conversations, we touched on a number of topics that elicited a range of emotions—from joy, sadness, and embarrassment to anger, frustration, and hope. I am grateful to them for their bravery, honesty, and openness.

Let their stories sing and pay homage to the ancestors that came before—who faced adversity and sacrificed much with the hopes of them achieving the highly sought after *American Dream*. Let their stories sing in the present about the enduring ways they grapple with race, ethnicity, gender, and class in their public and private lives. And, let their stories sing their hopes for the future and what lies ahead for their next generation as they say, *We, Too, Sing America*.

CONTENTS

CHAPTER 1

Introduction: My Personal and Scholarly Journey

Scholars like myself are often concerned with exploring the shifting and complex dynamics and changes that occur across racial and ethnic communities over time. Readers in this topic area may be most familiar with works by William Julius Wilson, Elijah Anderson, Thomas Shapiro, Melvin Oliver, Amanda E. Lewis, Douglas Massey and Nancy Denton and Mary C. Waters, to name a few, who have focused on the experiences and outcomes for underserved communities, working class African Americans, and/or new immigrants. As these racial and ethnic communities continue to expand and diversify a range of public and private, urban and suburban, social, economic, and political spaces, different lenses are needed to understand this complexity.

This book *Stories of Identity among Black Middle Class Second Generation Caribbeans: We, Too, Sing America* is a sociological exploration (albeit a self-exploration, too) that examines the salience of race and ethnic identity in the stories children of Caribbean immigrants tell about their complex experiences navigating public and private spaces. Inspired by Langston Hughes' 1945 poem "I, Too, Sing America," my research points to the continued struggle blacks experience to be heard and seen as a valued, vital part of America's cultural, social, political, and economic fabric.

As folklore suggests, Langston Hughes was compelled to write a response to Walt Whitman's (1886) poem "I Hear America Singing." For many, Whitman's poem celebrates America and the individuals that make

© The Author(s) 2018
Y.S. Lorick-Wilmot, *Stories of Identity among Black,*
Middle Class, Second Generation Caribbeans,
DOI 10.1007/978-3-319-62208-8_1

the country great. Line by line, Whitman lists different Americans by their occupations such as carpenter, mechanic, boatmen, shoemaker, and girl sewing, each singing "with open mouths, their strong melodious songs." Yet, Whitman's patriotic poem was one that reflected a particular vision of America; a vision that celebrates the working class men and women whom he saw as striving to build the country at the end of the nineteenth century. By my own analysis, Whitman imagines America as a chorus comprising a multitude of voices singing together for a common good.

In contrast, Langston Hughes' poem, I assert, challenges Whitman's vision of America by pointing out there are many other voices, particularly the black voice, that should be included in this great vision. For Hughes, the contributions blacks have made (and continue to make) toward building America are equally great but are rendered invisible because of their "blackness" and subsequent subjugation. Hughes' poem confronts continued racism, segregation, and oppression experienced by African Americans and the first wave of voluntary Caribbean immigrants (pre-1950s) by declaring that such injustices will not render blacks undeserving of the freedoms and inalienable rights afforded to all.[1] In effect, Hughes asserts "I, too, Sing America" as an equally important voice in America's chorus that should be heard when Whitman "hears" America singing. It is my intention that this book confronts the persisting invisibility of people of African descent in the United States in the twenty-first century. In particular, I intend to celebrate the "songs" or narratives of middle class, adult children of self-identified Black Caribbean immigrants who contribute to the building of contemporary society but are often invisible in the "chorus" of America. In effect, these stories represent their heart song, "We, Too, Sing America."

In the social science literature, this generation of middle class black Caribbean immigrants is a segment of the African American community that is often under-researched/documented and represented as "America." I contend this population has very similar experiences with racism and classism, prejudice and discrimination as any other groupings of people of color living in the United States, but are often not examined because they have the "trappings" of middle class lifestyle—the idealized notion of the American Dream. The narrative analysis I employ throughout the book intends to bring to the forefront their everyday experiences in challenging structures of oppression, via their racial and ethnic identity assertions, as black people, as children of immigrants, and as part of an established black middle class.

More specifically, the purpose of *Stories of Identity among Black Middle Class Second Generation Caribbeans* is to share the stories of this generation of black immigrants and unveil the complexities that define black lives across the spectrum of the United States. These stories are important because they reveal nuances to the human experience as it relates to race and people's evolving sense of identity; the moments black people articulate the critical instances of self-discovery and expression. This book expands the focus of the black experience in the United States to include the intersections of race, class, ethnicity, gender, and sexuality: how race, class, gender, and immigrant ancestry plays out in the United States; the emotional trade-ins or the psychological expense involved with having access to "white resources" or being singular blacks in white spaces; and the kind of global experiences African descendants can have, are able to reflect on and develop strategies to navigate diverse places and racial heterogeneous spaces that are both welcoming and hostile to black people and broadly, people of color in the United States and elsewhere.

I am personally motivated to conduct and share this research because it is a challenge for me (to find an articulation of myself) and for others interested in this scholarly exploration to overcome the predominant cultural models about black people and specifically the second generation black immigrant in the United States. It is a cognitively accessible narrative most associate with black people, which was made popular by Daniel P. Moynihan over 50 years ago in the controversial report *The Negro Family: The Case for National Action* (also known as the Moynihan Report): that the majority of blacks are poor/low income/working class with negative pathologies (i.e., failure, powerlessness, and exploitation). I am sure I cannot be alone in reacting to this persisting American cultural framework—my frustration and loathing of such a myopic and denigrating racist ideology that suggests it is legitimate and true. My intention is to share the "other"/ unheard stories of the black experience in the United States that resonate for all people; stories that are apolitical but are not "race-free;" stories that defy the anti-black and pathological ways the diversity of black voice and personhood are traditionally portrayed in literature, research, and popular culture. These are stories of family, struggle, resistance and triumph, individuality and collectivity that speculate on the fate and destiny of black people across the United States and for generations to come.

THE PERSONAL AND SCHOLARLY JOURNEY

In her 2005 book *On Beauty*, Zadie Smith wrote, "the world does not deliver meaning to you. You have to make it meaningful...and decide what you want and need and must do." A few years after reading Zadie Smith's book, my mind could not help returning to that line; a line which resonated with me more strongly than when I first read the book.

One afternoon I was organizing my home's library when my daughter saw me perusing through several of my yearbooks and asked me about the people in the pictures. After a while, she made an observation and asked: Did many of your friends in high school and college have parents from the Caribbean like you? In fact, that was who I primarily lived among and went to school with. These same friends grew up in households where English, French, Spanish, or a creole of one of these languages was spoken on a daily basis; where some had to negotiate generational dynamics that required translating important documents for parents whose command of American English was not strong while others had parents who were para- and semi-professionals with high educational expectations for their children. Now of course, where I lived with my parents in Brooklyn and went to school was, in large part, consciously determined by economic factors. The Fort Greene, Eastern Parkway, Flatbush, and Crown Heights neighborhoods and communities were economically similar but also racial-ethnically and culturally distinct as compared to, say, Bay Ridge or Red Hook in the 1980s. Yet, as Bill Bishop argues in his 2008 book, the *Big Sort*, we all have a tendency to seek out and fraternize with others that are similar to us in a number of ways or at least, to cluster in communities of like-mindedness.

For those I have remained in contact with over the years, these friends have lived in major metropolitan cities, both in the United States and abroad. Many, if not all, own their own homes, either condos or single-families, graduated from college, and earned an advanced or professional degree. These friends also remain connected to their parents' home country, whether they are planning to "play mas" at an upcoming carnival, are feverishly referencing their carnival tabanca post-carnival festivities, or are visiting relatives and actively supporting family members or school communities in the Caribbean.

On social media, I would see signifiers of middle class material culture and social status in their pictures, which point to my friends' access to disposable income: designer handbags, luxury cars, and collections of art are seen in the background. Of course, it would be remiss of me not to consider Erving Goffman's theories of identity and presentation of self in social media and the ways people communicate status and position in public spaces. There is a certain degree to which people generally present an idealized version of themselves in terms of how they want to be perceived by others—a "front-stage" persona. Yet in their same posts on social media, I also see glimpses of the kind of intellectual, personal, and professional work my friends engage in around issues that affect them and matter to them—a "back stage" persona. In fact, these same friends post articles, essays, videos, and even, well articulated rants on a variety of social justice topics often related to issues of race, class, and gender inequality and how they see these issues impacting their home lives, work, and well-being in the United States, the Caribbean, and across the world.

In my mind's eye, I return to my daughter's observation and consider the ways these "front-stage" and "back stage" personas interact on a daily basis; the constant negotiations we all make in our interactions with others and across contexts, such as in our home, work, and community lives. I began to deeply consider my own presentation of self; the ways I learned as a child to identify with my parents' Caribbean culture. And then learning as an adult how I, too, must do the work to balance how I perceive myself with the ways others perceive me in public and private spaces—as a woman, black person, an American, a child of Caribbean immigrants, an educated woman of color with a PhD, and a person who occupies a middle class social and economic space.

Then the idea came to me like a bright light in a dark tunnel. I listened carefully as my girlfriend spoke. It was then I was reminded of Zadie Smith's quote. I wondered how is it that we all make meaning in our everyday lives? How do we make life meaningful in the midst of balancing multiple identities of race, gender, class, and ethnicity? What are the stories we tell ourselves and tell others about these negotiations? How can stories help to rid ourselves of the isolation and pressure we may feel when balancing these front and back stage personas? How do these performances become complicated by the fluidity of one's own assertions of racial, ethnic, gender, and class identities?

Often academics, including myself, will frame this kind of meaning-making process as being "between two worlds," a model where individuals' racial and ethnic identities and social location are positioned between being invisible and visible, as seen in Benjamin Giguere, Richard Lalonde, and Eveline Lou's article, *Living at the Crossroads of Cultural Worlds*, June

Jordan's poem, *Moving Towards Home*, Laura Moss', *The Politics of Everyday Hybridity*, Stuart Hall's, *A Place Called Home*, Pauli Murray's, *Proud Shoes: The Story of an American Family*, and Roy Bryce-Laporte's seminal article, *Black Immigrants: The Experience of Invisibility and Inequality*, to name a few. By all accounts, population studies such as the Pew Research Center's 2013 report *Second-Generation Americans: A Portrait of the Adult Children of Immigrants* indicate that I and others like me are a part of the overall population that is responsible for changing the face of America, equally impacting the nation's economic landscape. And yet our stories, filled with the nuance of struggle and triumph—for confronting inequities, clearly intending to assert voice, position, visibility as experienced everyday—are often unheard or marginalized. In my small attempt, I aim to help make the world meaningful; I decided what I want and need and must do is to share the stories of people that are like me, second generation Caribbean immigrant, middle class, and who self-identify racially as black.

I will be transparent and admit that my presentation of these narratives takes on a postcolonial lens. Importantly—at least from an ethnographic and sociological standpoint, I intend to reject European or Western world cultural traditions of storytelling (read: white) as conceptualized and espoused by modernist philosophers such as Joseph Ernest Renan and Georg Wihelm Friedrich Hegel who edify ideologies that support the suppression of non-Western voice and subjectivity, as evidenced in essays like *The African Character* (Hegel 1830/2006). Instead, Michel Foucault's (1986:23) *Of Other Spaces* raises an important nuance to employing a post-colonial approach, which I appreciate and hope to bring forth in this research:

> The space in which we live, which draws us out of ourselves, in which the erosion of our lives, our time and our history occurs, the space that claws and knaws at us, is also, in itself a heterogeneous space. In other words, we do not live in a kind of void, inside of which we could place individuals and things. We do not live inside a void that could be colored with diverse shades of light, we live inside a set of relations that delineates sites, which are irreducible to one another and absolutely not superimposable on one another.

In other words, the spaces and places people inhabit do not exist in a vacuum. Instead the human world is intricate, constantly interacting, overlapping, informing, and being influenced by culture, laws, and policies—constituting complex power relations in the process. As Homi Bhabha (1994:175) insists:

The postcolonial perspective forces us to rethink the profound limitations of a consensual and collusive "liberal" sense of cultural community. It insists that cultural and political identities are constructed through a process of alterity. Questions of race and cultural difference overlay issues of sexuality and gender and over-determine the social alliances of class and democratic socialism. The time for "assimilating" minorities to holistic and organic notions of cultural value has dramatically passed.

For the purpose of my exploration, the socially constructed categories of race, ethnic, class, and gender identifications are tools indicative of social relationships of power, or as Michael Omi and Howard Winant put it—are tools of hegemony (used by some in an attempt to maintain their dominance and position over others), dispersed in all social relations and lodged in taken-for-granted practices and understandings (see also Hill Collins 1993). As such, I strategically borrow from Antonio Gramsci's theory on cultural hegemony to argue that the second generation Caribbean immigrant experience in the United States would be one of a subaltern existence (being socially, politically, and economically outside of the hegemonic power structure) and whose race, ethnic, class, and gender experiences ideologically challenge the assumption that we live in a society that has overcome racism since the Civil Rights Movement.

For me, a postcolonial lens requires examining the ways in which groups that have been historically disenfranchised, particularly people of African descent, have agency. With reminders set forth in the post-colonial works of Chinua Achebe, Ajit Maan, Gayatri Spivak, and bell hooks, I recognize the important role agency has when it comes to those who share their stories with me. As a researcher trained in traditional Western methods, I must consciously ensure that I do not "other" or subjugate the voice of the subaltern experience while avoiding essentializing them (see also Henry Louis Gates, Jr.'s' *The Signifying Monkey*). By bringing forth these stories, I intend to provide the platform by which the second generation's own words, stories, and experiences richly contextualize the impact and legacies of colonialism on their own construction and assertion of postcolonial identities as interacting with and participating in social, political, cultural, and economic institutions around them.

Notes

1. Much of Langston Hughes' commentary in his work often looked to the experiences of both African Americans and Caribbean-descended people in the United States and their role in building contemporary America. At the

time of Hughes' writing, the presence of Caribbean-descended people in the United States were attributed to those who emigrated voluntarily from the Caribbean to the United States between 1866 and 1910, as well as the generations of formerly enslaved Africans who were brought from the Caribbean to the United States during the seventeenth and eighteenth centuries. In the seventeenth century, for example, most of the African slaves in the states of South Carolina and Virginia were actually from the islands of Barbados, Jamaica, and Antigua. By the eighteenth century, the number of Africans from the Caribbean significantly increased throughout the country, with many being sent to northern states like New York. For writers like Hughes, it was important to give voice to the experiences of all of these blacks—African American, Caribbean-descended, and the newly arrived immigrant as these groups struggled for equality, respect, and economic advancement.

BIBLIOGRAPHY

Bhabha, H. (1994). *The Location of Culture*. New York: Routledge.

Collins, P. H. (1993). Toward a New Vision: Race, Class and Gender as Categories of Analysis and Connection. *Race, Sex & Class, Fall*(1), 25–45.

Foucault, M. (1986). Of Other Spaces. *Diacritics, Spring*(16), 22–27.

Hegel, G. W. (1830/2006). The African Character. In J. Conrad, & P. B. Armstrong, *Heart of Darkness* (4th ed., pp. 208–212). New York: WW Norton.

Whitman, W. (1886). *Leaves of Grass: The Poems of Walt Whitman [Selected] with Introduction by Ernest Rhys* (The Walt Whitman Archives http://whitmanarchive.org/published/books/other/rhys.html ed.). London, UK: Newcastle-on-Tyne.

CHAPTER 2

Un-*Othering* the Black Experience: Storytelling and Sociology

This book is about stories. I once wrote elsewhere that stories are the mediums through which people connect to one another. We tell stories because they appeal to our social intelligence—our ability to understand and navigate through the psychology and history of complex social interactions. In the narrative process, the storyteller is a problem-solver; he or she points to the challenges faced, choices made, and outcomes learned that could, ultimately, inspire the listener toward some action. As such, stories are powerful. Because stories also communicate emotions that are contextualized in events with a before and after that are often familiar to the listener, the "I's," "we's," and "they's" actively bring people into being, and channel individual and collective sentiments.

When I started this book project almost seven years ago, I wanted to share stories about the middle class second generation, self-identified black Caribbean immigrant (MSGCI) experience in the United States but did not want it to be a book just about the immigrant experience, as if that were the only kind of story someone like me could share. After spending scores of hours with English, French, and Spanish-speaking adult children of Caribbean immigrants, I listened to their stories about the persistence of racism and other forms of subordination. The stories I was hearing were not only voices of authority in relating these experiences but they also documented experiences from the margins of race, ethnicity, class, gender, and immigrant discourses. Looking to Ralph Ellison's commentary in the book *Invisible Man* and Langston Hughes' poem, "I, Too, Sing America,"

© The Author(s) 2018
Y.S. Lorick-Wilmot, *Stories of Identity among Black,*
Middle Class, Second Generation Caribbeans,
DOI 10.1007/978-3-319-62208-8_2

I contend the persisting invisibility of the black middle class (e.g., broadly defined as those who earn incomes above the poverty line, attained a college degree or higher, and are employed in semi-professional and professional occupations) in the American consciousness distorts and devalues the group's social, political, and cultural obstacles and contributions to the society at large. And while prevailing race-based assumptions about all blacks in America often trigger cultural models and images of the "young thug black male" and "black welfare queen," I argue that the systematic devaluation also hinders society from seeing and hearing how the black middle class defines itself and what it has had to endure, including the effect of internalized racism and psychological costs of constantly being measured only by material wealth and acquisition as a sign of well-being and success.

Stories of Identity among Black Middle Class Second Generation Caribbeans examines these issues by exploring the social constructs of race, ethnicity, class, and gender as created and performed at macro- and micro-levels for this MSGCI population. Along the same vein, I am concerned with exploring the everyday experiences of this population that may often find themselves embracing while negotiating ways to resist negative perceptions of blackness as encouraged by the dominant culture (see hooks 2001). In part, the research explores how identities often emerge from negotiations between imposed and chosen meanings individuals describe as influencing the MSGCIs' lived experiences in their home, work, and community lives.

WHY IS THIS RESEARCH IMPORTANT?
HOW DOES IT CONTRIBUTE TO THE FIELD

A particular contribution I wish to make with *Stories of Identity among Black Middle Class Second Generation Caribbeans* is to elucidate the subject and reality of the diverse black middle class and immigrant experience in America. I endeavor to demonstrate the cognitive frameworks they use and the stories they tell about how they navigate their individual aspects of reality, in its fullness and intrinsic-ness—that their black ethnicity, black racial identity, and black middle class-ness are not necessarily antagonistic realities—serve as a critical voice in contemporary America as it relates to racial and economic progress. In the social sciences and across other academic disciplines, there is a growing interest in the multiple consciousness and anti-essentialism of the diverse histories and voices of people of color throughout the Americas and the Africa diaspora. Because scholars now realize what people of color and other social groups that experience subjugation have long understood: there are multiple and intersecting locations of class, gender, religious, linguistic differences that affect an individual's social class mobility, ability to work, ability to live in particular neighborhoods, and cultural production. And, by telling their own stories, society can gain a deeper understanding and appreciation for the rendering of social reality for all.

The significance of my point here is also evident in W.E.B. Du Bois' (1903) *Souls of Black Folk* in a chapter entitled "The Training of Black Men," where he remarked on the "soul" and voice of the black person in America. Du Bois (1903:66–67) writes,

> Herein the longing of black [wo] men must have respect: the rich and bitter depth of their experience, the unknown treasures of their inner life, the strange renderings of nature they have seen, may give the world new points of view and make their loving, living and doing precious to all human hearts. And to themselves in these the days that try their soul, the chance to soar in the dim blue air above the smoke is to their finer spirits boon and guerdon for what they lose on earth by being black.

As a demonstration, too, of their strength and ability to tell their stories as Du Bois himself saw as important, *Stories of Identity among Black Middle Class Second Generation Caribbeans* offers tangible solidarity to the African descended voice in contemporary United States. Because white hegemonic forces via racialization insidiously work to categorize whiteness as normal and all else as an "other," it reinforces its normalcy as invisible. Hegemony easily creates a culture of exclusion and obfuscation that denies the existence and undervalues the experiences of those who do not embody "whiteness" (white, cis male, heterosexual, and middle class). As such, white hegemony creates the black monolith because it does not need or want to interrogate blackness or non-whiteness and the impact of systematized forms of oppression, or consider nonwhite articulations and interpretations of a broad black nationalism that is not only global but also aware of the oppression and privilege of black personhood across various societies.

In *Stories of Identity among Black Middle Class Second Generation Caribbeans,* the tangible solidarity highlighted by the MSGCIs' stories point to the ways they talk about their identities—their blackness, their middle class social status, and their immigrant upbringing, for example—to forge alliances and develop strategies for developing spaces of shared understanding and empowerment across various social boundaries and within the context of global forces and diasporas. Indeed, critical race scholars agree identity and personhood is linked to one's race and politics of personhood and, especially for people of color, it is related to the socio-political and economic disadvantages associated with being of African descent. We see this in the ways race remains a significant predictor of income, wealth, employment, health, educational attainment, and a number of other social and economic outcomes (post Civil Rights) and how blacks (both native and foreign-born) lag behind whites in these areas. For this reason, *Stories of Identity among Black Middle Class Second Generation Caribbeans* makes the case that there is a small subset of American-born blacks that are both middle class and post-1965 second generation Caribbean immigrant who also face similar barriers to equality despite anti-discrimination legislation over the last 50 years. I use critical race theory (CRT), racialization, and postcolonial frameworks to illustrate the manner in which race (and ethnicity) is embedded not only in social relationships, practices, and institutions but also shapes individual identities and impacts an allocation of and individual's access to economic, political, and social resources.

More broadly speaking, *Stories of Identity among Black Middle Class Second Generation Caribbeans* intends to challenge how society understands "Black" as a racial category, "Caribbean/ African American" as an ethnic category, and notions of "middle class" as labels used to generalize, limit, and box-in people according to preset social definitions. Instead, the research posits "Black," "Caribbean/African American," and middle class are experiences individuals have in interaction with other people and institutions across context, time, and space. For instance, the experience of being black, middle class, and of Caribbean may differ for one person who lived in the Midwest United States in the 1930s as opposed to another person living in the southeastern United States in the 2010s. My concern with society's assumption of a black monolith in the United States draws attention to the forces of hegemonic authority and oppression as it relates to cultural difference and discrimination for the people who identify with and are identified by such ethnic labels and racial categories. Therefore, the MSGCIs' stories provide an opportunity to expose these interrogations and re-articulations of the meanings of these experiences explicitly.

Conceptually, I define identity as the various meanings attached to oneself and others, and in various social spaces through relationships implied by that identity (Gecas and Burke 1995). Each of us maintains a collection of self-identities, each of which is based on occupying particular roles at particular times (Stryker 1968; Burke and Reitzes 1981). These various roles influence behavior and experiences since each role has a set of associated societal meanings and expectations, which render particular social outcomes and experiences. In addition to one's individual self-identity, most people also occupy social group memberships through which they simultaneously identify, negotiate, find, and make meaning. While most will agree there is a situational aspect to one's identity constructions and assertions because identities are essentially intersectional, attempting to isolate one identity over another is what Sherry Ortner, and Elizabeth Cole and Sayari Omari contend is a "hollow project in terms of individuals' lived experiences" (2003:786). For this reason, the narratives of the MSGCI population in the United States are instructive to understanding race relations and class mobility in the larger public discourse on American immigration and "strategic" assimilation.

In terms of academic discourse, there is a paucity of information as to how adult children of Caribbean immigrants cope with, resolve, and make meaning of what they experience as both middle class Americans and as the children of black immigrants. It has been argued that second generation black Caribbean immigrant identity is relatively unstable, and that over time these individuals either choose to become American-identified or ethnic-identified. Scholars such as Mary C. Waters, Tekle Mariam Woldemikael, Herbert Gans, Alejandro Portes, and Ruben Rumbaut agree that no other racial or ethnic minority group feels these paradoxes more acutely than black immigrants and their children, for whom assimilation (repression of psychological connections to the Caribbean required for successful social incorporation) means joining the ranks of America's historically disenfranchised racial-ethnic group—African Americans. Yet, this binary does not clearly tell a story about the factors, the interpretation of events and experiences, and the enmeshment of transnational networks and community that impact the lived experiences for this second generation. Using critical race and postcolonial theories, I posit this binary inadvertently reifies the "model minority" framework of post-1965 immigrant incorporation and success by using Caribbean immigrants and their adult children's purported ethnic identification to further an insidious discourse about American-born blacks that avoids addressing the persistence of racial inequality and injustice at macro- and micro-levels of social interaction and further perpetuates intragroup conflict between African Americans and blacks of Caribbean descent.

Similar to Karyn Lacy's (2004, 2007) exploration of middle and upper middle class blacks' construction, navigation, and maintenance of "middle class-ness," and her contribution to the field's understanding of the intersections between race and social class performances and cultural production of class, *Stories of Identity among Black Middle Class Second Generation Caribbeans* contributes to the social sciences by looking at these social categories within the context of black ethnicity and immigrant generation. *Stories of Identity among Black Middle Class Second Generation Caribbeans* explores how the MSGCI, who arguably, live in a world of shifting racial-ethnic, class, gender, and economic divisions of which outsiders to this position may be only barely aware, also grapple with negotiating race, ethnic, and class identities within contexts that are complicit in reproducing social order and reifying the "model minority" framework. Specifically, I ask: How do second generation black Caribbean immigrants vary in their definitions and expectations of what it means to be "Black in America," "second generation Caribbean immigrant," and "middle class"? Are there other social identities that emerge as part of their identity construction and negotiation process? How do these identities and identity performances vary and evolve among individuals, and intersect across space and social contexts of home and family life, work and community? And, what is the impact of these identities and performances, if any, on the third generation? Whether their stories pointed to events that seemed to conflict with previous racial-ethnic, gender, and social identity assertions or to events that required them to assert, define, and/or redefine their racial and ethnic identity, the MSGCIs are able to reflect on and develop strategies to navigate racial heterogeneous spaces and places that are both welcoming and hostile to black people and broadly, people of color in the United States and elsewhere.

Theoretical Orientations: Situating Race and Ethnic Identity for the Second Generation Caribbean Immigrant

Brief Overview of Race and American Immigration Literature

Over the past century, the study of race and ethnicity among immigrant generations has received considerable attention, particularly in academia. At the turn of the twentieth century and through the 1950s, race and immigration scholars used assimilation theories to highlight the process of assimilation and ethnic identity construction to discern whether immigrants can fully assimilate in accordance to an American ethos (see Park and Burgess 1921/1924; Warner and Srole 1945; Park 1950). Researchers like Robert E. Park, for example, developed the paradigm "race relations cycle" to postulate the immigrant assimilation process is linear; whereby immigrants over time will become more "Americanized" by unlearning their "inferior" cultural traits to successfully learn the new way of life necessary for full acceptance ("straight-line assimilation").

By the 1960s, the rise of globalism and the passage of immigration reform led to the ongoing study of assimilation. Some scholars such as Milton Gordon (1964) in *Assimilation in American Life* elaborated on Park's construct of assimilation into a conceptual framework. Gordon described seven dimensions of assimilation: cultural, marital, identification, attitude-receptional, behavior-receptional, civic, and structural. Together, Park and Gordon's work argued that assimilation requires the acquisition of cultural characteristics of American society and the participation of the entire society, including the immigrant population. They also assumed the greater the congruence between native-born and immigrant populations, the less likely conflict will exist. This point is critical to the analysis of classical assimilation theory: it reveals assimilation is very dependent on the view American society has of the immigrant population and how well American society, with the use of power and resources, can easily mesh immigrants into its general population.

Other scholars felt much of the American immigration scholarship to this point did not fully explore the paradox of American society with regard to race, racialization, and immigrant status for people of color. Scholars such as Gunnar Myrdal (1944), Oscar Handlin (1973), and Werner Sollors (1986) observed shifting social dynamics—how waves of migration of new immigrants, especially those from majority nonwhite nations, coincided with US civil rights and pan-ethnic identity movements—and began to rethink scholarship in the field. With a focus on resistance and the existence of binaries (e.g., black-white, rich-poor, or male-female), scholars emphasized ethnicity, pluralism, and hybrid cultural multiplicities in an attempt to shift the discourse away from classic assimilation theories.

A common argument against the "inevitability" of the assimilation model for post-1965 immigrants of color is that it is less available to racial-ethnic immigrants because of their racialization and nonwhite European origins.

In fact, several postcolonial scholars, including Chandra Talpade Mohanty (1991:24), draw parallels between the history and scope of theories that champion European immigration and to the process of racialization of immigrants of color by asserting: "the patterns of immigration and citizenship laws for both groups (European and non-European) are based on racial heritage and the 'economic exigencies' of the state." To counter the predominance of the straight-line assimilation perspective, scholars such as Werner Sollors examined complexity of identity construction, particularly for immigrants of color as they assert identities related to their nativity, self-identity, and imagined communities simultaneously while fashioning a new identity as "newcomer" in the United States.

By the end of the twentieth century, most scholars in the field of race and American immigration recognized that

> Whatever the deficiencies of earlier formulations and application, this social science concept [assimilation] offers the best way to understand and describe the integration into mainstream experiences across generations...even if it cannot be regarded as a universal outcome of American life. (Alba and Nee 1997:827)

At which point, scholars began to conceptualize assimilation, not as a linear process of ethnic obliteration but a dynamic one in which minority and majority cultures influence one another. Scholars Alejandro Portes, Ruben Rumbaut, Min Zhou, Michael Omi, and Howard Winant, for example, looked at segmented assimilation as a more fluid and reflexive relationship between immigrants and American society by contending that racial identities are not fixed but are social constructions "produced through the interaction of societal systems of racial classification and human agency" (Benson 2006:222).

For these scholars, segmented assimilation can occur along multiple dimensions (i.e., socio-economic, spatial/residential, structural) with different segments of the population, and at varying rates, depending both on the characteristics of the immigrant group and how the group is received in society (Benson 2006; Massey 1995; Portes and Zhou 1993; Vickerman 1999). Portes and Zhou (1993), Portes and Rumbaut (2006), and Mary C. Waters, for example, found immigrants of color are not uniformly incorporated and their incorporation varied specifically in terms of how these groups are racialized and construct their own racial identities. In particular, Portes and Zhou (1993) observed Asian immigrants develop strategies for passing and/or assimilating, while Waters (1999) examined narratives of ethnic difference among West Indian immigrants, who despite their efforts, their black master status relegated them to the bottom of the social strata.

And still, there were scholars who remained skeptical about the modes of incorporation and assimilation for the US born child of immigrants—the second generation immigrants. Herbert Gans (1992:172–173), for instance, believed the second generation could experience a "decline" or downward mobility. Gans argued that the second generation may find themselves unable to escape poverty because of their refusal or reluctance to work immigrant jobs for immigrant wages but lack the skills and network to improve their life outcomes (the native disadvantage). He also argued that, by contrast, those who remain tied to their parents' immigrant generation were more likely to have better life outcomes (the immigrant advantage). Following Gan's (1992) and Portes and Zhous's (1993) analysis, it is easy to make the prognosis that if immigrant parents encourage their children to maintain ethnic ties and connections to their racial-ethnic immigrant community, then the second generation will have better means to get ahead socially and economically.

When I consider these theories in its totality and their potential utility for understanding the experiences and identity assertions of the MSGCI, I am compelled to consider theoretical perspectives that go beyond the binary of cultural explanations (immigrant culture versus American culture) in the assimilation process for the second generation. Take for instance Kasinitz et al. (2008:20) assertion in *Inheriting the City,* which argues that members of the second generation can

> sometimes negotiate among different combinations of immigrant and native advantage and disadvantage to choose the best combination for themselves. In other words [,...] the ability to select the best traits from their immigrant parents and their native-born peers yields a distinct *second generation advantage.*

Their research findings present a positive picture of second generation advantage, for the most part, which allows the authors to successfully debunk theorists who favor downward assimilation and segmented assimilation explanations for the children of immigrants. A critique of their work and its theoretical contribution to the field, however, is that its arguments remain wedded to longstanding debates on immigrant integration without pointing to a new theory that captures the complexity and nuances of race, ethnicity, and other identity developmental processes among the second immigrant generation, and especially those of African descent.

I contend there is a great need for theories to re-conceptualize the issues and realities that the second generation grapples with as it relates to their ongoing responses to, understanding of and navigations within and between social spaces and places. In other words, are there theoretical orientations that can better situate scholars' interpretations of the juxta-positions of perceptions and experiences the MSGCIs articulate for them-selves around prejudice, racism, and other forms of discrimination? How can other theoretical models help explain the second generations' inter-nalization of particular racial and cultural scripts of their families, peers, and media representations as constantly informing their ideological frame-works, identity constructions and assertions, and strategies for their mobility? As such, I rely on the theoretical tenets of racialization, CRT, and postcolonialism as part of my analysis of MSGCI narratives.

Racialization, CRT, and Postcolonial Frameworks

Racialization is a framework used to explore how MSGCI identity is consid-ered and expressed. Embedded within the concept of racialization is the nature of identity: identity that inscribes particular individuals' and groups' socio-political status in the world versus external groups' formulations about these individuals about who they are and their cultural significance. In this regard, identity is conceived as a complex construct influenced by hegemonic discourse around race, class, ethnicity, gender, and immigrant generation. According to Kenneth Mostern (1999:6), this is the case since race,

> has remained an ever present lens by which the world is viewed and has continued to be a primary force in social struggle. That something is bio-logically insignificant as skin color has in becoming raced, maintained such a role is precisely what should provide the impetus for an inquiry into the historical interrelations between the socioeconomic and psychological meanings of identity as it structures and determines politics.

Therefore, I contemplate the ways in which MSGCIs develop an acute awareness of their racialized position and status and are constantly negoti-ating and rethinking about their race and ethnicity in relationship to other aspects of their identities across various contexts.

In particular, *Stories of Identity among Black Middle Class Second Generation Caribbeans* considers how racial and ethnic constructions of identity, class, and gender is constructed for the MSGCIs themselves in contrast to how mainstream society [read: white] construct and racialize black identities. In doing so, tenets of racialization are utilized to explore the ways the MSGCIs respond to, reject, and develop alternative meanings around blackness, middle class-ness, and immigrant generation-ness through sociopolitical and cultural terms.

CRT, which evolved out of critical legal studies in the 1980s, is considered an interdisciplinary approach that employs theories and practices from ethnic studies, women's studies, sociology, history, humanities, and legal fields to account for the role race and racism play in US society. CRT foregrounds issues of race and racism in all aspects of social life: its normative function (as an institutional and systemic phenomenon) and its impact on the racial, gender, and class subordination of people of color. For instance, critical race theorists such as Bonilla-Silva (2009) use its tenets to argue that racism is not only normative and perpetual in the United States, but it continues to adapt to cultural standards that prevent racism's victims from easily identifying race as the cause of their plight. CRT is often used in the development of theory and praxis that seek to challenge systems of oppression that hinder the social progress and mobility of nonwhites and to develop strategies to dismantle its persistence (see works of hooks 1990a, b; Delgado and Stefancic 2012; Crenshaw et al. 1996).

Intersectionality, another aspect of CRT, acknowledges the multiple forms of oppression (as opposed to binaries of opposition) as interacting with race and racism and its influence on the experiences of people of color. As such, several scholars have used CRT methods, such as counter-narrative storytelling to present the viewpoints of oppressed minorities as opposed to the dominant [read: white] narrative, which is often portrayed by mainstream media outlets (Cook and Dixon 2013; Delgado and Stefancic 2012; Wing Sue et al. 2008).

CRT's methodological orientation toward narratives or storytelling activities is relevant to this study because it provides a platform of agency for the MSGCIs to confront the effects of racialization, to describe their experiences, and to showcase their responses to and resistance of racism and other intersectional forms of oppression. This is an important feat because storytelling is a vehicle for the MSGCI to express their voice and to clearly identify their racialized experiences. Further, it is a necessary academic endeavor to increase scholars' understanding of racism's multilayered effect on second generation immigrant identity and mobility.

Postcolonialism provides an interesting lens to understanding the persistence of binary distinctions (I/other, we/they, man/woman, black/white) and classifications, which serve as the basis of social norms and values, that constitute western/European structures of domination that have become globalized. At its crux, postcolonialism interrogates the construction of knowledge with the positioning of European modern society as the universal representation whereas societies who are non-European are positioned as "other." In this regard, the development of knowledge becomes racialized; whiteness and/or Eurocentric tradition gains strength and identity by setting itself against the "other" as a surrogate (Morley and Kuan-Hsing 1996). Because this newly constituted Eurocentric knowledge becomes a universal practice or the norm, the "other's" ability for self-identification and articulation are often challenged by hegemonic practices that prefer to maintain its binary power relations. Homi Bhabha (1994:6) in *Location of Culture* asserts that,

> Postcoloniality is a salutary reminder of the persistent neo-colonial relationship within the new world order and the multinational divisions of labour. Such a perspective enables the authentication of histories of exploitation, and the evolution and the evolution of strategies of resistance. Beyond this, however, postcolonial critique bears witness to those countries and communities...constituted...otherwise than modernity.

As such, postcolonial theories intend to privilege the voice, perspectives, and experiences of the marginalized because it recognizes the influence colonial legacies have on shaping expression and performance of all aspects of identity and self-hood (see Hall 1990; Maan 2005; Spivak 1999).

Because this project also looks to MSGCI identity in terms of race, ethnicity, social class, and gender/sexuality, postcolonialism is useful in understanding how the identities defined within these categories are simultaneously subjective and

> structure interactions, opportunities, consciousness, ideology and the forms of resistance that characterize American life ...[and shape] the social location of different groups in contemporary society. (Andersen 1996: ix; see also Mclintock 1995)

Therefore, I look to postcolonialist Stuart Hall's "de-centered subject" when it comes to understanding the identity development process of the MSGCIs.

Stuart Hall's conception of the de-centered subject/"other" derives from the notion that hegemonic systems create a place for the "other" by classifying and positioning the "other" in relationship to itself. Interestingly, Hall asserts the "other" also classifies and positions him or herself, thereby becoming the subject that is established in the system. For Hall, there is a "de-centering" that occurs during the positioning process that allows for an identifying moment, where self-identity is marked by self-constitution and by subjectification. He explains the process of de-centering as,

> [...] how they fashion, stylize, produce and perform these positions, and why they never do, or are in a constant, agonistic process of struggling with, resisting, negotiating and accommodating the normative or regulative rules with which they confront and regulate themselves. (Hall 1996)

For the purpose of this research, Hall's and other postcolonial scholars' work on the process of identity or identity making (e.g., the construction, articulation, and assertion) can provide insight into considering how MSGCI identities are produced in specific historical and institutional sites and emerge within particular power dynamics that go beyond the cultural binary of immigrant advantage versus native disadvantage.

INTRODUCING AN ALTERNATE FRAMEWORK: TRIPLE IDENTITY CONSCIOUSNESS

For the purpose of this project, I also contend, there was a need to develop a new operational framework to identify and understand the complex and nuanced phenomena of MSGCI identity: triple identity consciousness. The MSGCI stories shared with me reveal subtleties about the intersectionality of identity that, I contend, cannot solely be contexualized by one particular discursive paradigm discussed above. As part of my reflection and analysis, the goal is not to make any attempts to obscure other axes of affiliation (such as class, religion, gender, and sexuality) in my discussion of race and ethnic identity assertions and racialization of MSGCIs, but to highlight their intricacies. There are, of course, implications for how I discuss issues of immigrant generation, race, class, gender, and selfhood. Hence, the concept of triple identity consciousness intends to serve as a useful analytic tool to understand the development processes of identity, including how the second generations' diasporic journeys and/or transnational connections both local and global inform their articulation and expression of identity. Thus, there are three key ideological orientations that specifically informed my conceptualization of a triple identity consciousness framework: postcolonialism, CRT's intersectionality, and W.E.B. Du Bois' concept of double consciousness. Postcolonialism and CRT's notion of intersectionality, I contend, undergirds the operational framework of triple identity consciousness, whereas Du Bois' concept of "double consciousness" serves as the theoretical platform from which this framework developed. Let me elaborate further.

As mentioned previously, theories of postcolonialism can help us understand the "decentering" process in which the MSGCIs intentionally choose to assert specific aspects of their identities in various situations. For instance, scholars Gayatri Chakravorty Spivak, bell hooks, and Homi Bhabha, often emphasize the critical awareness that the "other" understands his or her subjectivity, objectivity, consciousness, and unconsciousness as something distinct, almost transcendental. As such, it is this awareness or consciousness that not only guides MSGCIs' thoughts and actions but helps them to create a new "space" in which they negotiate meaning and representation for themselves as something different than the version of them that is proscribed. Such awareness, I consider, to be a type of social protest against the projection of being the "other" subaltern voice, which is defined by systems of oppression.

CRT also provides another way of understanding how the MSGCIs examine and critique the systems of oppression that purposefully devalue them and their voice, and subsequently develop approaches to dismantle such systems. Applying a CRT lens to MSGCI narratives, the concept of intersectionality reveals how racialization, subjugation, and oppression function. Avtar Brah and Ann Phoenix (2004:76) assert

> the concept of 'intersectionality' as signifying the complex, irreducible, varied, and variable effects which ensue when multiple axis of differentiation—economic political, cultural, psychic, subjective and experiential—intersect in historically specific contexts.

Therefore, the notion of intersectionality emphasizes that different dimensions of social life cannot be separated out into discrete and pure "strands" or experiences. Instead, these strands inform and are informed by one another. When the MSGCIs express their own understanding of their identities across varied and historically specific contexts, they describe and explicitly point out their own awareness of the multiplicity of their social identity (e.g., their gender, sexuality, ethnicity) exists simultaneously and is conferred, asserted, and realized in various contexts.

My consideration and subsequent development of the triple identity consciousness framework also came from the notion that there is a deeper and nuanced level of awareness—a "third consciousness"—that enables the MSGCIs to engage in the intersectionalities of themselves, as it relates to their acknowledgment of racial meanings and black subjectivity. It is this "third level of awareness," I argue is the space that incites the MSGCIs to develop strategies to transcend oppressive definitions. In this regard, I consider W.E.B. Du Bois' concept of "double consciousness" to illustrate this point.

Though triple identity consciousness as a framework is in its infancy, my conceptualization of it, I contend, extends W.E.B. Du Bois's concept of the "veil" or double consciousness[1] of racial dualism, which he first articulated in the book, *The Souls of Black Folk* (1903). In his book, Du Bois explains the condition of racism in America is one in which those trapped by it are forced to live a life within it. He then describes the divide between experience and self-awareness, "introjecting racism into the racially oppressed self." Similarly, I also conceive triple identity consciousness dialectically,[2] in that it "operates both at the level of the personal or intrapsychic (micro) and at the institutional or structural (macro) level of social interaction" (Winant 2004:1). The difference between Du Bois' "veil's" expression of double consciousness both on the macro and on the micro-level and my conceptualization and operationalization of triple identity consciousness is in how Du Bois and I demonstrate the veil's operation on the micro and micro level of interaction.

In my opinion, Du Bois (1903) is at pains to show the veil's operation beyond an instance—though an important instance, in which he describes the case of John, a young black scholar on leave from school who becomes aware of the shroud of an imposed racial dualism. In the book, Du Bois asserts that John had a transcendental moment when he had the opportunity to experience an aspect of social life that had been denied to people of color. Hence, Du Bois makes the argument that if one can transcend it (the veil), and can live beyond it, there is an experience of being that is no longer limited by it. For me, the triple identity consciousness framework extends the singular instance of John's awareness, which Du Bois describes. Instead, this framework can be applied to the multiple situations in which the MSGCIs not only demonstrate an awareness of the world, its complexities and the way racism does not have to define their being and/or their view of themselves similar to John, but how their awareness becomes consistently expressed in social action both on an individual and group level.

Therefore, I conceptualize triple identity consciousness as an awareness in which the MSGCIs simultaneously connect themselves by invoking a collective history of struggle against racism. Although identity is contextual and depending on the situation, where one aspect of identity may be made more salient and dominant than others, there are aspects of identity that are historically hegemonic over others. And still an awareness about how one's identity is conceptualized; ways in which a person is able to make disconnections or (emphasizing difference) from others in these situations. I contend, it is this difference and sameness that makes the construct of identity fluid, complex, and contingent upon the moment—social economic, political, historical, geographical, and so on. The singularity of certain aspects of identity (e.g., woman, gay, person of color) rears itself in the multiplicity of these situations or moments. Hence, it is through triple identity consciousness framework that we can understand how the multiple versions of identity for the MSGCI exist and are ultimately articulated and expressed in daily experiences.

METHODOLOGY OF RESEARCH
AND PROFILE OF PARTICIPANTS

Researchers Carol A.B. Warren (2002) and Nicholas Mays and Catherine Pope (1995) once argued that the selection of participants in a typical ethnographic, qualitative study always differs from that of quantitative research because its, "purpose is not to establish a random or representative sample drawn from a population but to identify specific groups of people who either possess characteristics or live in a circumstances relevant to the social phenomenon being studied" (Mays and Pope 1995:110). To help share the stories of this second generation, I refused to take on the traditional social science preoccupation with sample randomization and representation per se and decided to employ tenets of an ethnographic and case study methodological approach. In fact, cultural theorists such as bell hooks (1990b:152) point to the groundbreaking work of James Clifford and George Marcus' *Writing Culture* and the changing role of ethnography and its utility in culture and identity politics research by arguing:

> Ethnography is actively situated between powerful systems of meaning. It poses its questions at the boundaries of civilizations, cultures, classes, races, and genders. Ethnography decodes and recodes, telling the grounds of collective order and diversity, inclusion and exclusion. It describes processes of innovation and structuration, and is itself part of these processes.

Because this project is one that explores narratives and, in essence, the power of the narrative structure and what it reveals about the experiences of this second generation population, I am preoccupied with its presentation as being both reflexive and respectful. Hence, in the same way my initial conceptualization of this project was sparked by conversations with my daughter and my girlfriend, it made sense to begin the project by speaking with and soliciting the cooperation of family, family friends, and former schoolmates.

I relied on these personal relationships to provide entrée into informal networks of people who were both middle class and second generation, self-identified Black Caribbean immigrants. These networks turned out to be particularly crucial in gaining access to a population regarded as relatively "invisible" because of their in-between status (i.e., not first-generation immigrant, American-born but not necessarily African American identified, and not poor or working class)—without basing specific selection criteria in particular racial-ethnic identity outcomes. Further, this MSGCI population is not easily accessible via traditional channels of affinity associations and community and service organizations because the label of "second generation Caribbean immigrant" is not one widely used to identify and interact with the adult children of black Caribbean immigrants. A few members of my family agreed to be interviewed and to provide names of other relatives, friends, colleagues, neighbors, and fellow church parishioners. I also identified MSGCIs with the assistance of fellow academics engaged in their own research around race and the immigrant experience. The snowball sampling technique was achieved by asking each participant to recommend others as potential participants.

In most cases, participants contacted the person they recommended first and then gave me his or her name, telephone number, and/or email address. I found this approach to be quite helpful and nonintrusive. Potential participants had heard about my project from someone they knew, oftentimes trusted and had already contributed themselves. Participants had a general idea about my project prior to my speaking with them. In addition to speaking with each potential participant, I also prepared a one-page summary about the project in the event that he or she had additional questions or needed to be reminded about the purpose of my project. Some asked me to email or provide them with a hard copy of the summary so that they would have something on hand in case the potential participant they recommended had questions.

Overall, participants were very willing to contribute in any way I needed them for my project. There were several participants, however, who refused to sign a written consent form and were only willing to participate as long as I provided them with a pseudonym and did not share identifiable information about them, specifically regarding their employer's name and details of the schools they attended. In some instances, these participants specifically stated which events or stories they did not feel comfortable with me sharing in the book. In this regard, I am unapologetic for placing the interests of my participants as paramount in the "data collection" process. In order to maintain the trust, confidence, and privacy of participants, I contend, "researchers need to proceed with sensitivity and concern for their needs and desires" (Polkinghorne 2005:144). As such, I indeed followed customary ethical procedures to address participants' concerns regarding consent and confidentiality and in other cases, anonymity for those who expressed confidentiality concerns. It was very important that each participant felt untethered to any sort of expectations I had of them in the way they told their own stories as well as felt relieved of their anxiety about personal information, "being shared with all the world to see"—as one participant expressed as a concern.

From the outset, I divided the interview process into two parts: a demographic questionnaire, which gathered basic information such as age, gender and place of birth, and an interview, which loosely followed a semi-structured interview protocol to ensure consistency of general questions asked across all interviews. While this process had some structure, the conversations with participants themselves were often free flowing with several open-ended questions that allowed for the participants to tell their own internarrative in a way that defies a "western normative ideal for autobiographical narrative" (Maan 2005). The internarrative is the space in which the marginalized voice is heard and stories are told. In her book *Internarrative Identity*, Ajit Maan argues that the story a person shares expresses identities of self in ways that are contextualized and highly relational, so that—in a postmodern view—its inconsistency is not a threat to one's self but makes sense in defining "Who am I?" As a result, the story structure becomes less about being linear, chronological or adhering to Western ideals regarding universalist principals of behavior and identity assertion, but rather more about the person's control over his or her own story without necessarily changing the subject.

Approximately half of the interviews were conducted over the phone or using Skype and FaceTime during the evening hours; the other half were conducted in person, either at a local café during mid-morning hours or at the person's home on the weekends. Although all interview locales were subject to either family members peeking in or the inquisitive café patron eavesdropping, for the most part, there were few interruptions other than the occasional phone call. The average interview lasted about one hour and half but I often stayed around longer to chat after the interview was over. During these conversations, some talked about the latest happenings at their jobs or in their families' lives like vacations and birthday parties. Others shared their opinions on the latest current event story and asked me to share my opinions with them. One or two people showed me their photo albums or portraits that hung in their homes. In these post-interview conversations, I had an additional opportunity to learn more about their lives.

For this project, I conducted a total of 20 interviews with English-, Spanish, and French speaking MSGCIs. Because of its sample size, there are important issues to contend with when it comes to conducting qualitative ethnographies and especially in the social sciences where large data sets and quantitative survey methods are often privileged. An important feature of qualitative research and specifically qualitative ethnography such as *Stories of Identity among Black Middle Class Second Generation Caribbeans* is to study phenomenon in a particular context. Therefore, the intent is not to generalize from my sample of MSGCIs to the entire US MSGCI population (as it can be the case for statistical analysis of large data sets). Instead, the intent is to explain, describe, and interpret the essence of experience for this shared group and the potentiality of a developing collective story around racial-ethnic identity, including social class and gender. Hence, sample size is not about having reliable and representative opinions per se; the focus is on the richness and depth of the information shared as being valid and the high quality of its scholarship and interpretations presented. Notwithstanding the longstanding methodological debate between qualitative and quantitative research, several qualitative scholars have provided some recommendations of sample size ranges for various qualitative research, including the ones I use for this project: ethnography, a minimum of 4–5 cases; grounded theory, 20–50 cases; and narrative analysis, a minimum of 1–2 cases to a maximum of 325 cases. These recommendations, I presume, intend to help both qualitative and quantitative researchers resist the urge to think about qualitative sampling from a quantitative view (see works by Creswell 2013; Maxwell 2013; Morse 1994).

I conducted interviews with seven men and thirteen women, born in the United States between the late 1960s and 1987, and ranged in age from 25 to 45 at the time of interview (years 2010 through 2014). The majority of participants were married and/or in domestic partnerships, whereas two were divorced and three were single. In addition, 13 participants reported having children between the ages of three and seventeen, two reported having children over the age of eighteen and five reported having no children. In terms of their parents' countries of origin, these represent the racial, ethnic, cultural, and linguistic diversity of the Caribbean (i.e., Jamaica, Haiti, Cuba, Panama, Honduras, Puerto Rico, the Dominican Republic, Dominica, Costa Rica, Antigua, Trinidad, Grenada, and Barbados). Participants had at least one biological parent who came to the United States during the years shortly after the passing of the Immigration Act of 1965, which was approximately from 1966/1967 to 1985. The timing of parents' arrival is significant for this research because black immigrants, and particularly those that came to the United States between the mid-1960s and the early 1990s from the Caribbean, contributed to a 25% growth of the black population in the United States (see Kent 2007).

An interesting nuance to the analysis presented in this study is in the way particular Caribbean cultural tropes and themes that are readily identified by first generation Caribbean immigrants (their parents' generation) did not come across as equally distinctive for the participants in this study. In other words, most distinctions participants made regarding Caribbean cultural practices were talked about more broadly as being either "Caribbean" or "West Indian" as opposed to an explicit expression that reflect the nuance of country-specific cultures of their parents. This finding was evident when participants often shared childhood stories that seem to blend and present their individual parents' cultural practices into one. As such, it was not always clear whether certain discernible Caribbean cultural practices were adopted in their childhood households because it was perceived clearly to be more Panamanian than from the Commonwealth of Dominica, for example. Also, many participants were raised in households where their parents were born in locales that shared similar linguistic and colonial histories. Therefore, any linguistic and religious cultural differences readily discussed as nuanced and distinct for the participants largely occurred among those who also speak Spanish, French, and Dutch creole and/or celebrate aspects of non-Christian background (i.e., Hindu culture and religion). Such country-specific and cultural distinctions are more significant among the participants since they were born in and reared in the United States, which has had a long tradition of being a Judeo-Christian and Anglophone country.

Participants also discussed having traveled at least once to their parent(s)' country of birth during their childhood and adolescence, and their continued travel to these countries as an adult, spending time visiting with extended family members who remained behind. Over their life course, participants mentioned living in various major cities across the United States as well as in the Caribbean, Europe, and parts of Africa. At the time of the interview, many resided in major American cities including those along the Eastern Seaboard (i.e., the Greater Boston, Massachusetts area, the Greater Hartford, Connecticut area, the Greater New York City/New Jersey area, Philadelphia, Pennsylvania, Washington, D.C., the Greater Atlanta, Georgia area, and the Greater Orlando, Fort Lauderdale and Miami areas in Florida). These cities embody many of the economic, educational, and social forces that frame the settlement motivations of post-1965 immigrants from the Caribbean to the United States as well as the economic and educational outcomes for their children.

When it comes to talking about socio-economic status, and specifically social class, there is no official government definition of who belongs to the middle class nor is there a universally recognized definition of "middle class" socio-economic status; in fact, the term means different things to different people. The middle class may refer to a group with a common point of view or values, or to those having similar incomes, educational levels, and occupations, for example. For others, definitions may point to absolute income amounts that determine who belongs to the middle class. According to Craig Elwell's 2014 CRS report *The Distribution of Household Income and the Middle Class*, which highlights data from the 2012 Annual Social and Economic Supplement to the Current Population Survey, he argues that the "middle class" may refer to households with income levels that started from $39,736 (the bottom of the middle quintile, 20%, of households) and extended into the top quintile (households with income of $104,087 or more)—perhaps including households with incomes slightly over $200,000.

Participants self-identified as middle class using the following character-istics: household income earnings of $40,000 or more annually, earning a college degree or higher, and working within semi- and professional occu-pations. More specifically, participants reported having annual household incomes between mid $50,000s and $90,000s, with an exception of a few whose annual household incomes were slightly under $150,000 per year. I probed participants for detailed information on their performance and expression of their "middle class-ness"—how they engaged in specific activities they think reproduce their social, ethnic, and economic position, and which ones they feel allow them to bequeath cultural capital to their children and/or future generations. Such activities included collecting black art, navigating the higher education system, idyllic vacationing in La Jolla, Martha's Vineyard, the Hamptons, and the Caribbean, sending bar-rels to Central America and the Caribbean, establishing dual citizenship, developing patterns of homeownership, and engaging in community activ-ism and black philanthropy. Their accounts included how they engage in a process whereby they create a habitus of Blackness to avoid extreme mar-ginalization and to navigate situations of colorism, and racial, ethnic, and linguistic discrimination. For many participants, being a part of a larger black community (a diaspora of sorts) constitutes a racial and cultural soli-darity between African Americans and those from the Caribbean and Central America. Further, many participants described having adopted a transnational racial consciousness (see Quintana and Segura-Herrera 2003; Quintana 2007) or as W.E.B. Du Bois (1903/1990) purports "a double consciousness." Another interesting nuance to the analysis presented sug-gests the process of creating a habitus of blackness is informed by their perceived contours of middle class identity (measures of middle class well-being and material expression) for challenging structures of oppression.

RESEARCH FOCI AND THE STUDY OF MSGCIs IN THE UNITED STATES

Two central foci anchor this analysis. The first is the role colorblind dis-course plays on the second generation Black immigrant's race awareness and middle class experience in the United States. Following the works of Lawrence Bobo et al.'s (1997) *Laissez-Faire Racism* and Eduardo Bonilla-Silva's (2009) *Racism Without Racists*, I argue that the "new racism" of these second generation experiences serves as an important tool for the maintenance of racial order and limits their ability to truly transcend the developing three tier hierarchy that relegates, "a collective black" group—despite their achievement of aspiring and acquiring the American Dream of middle class-ness—toward the bottom. Bonilla-Silva argues that America's racial and ethnic stratification system will soon resemble the complex patterns of race and ethnic classification systems in Latin America. He contends there will be at least a three tier racial hierarchy with: "white" at the top (e.g., descendants of or recent immigrants from Eastern and Western Europe and certain members from Argentina and Cuba), "honorary white" which includes some lighter skinned Asian and Latino groups (e.g., China, Japan, and Korea) and multiracial people in the middle, and the "collective black" at the bottom, which includes African-Americans, Native Americans on reservations, first and second generation Caribbeans and Africans, and darker-skinned members of Latino and Asian populations (e.g., Puerto Ricans and Dominicans, Cuba, Cambodians, and Laotians).

I argue this re-articulation of or the shift from the longstanding black-white racial binary to a more "expansive" racial hierarchy model, which includes the growing Asian and Latino population in the United States, still reinforces blacks' relegation (albeit the "collective black") to the bottom. As such, this relegation reifies the long-term effects of white supremacy on the lives of those who are not allowed to move up toward the top of the racial hierarchy, despite their own fluid notions of race and ethnic identity and class mobility (see Lewis Gordon 1997). In many regards, this line of analysis points to the fundamental issue about what we as a society understand as social (in)justice. It speaks clearly to the comfort and luxury of power and privilege afforded to some and the perpetual marginalization of people of color (particularly "the collective black") when it comes to education, housing, employment, health care, and its relationship with the criminal justice system.

Second, this book explores the rich insights critical race and postcolonial theories provide around the concept of intersectionality. As argued in Kimberle Crenshaw's (1991) *Mapping the Margins: Intersectionality, Identity Politics and Violence Against Women of Color*, intersectionality proves to be especially valuable in appreciating the relationship between race, ethnicity, gender, and class as experiences for MSGCI, and has proven to be an important tool for understanding how membership in more than one marginalized or invisible group (albeit black middle class) can complicate the impact of oppression for a population that experiences "insider-outsider" status in public and private spaces. Employing this layer of analysis has provided additional insight into the nuances of the "-isms," its various manifestations, and the complicated—perhaps damaging—consequences racism causes, which participants' stories tell.

Conducting research on the study of the MSGCI population poses interesting challenges. In addition to the existing limitations of accessing this segment of the "black identified" Caribbean immigrant population that is very much a part of the larger diaspora in the United States, there is an effort to actively resist reifying persisting stereotypes about the middle class, native-born blacks, and children of black immigrants. As previously discussed, current literature in sociology and migration studies continue to grapple with these issues, sometimes in contradictory ways, particularly around the second generation immigrants' assimilation process and their presumed "drive to succeed" or their downward assimilation away from the norms of the dominant, mainstream society (see the works of Perlmann and Waldinger 1997; Waldinger and Feliciano 2004; Kasinitz et al. 2008). Even before the work of Bryce-Laporte (1972), the literature would often offer at least three different explanations for the rise of a growing black Caribbean middle class: cultural superiority, stronger human capital, and a more favorable standing among whites. Subsequent work by Thomas Sowell, for example, provides a cultural explanation that suggests the children of black Caribbean immigrants are socialized to develop different value systems from African Americans. Such explanations are still cited to explain why there are slightly higher proportions of educated skilled workers among first and second generation Caribbean immigrants than native-born African Americans. As stated earlier, this book rejects these assumptions or explanations that reify white favoritism in order to promote "superiority of" Caribbean culture.

I contend, however, the middle class for this population interprets and internalizes race, ethnic, gender, and class in ways that differ from what the previous research in the field does not effectively illustrate. The question that still remains is: how does the middle class, second generation Caribbean immigrant population engage, negotiate, and perhaps cope with predominant race, ethnic, and gender identity discourses in everyday life? When we look to health outcomes of this population, for example, from recent National Institute of Health reports (see Borell 2006; Jackson and Antonucci 2005; Williams et al. 2007), we can see the ways in which race, ethnicity, class, and gender strongly impact their home, work, family, and community life as well as their health and wellbeing outcomes. Research has found that:

- Self-identified black men of Caribbean ancestry in the United States had higher risks for 12-month rates of mood and anxiety disorders (including but not limited to clinical depression, anxiety and panic attacks, and bipolar disorder) in comparison to African American men.
- Self-identified black women of Caribbean ancestry reported experiencing stressors associated with racism and migration as well as those related to their gender—greater work opportunities, financial and personal independence, and increased power in the domestic sphere.
- Self-identified black Hispanic/Latino women had higher rates of mood and anxiety disorders compared with women from the English-speaking Caribbean.
- Self-identified black Hispanic/Latino women more often report feeling greater pressure to stop working because codes of middle class respectability in their culture are more closely tied to women remaining in the domestic sphere in comparison to US born women and white immigrants.
- Self-identified black Hispanic/Latino (or Afro-Latino) men and women tend to have poorer health compared with individuals of lighter complexion, because they face discrimination on the basis of their shade of skin color from both within and outside their ethnic community.
- Social and psychological consequences of having a darker skin tone not only have negative effects but also are more consequential among women than among men for this group.

Because race, ethnicity, and gender are powerful stratification factors in the United States, the aforementioned physical and mental health findings point to the negative impacts these factors have on life circumstances and outcomes, and exposures to race-related treatment for this generation are—similar in the ways these impacts, too, have a negative effect on African Americans outcomes (Model 1991, 1995). And yet, there is paucity of research on why, too, the children of the second generation Caribbean immigrants are beginning to display the same or even worse health outcomes than African Americans—a group often assumed they should resemble given their parents' American birth, and regardless of their middle class status.

In the following chapters, I explore the social constructs of race, ethnicity, class, and gender and uncover the costs and benefits of being middle class, self-identified as black, adult child of Caribbean immigrants as told by this generation. In effect, I also examine: how these experiences impact a host of life outcomes, including home life, community, and work experience, and shape identity for the MSGCI both locally and globally.

NOTES

1. According to Howard Winant (2004:4), "The whole framework of double consciousness draws upon this legacy: it describes a subjectivity both sundered and fused, an identity divided by forces originating both within and outside the self. The concept of the veil also recognizes the black soul's striving for wholeness, for synthesis and integration: after all its "dogged strength alone keeps it from being torn asunder."
2. The concept of "dialectic" refers to a relationship that simultaneously embodies both antagonism and interdependence that develops over historical time and that links the small-scale and large-scale dimensions of social life.

BIBLIOGRAPHY

Alba, R., & Nee, V. (1997). Rethinking Assimilation Theory for a New Era of Immigration. *International Migration Review, 31*(4), 826–874.

Andersen, M. (1996). Foreword. In E. N.-L. Chow, D. Wilkinson, & M. B. Zinn (Eds.), *Race, Class and Gender: Common Bonds, Different Voices* (pp. i–ii). Thousand Oaks: Sage Publications.

Benson, J. (2006). Exploring the Racial Identity of Black Immigrants in the United States. *Sociological Forum, 21*(2), 219–243.

Bhabha, H. (1994). *The Location of Culture.* New York: Routledge.

Bobo, L., Kluegel, J. R., & Smith, R. A. (1997). *Laissez-Faire Racism: The Crystallization of a Kindler, Gentler Anti-black Ideology.* New York: Russell Sage Foundation.

Bonilla-Silva, E. (2009). *Racism without Racists: Color-blind Racism and the Persistence of Racial Inequality.* Lanham: Rowan Littlefield.

Borell, L. N. (2006). Self-reported Hypertension and Race Among Hispanics in the National Health Interview Survey. *Ethnicity and Disease, 16,* 71–77.

Brah, A., & Phoenix, A. (2004). Ain't I a Woman? Revisiting Intersectionality. *Journal of International Women's Studies, 5*(3), 75–86.

Bryce-Laporte, R. (1972). Black Immigrants: The Experience of Invisibility and Inequality. *Journal of Black Studies, 3,* 20–56.

Burke, P. J., & Reitzes, D. C. (1981). The Link Between Identity and Role Performance. *Social Psychology Quarterly, 44*(2), 83–91.

Cole, E., & Omari, S. (2003). Race, Class and the Dilemmas of Upward Mobility for African Americans. *Journal of Social Issues, 59*, 785–802.

Cook, D., & Dixon, A. (2013). Writing Critical Race Theory and Method: A Composite Counterstory on the Experiences of Black Teachers in New Orleans post-Katrina. *International Journal of Qualitative Studies in Education, 26*(10), 1238–1258.

Crenshaw, K. (1991). Mapping the margins: Intersectionality, Identity Politics, and Violence against Women of Color. *Stanford Law Review, 43*(6), 1241–1299.

Crenshaw, K., Gotanda, N., Peller, G., & Thomas, K. (1996). *Critical Race Theory: Key Writings that Formed the Movement.* New York: The New Press.

Creswell, J. W. (2013). *Qualitative Inquiry and Research Design: Choosing among Five Approaches.* Thousand Oaks: Sage Publications.

Delgado, R., & Stefancic, J. (2012). *Critical Race Theory: An Introduction* (2nd ed.). New York: New York University Press.

Du Bois, W. (1903/1990). *Souls of Black Folk.* New York: Vintage Books.

Elwell, C. K. (2014). *Distribution of Household Income and the Middle Class.* Washington, DC: Congressional Research Service.

Gans, H. J. (1992). Second Generation Decline: Scenarios for the Economic and Ethnic Future of the Post-1965 American Immigrants. *Ethnic and Racial Studies, 15*(2), 173–192.

Gecas, V., & Burke, P. J. (1995). Self and Identity. In K. S. Cook, G. A. Fine, & J. S. House (Eds.), *Sociological Perspectives on Social Psychology* (pp. 41–67). Boston: Allyn and Bacon.

Gordon, M. (1964). *Assimilation in American Life: The Role of Race, Religion and National Origins.* New York: Oxford University Press.

Gordon, L. R. (1997). *Her Majesty's Other Children: Sketches of Racism from a Neocolonial Age.* New York: Rowman and Littlefield.

Hall, S. (1990). Cultural Identity and Diaspora. In J. Rutherford (Ed.), *Identity: Community, Culture, Difference* (1st ed., pp. 222–237). London: Lawrence and Wishart.

Hall, S. (1996). Introduction: Who Needs "Identity"? In S. Hall & P. du Gay (eds.), *Questions of Cultural Identity* (pp. 1–17). New York: SAGE.

Handlin, O. (1973). *The Uprooted: The Epic Story of the Great Migration that made the American People.* Boston: Little Brown.

hooks, b. (1990a). Marginality as a Site of Resistance. In R. Ferguson (Ed.), *Out There: Marginalization and Contemporary Cultures.* London: MIT Press.

hooks, b. (1990b). *Yearning: Race, Gender and Cultural Politics.* Boston: South End Press.

hooks, b. (2001). *Salvation: Black People and Love.* New York: Harper Perennial.

Jackson, J., & Antonucci, T. C. (2005). Physical and Mental Health Consequences of Aging in Place and Aging Out of Place Among Black Caribbean immigrants. *Research in Human Development, 2*(4), 229–244.

Kasinitz, P., Mollenkopf, J., Waters, M. C., & Holdaway, J. (2008). *Inheriting the City: The Children of Immigrants Come of Age*. New York: Harvard University Press.

Kent, M. M. (2007, December 01). Immigration and America's Black Population. *Population Bulletin, 62*(4), 1–20.

Lacy, K. R. (2004). Black Spaces, Black Places: Strategic Assimilation and Identity Construction in Middle Class Suburbia. *Ethnic and Racial Studies, 27*(6), 908–930.

Lacy, K. R. (2007). *Blue Chip Black: Race, Class and Status in the New Black Middle Class*. Berkeley: University of California Press.

Maan, A. K. (2005). Post Colonial Practices and Narrative Nomads: Thinking Sikhism Beyond Metaphysics. *Sikh Formations, 1*(1), 217–227.

Massey, D. (1995). The New Immigration and Ethnicity in the United States. *Population and Development Review, 21*(3), 631–652.

Maxwell, J. A. (2013). *Qualitative Research Design: An Interactive Approach* (3rd ed.). Thousand Oaks: Sage Publications.

Mays, N., & Pope, C. (1995). Qualitative Research: Rigour and Qualitative Research. *British Medical Journal (BMJ), 311*(6997), 109–112.

Mclintock, A. (1995). *Imperial Leather: Race, Gender, and Sexuality in the Colonial Context*. New York: Routledge.

Model, S. (1991). Caribbean Immigrants: A Black Success Story? *International Migration Review, 25*, 248–276.

Model, S. (1995). West Indian Prosperity: Fact or Fiction? *Social Problems, 42*, 535–553.

Mohanty, C. T. (1991). Cartographies of Struggle: Third World Women and the Politics of Feminism. In C. T. Mohanty, A. Russo, & L. Torres (Eds.), *Third World Women and the Politics of Feminism* (pp. 2–47). Bloomington: Indiana University Press.

Morley, D., & Kuan-Hsing, C. (1996). *Stuart Hall: Critical Dialogs in Cultural Studies*. New York: Routledge.

Morse, J. M. (1994). Designing Funded Qualitative Research. In N. K. Denzin & Y. S. Lincoln (Eds.), *Handbook of Qualitative Research* (pp. 220–235). Thousand Oaks: Sage Publications.

Mostern, K. (1999). *Cultural Margins: Autobiography and Black Identity Politics: Racialization in Twentieth Century America* (T. Brennan, Ed.). Cambridge, UK: Cambridge University Press.

Myrdal, G. (1944). *An American Dilemma*. New York: Harper & Row.

Park, R. E. (1950). *Race and Culture* (E. Hughes, Ed.). Glencoe, IL: The Free Press.

Park, R. E., & Burgess, E. W. (1924). *Introduction to the Science of Sociology*. Chicago: University of Chicago Press.

Perlmann, J., & Waldinger, R. (1997). Second Generation Decline? Immigrant Children Past and Present- A Reconsideration. *International Migration Review, 31*(4), 893–922.

Polkinghorne, D. E. (2005). Language and Meaning: Data Collection in Qualitative Research. *Journal of Counseling Psychology, 52*(2), 137–145.

Portes, A., & Rumbaut, R. (2006). *Immigrant America: A Portrait* (3rd ed.). Berkeley: University of California Press.

Portes, A., & Zhou, M. (1993). The New Second Generation: Segmented Assimilation and Its Variant. *Annals, 530*(1), 74–96.

Quintana, S. M. (2007). Racial and Ethnic Identity: Developmental Perspectives and Research. *Journal of Counseling Psychology, 54*, 259–270.

Quintana, S. M., & Segura-Herrera, T. (2003). Developmental Transformations of Self and Identity in the Context of Oppression. *Self and Identity, 2*, 269–285.

Sollors, W. (1986). *Beyond Ethnicity: Consent and Descent in American Culture.* New York: Oxford University Press.

Spivak, G. C. (1999). *A Critique of Post Colonial Reason: Toward a History of the Vanishing Present.* Cambridge, MA: Harvard University Press.

Stryker, S. (1968). Identity Salience and Role Performance: The Importance of Symbolic Interaction Theory for Family Research. *Journal of Marriage and the Family, 30*(4), 558–564.

Vickerman, M. (1999). *Crosscurrents: West Indian Immigrants and Race.* Oxford: Oxford University Press.

Waldinger, R., & Feliciano, C. (2004). Will the New Second Generation Experience 'Downward Assimilation'? Segmented Assimilation Re-assessed. *Ethnic and Racial Studies, 27*(3), 376–402.

Warner, W. L., & Srole, L. (1945). *The Social Systems of American Ethnic Groups.* New Haven: Yale University Press.

Warren, C. A. (2002). Qualitative Interviewing. In J. F. Gubrium & J. A. Holstein (Eds.), *Handbook of Interview Research: Context and Method* (pp. 83–101). Thousand Oaks: Sage.

Waters, M. C. (1999). *Black Identities: West Indian Immigrant Dreams and American Realities.* New York: Russell Sage Foundation.

Williams, D., Haile, R., Gonzalez, H. M., Neighbors, H., Baser, R., & Jackson, J. S. (2007). The Mental Health of Caribbean Immigrants: Results from the National Survey of American Life. *American Journal of Public Health, 97*(1), 52–59.

Winant, H. (2004). *The New Politics of Race: Globalism, Difference, and Justice.* Minneapolis: University of Minnesota Press.

Wing Sue, D., Nadal, K. L., Capdilupo, C. M., Lin, A. I., Rivera, D. P., & Torino, G. C. (2008). Racial Microaggressions Against Black Americans: Implications for Counseling. *Journal of Counseling and Development, 86*(3), 330–338.

CHAPTER 3

What Does *Race* Have to Do with It?

What's wrong with black people anyway? Why is it important for society to culturally appropriate our music, our style, and vernacular and at the same time tell us that our cultures are deviant, that we are poor, lesser than and not worthy of respect, humanity, and adoration like other people in America? Black people from all over the world come here and are loved and hated at the same time. It makes no sense but makes me strongly believe race and racism is very much alive and well.

—*Joachim, 34 years old, Family Therapist
and Community Health Worker*

We live in a "post-racial" United States, right? Not so. Some would assume Dr. Martin Luther King Jr.'s prophetic proclamation—"I Have a Dream that…one day this nation will rise up and live out the true meaning of its creed: …that all men are created equal" came to fruition with the presidency of Barack H. Obama. Proponents of post-racialism believe the country has entered a new era where race is no longer a determinant in shaping the lives, fortunes, and experiences of people of color (Brown and Donnor 2011; Crowley 2008; Givhan 2008; Iweala 2008; Terry 2004; Williams et al. 2007).

Quite frankly, "post-racialism" is one of the biggest farces of the twenty-first century. As Frank Rich wrote in his 2012 *New York* Magazine article "Post-Racial Farce" on the current state of American race relations:

So much for the better or the worse, but a shift into a kind of twilight zone where the nation's racial conversation has moved from its usual gears of intractability,

© The Author(s) 2018
Y.S. Lorick-Wilmot, *Stories of Identity among Black,
Middle Class, Second Generation Caribbeans,*
DOI 10.1007/978-3-319-62208-8_3

obfuscation, angry debate, and platitudinous sentimentality to the truly unhinged. It's as if everyone can now say, well, that's that, we've elected our first African-American president, we can pat ourselves on the back for doing so.

Race (and ethnicity) continues to be an undercurrent issue in US society. Sociologically speaking, race is an ideological construct in which its categories are imposed and infused with stereotypical moral meaning, all the more when they become master statuses affecting all aspects of social life (Feagin 2006). Moreover, it is a product of history—a contextual variable which sets apart who is considered of dominant and subordinate taxonomies and connotes social worth—that has informed structures of inequality through institutions and cultural practices that still exist today.

And still, notwithstanding data that point to generations of native and foreign-born blacks making economic and educational progress over the last 20 years or so, this segment of the US population still continues to lag behind whites in jobs, health outcomes, education, housing options, and wealth. In fact, a Federal Reserve's 2010–2013 *Survey of Consumer Finances* report on wealth and income disparity reveal this dismal reality:

- One in three blacks has less than $1000 in wealth (assets minus debts).
  - In comparison, for whites it is one in nine; Asians, one in eight; and Latinos, one in four.
- At the top end of the distribution, the odds of having $1 million in wealth are one in eight for whites and one in nine for Asians but about one in 100 for those who are Latino or black.
- Not surprisingly, median (or typical) wealth levels mirror these disparities: $134,000 for whites, $91,000 for Asians, $14,000 for Hispanics, and $11,000 for blacks.

When it comes to examining whether the wealth gap between whites and people of color in the United States are closing, income is also considered a major source of wealth accumulation for many families. Income gains, however, for white households added $5.19 wealth while the same income gain only added 0.69 cents of wealth for black households over the last 25 years (Shapiro et al. 2013). These findings ask us to consider the question: why has inequality become so entrenched in our post-Civil Rights era of supposed legal equality? In effect, what does race have to do with it? And, how does race impact the lives of blacks, especially the Middle Class Second Generation Caribbean Immigrant (MSGCI) today?

Scholars and policy analysts often look to macro social structures to explain what may be driving this inequality. In recent years, education researchers such as those from the UCLA Civil Rights Project[1] posit that because of job decentralization and housing segregation, public schools across the country and especially those in northeastern states' metropolitan areas (i.e., New York, New Jersey, Connecticut, Delaware, Virginia, Maryland, Massachusetts, North Carolina, and Pennsylvania) are more segregated now than before integration. In fact, six decades after the landmark Supreme Court case *Brown v. Board of Education of Topeka* 1954, many schools in these areas have become racially isolated with more than 99% of its student body as people of color. When it comes to higher education, the Supreme Court in 2014 upheld the ruling that the state of Michigan (like California and Florida) can choose to ban affirmative action in admissions selection policies in their public universities and, at the very least, is encouraged to consider race-neutral alternatives to ensure diversity on its campuses. The effects of such rulings are significant: these states have seen a significant drop in black and Latino enrollment rates at their public universities and a growth in a number of apartheid schools that are high in poverty, tend to have lower expectations than at middle class schools, and tend to have more Caribbean immigrant children (including Latinos)—which all translates to lower levels of academic achievement and limited access to higher education options. But whether state universities choose to ban race-conscious selection, outreach, and financial aid in their admissions process or that children of color in predominately metro-areas attend apartheid schools, there are implications of race in our current educational system. The education system is impacted by de jure and de facto discrimination policies and segregation by ethnicity, class (poverty), and language that are set against the historical backdrop of centuries of explicit and persistent racial discrimination in the United States.

Scholars also look to our criminal justice system for explanations. And in spite of recent public campaigns, uprisings, and social movements such as #BlackLivesMatter, we should not be surprised that criminal justice advocates report blacks and Latinos are incarcerated at a rate double their share of the population and are more likely to experience racial profiling by police. Even the Department of Justice's 2015 investigative report following the killing of youth Michael Brown by white police officer Darren Wilson of the Fergusson, Missouri police department found a, "pattern and practice" of discrimination against African Americans. The report found that the Ferguson police and municipal courts used minor traffic and other violations to raise money for the city by targeting African-American motorists for traffic infractions. It was also found that black residents were disproportionately cited for jay walking violations, had police force used against them, and were handed out harsher and longer jail sentences (US Department of Justice 2015). With high-profile police-involved murders that took place in 2016 of Freddie Gray, Sandra Bland, Tamir Rice, and Terrance Crutcher, to name a few, the Department of Justice continues to conduct investigations of local police departments. The Department of Justice has found consistent patterns of civil rights and 4th amendment violations, where officers engage in patterns or practices of force and use of deadly force, often toward communities of color, in cities of Cleveland, Tulsa, Baltimore, and most recently, Chicago (US Department of Justice 2017).

And to what end do we, society, work to remediate such inequality in the United States? Often, we look to social mobility as the measure of "making it in America." In other words, if people, regardless of race, are able to pull themselves by their bootstraps—go to school, get a good paying job, work hard, save money, and buy a home of their own in a minimal crime-ridden area with great schools, access to green spaces, health care options, and healthy food sources, they can overcome their circumstances and set the path for their future generations. While most will agree that a healthy dose of individual responsibility is necessary to being successful, the notion of the American Dream remains elusive or, at best, an illusion for many, especially for people of color.

In his 2014 Council on Foreign Relations article *The American Dream is an Illusion*, Gregory Clark argues that social mobility in the United States today is no easier than medieval England and that the status of people's children and subsequent generations (up to four generations out) will be quite closely related to their own social status currently. In this regard, ancestry predicts social class for future generations. If you are working class today, your great-great grandchildren are more likely to have a working class experience as well. Most people do not want to resign to such stagnation unless they are already a part of the population that amasses the top 1% of wealth in the United States and are looking to maintain it. Still, the majority of people look to social mobility tracts to improve their outcomes and those of their future generation. One such tract is the pathway to homeownership.

Homeownership is part of the American Dream because, to many, it exemplifies a sense of accomplishment and a higher status of social wealth within society's values and expectationsof people. Therefore, being a person of color and a homeowner means that you have successfully assimilated into American culture and are no longer part of the stereotype associated with minorities—such as having bad credit, being poor, and uneducated. However, race is a continuing factor in real estate and subprime lending practices that carry poor provisions, high-interest rates, and undisclosed terms and lending discrimination make it hard for people of color to successfully progress in the housing market and increase their home equity, which is a disadvantage to both the market and the people. Even still, economists also find black homeowners are still poorer than whites, despite federal policies over the last decade that attempt to increase minority homeownership rates. Researchers at the Pew Research Center looked to the impact of the Great Recession (2007–2013) and found homeownership rates between 2010 and 2013 for white households fell 2% from 75.3% to 73.9% whereas the homeownership rate among black and Latino households decreased by 6.5% from 50.6% to 47.4% during this same period (Kochhar and Fry 2014).

Of course, the important connection between wealth and homeownership rates is not only the fact that homes are financial assets or vehicles for the middle class to transmit wealth across generations and/or can leverage in times of crisis but, equally as important, are the neighborhoods these homes are located and their assessed market values. Research shows blacks and whites indeed buy homes in very different neighborhoods and that homes in majority black neighborhoods (>10% black) do not appreciate as much as homes in overwhelmingly white neighborhoods. According to a Brookings Institution study, "Segregation Tax: The Cost of Racial Segregation to Black Homeowners," which compared home values to homeowner incomes in the nation's 100 largest metropolitan areas, researchers found minority neighborhoods' home values (including those in affluent neighborhoods) were valued at 18% less than those located in white neighborhoods. Interestingly, these comparisons controlled for age, social class, household structure, and geographic location. And while these data suggest there are no gross financial benefits for blacks, there are still benefits to homeownership. While the few black homeowners in these white neighborhoods may generally experience lower crime rates and better access to schools and municipal services, what about the emotional and psychological price paid for those who move to these predominantly white neighborhoods versus those interested in creating spaces of community with other ethnics and/or remaining in communities of color? How do race, ethnicity, and immigrant heritage complicate social mobility for the MSGCI?

LOOKING AT THE DATA: THE ADULT FIRST AND SECOND GENERATION CARIBBEAN IMMIGRANT POPULATION IN THE UNITED STATES

Race still matters today, particularly when it comes to examining rapid shifts in US demographic patterns and the contributions of Latin American and Caribbean immigrants[2] and their children to society. From demographers and community organizers to practitioners and educators who work in diverse communities, demographic statistics on ethnicity and race are used for many important purposes. These include assessing disparities in health, education, employment, and housing, enforcing civil rights protections, developing state and local programming, and deciding who might qualify for special consideration as members of underrepresented racial-ethnic groups.

According to the United States Census Bureau's Department of Commerce *Projections of the U.S. Population 2014–2060* (Colby and Ortman 2015), the country will become more racially and ethnically diverse in the coming years. Between 2014 and 2060, the population of those who identify as "Black Single Race" (a person having origins in any of the Black racial groups of Africa), on the US Census is projected to increase from 42 million to 60 million—an increase of 42%. In other words, the numbers of blacks in the United States is projected to increase from approximately 13% in 2014 to 14% in 2060. For the purpose of this book project, it is important to account for part of the black population that identifies as "Two or More Races" and of Hispanic or Latin origin, given the racial and ethnic diversity of people of Caribbean descent, born and living in the United States. While some will agree that categories such as "Two or More Races" are a catchall that is inadequately detailed, it is one place for which an individual who identifies as being of Caribbean black and East Indian descent, for example, may choose to classify him or herself. The Two or More Races population is projected to be the fastest growing, over the next 46 years with its population expected to triple in size (an increase of 226%). This group is projected to increase from 8 million to 26 million between 2014 and 2060. Its share of the total population is projected to increase from 2.5% in 2014 to 6.2% in 2060.

Because the US Census defines Hispanic or Latino origin as an ethnicity and not a race, the category is "considered to be a person belonging to any race but who classified themselves in one of the specific Spanish, Hispanic, or Latino categories" listed in the 2010 US Census. These included "Mexican," "Puerto Rican," or "Cuban" as well as "another Hispanic, Latino, or Spanish origin" whose origins are from Spanish-speaking countries of Central, South America, or the Dominican Republic. According to projections, the Hispanic/Latino population will be the third fastest growing population. This population is projected to increase from 55 million in 2014 to 119 million in 2060, an increase of 115% . In 2014, Hispanics/Latinos accounted for approximately 17% of the US population. By 2060, 29% of the United States is projected to be Hispanic/Latino—more than one-quarter of the total population.

In light of these statistics, the Census Bureau reports that 2.5% of the 54 million Hispanics/Latinos in the US also identified as black—a figure that many say is an undercount. Researchers found that, while over half of Hispanics/Latinos identified themselves as white on the last census, 36% checked "some other race" or "two or more races" (i.e., identifying as white, Peruvian, Chinese, and black). Demographic projections for year 2060 are significant in terms of the racial and ethnic diversity because the country will be majority people of color. As such, the racial and ethnic politics that will ensue will also continue to complicate discussions around race and social justice.

These projections, however, should not be surprising. Immigration reforms in 1965 (i.e., The Hart-Celler Act), which lifted national origin-country quotas and replaced them with a system based on family reunification and employment, exponentially increased the size of the racial-ethnic immigrant population in the United States that exists today. In particular, a decade after the 1965 reforms, the number of migrants from Latin America and the Caribbean (excluding Mexico) almost equaled the number of migrants arriving from Mexico and Canada combined. Demographic studies suggest that Jamaica, Haiti, Trinidad and Tobago, Cuba, the Dominican Republic, and Puerto Rico[3] are among the top countries of origin for Caribbean immigrants to the United States, and this trend continues from the 1970s through the present.

Implications of US Immigration Policy on Caribbean Immigrants' Race and Ethnic Identity Assertions

An interesting feature of the immigrant population from the Caribbean is that it is considered racially and ethnically diverse. This diversity is, indeed, a reflection of their histories of slavery and colonialism as experienced by each respective country as well as its migratory patterns of people passing through its borders. Depending on the country's colonial history, public narratives around race, racial classification systems, and meanings of "blackness," Caribbean immigrants tend to vary in their racial identity when asked in the United States.

According to the Migration Policy Institute's analysis of data from the American Community Survey (ACS)[4] in 2008–2009, black Caribbean immigrants are inclined to identify as "Black," either alone or in combination with any other race and/or ethnicity (e.g., "Black and Puerto Rican"; "Asian American and Black"). Estimates in 2009 indicated that 49% of all Caribbean immigrants identified themselves as Black or as having African ancestry. A significant portion of this population is made up of multi-racial and Indo-Caribbean people, especially in the Guyanese and Trinidadian communities, where there are people of African and Southeast Asian Caribbean descent. Over 90% of Caribbean immigrants in the United States are from several sending countries including the two largest — Jamaica and Haiti. These two countries along with Belize, the Bahamas, Barbados, and Grenada also have immigrants that tend to identify themselves as Black. On the other hand, Hispanic/Latino self-identified black immigrants accounted for only 3, 14, and 47% of immigrants from Cuba, the Dominican Republic, and Dominica, respectively. Black immigration from these three countries as well as from Puerto Rico, Panama, and Costa Rica has accelerated recently, further increasing the diversity of the Caribbean immigrant population (McCabe 2011). This increase can be attributed to migrants leaving their country of origin in search of economic opportunities not readily available or in search of additional educational opportunities in specific industries such as research. It is important to note, however, that accounting for the diversity of first and second generation immigrant populations from these countries becomes complicated as indicated by the 2010 census data.

While the likelihood of a Caribbean immigrant identifying as black and/or Hispanic/Latino varied greatly by country of origin, researchers have found that there is a tendency for some to downplay or intentionally ignore blackness in their heritage. This tendency is a result of the historical (and ongoing) application of the "one-drop" rule. According to this rule of hypo-descent, any person with "one-drop" of African blood is considered to be black regardless of the number of European or Asian or Indigenous ancestors. We still see how these definitions shape racial identification in the Caribbean, Central and South America, and in the US as evident in the self-identity trends surrounding persons of Hispanic and/or *mestizaje* background in these locations. In the US particularly, remnants of legal definitions used in immigration reforms of 1917 and 1924, which defined blackness as "having African nativity or being of African descent," helped to clarify the meaning of whiteness. As such, the US courts have denied naturalization to any person who was not a "free white person" being that of common speech and understanding, synonymous with the word "Caucasian"—as Supreme Court Justice George Sutherland argued (Johnson 2003). The application of this ruling can be seen in cases brought forth by multi-racial immigrants ("mixed race persons") and Asian immigrants classified as "not white" and therefore ineligible for naturalization (see the 1923 United States v. Bhagat Singh Thind, 261 U.S. 204 ruling in which the United States Supreme Court unanimously decided that Bhagat Singh Thind, an Indian Sikh man, was ineligible for naturalization). Therefore, an explicit rejection or downplaying of one's blackness over asserting a white identity is perceived as advantageous for ethnic groups—even for populations that arrived post-1965 immigration reforms.

Particularly citing those who identify as having Hispanic/Latino origins, as Pedro Noguera in *Anything But Black* (2003) and Nicholas Vargas' study on *Latina/o Whitening* (2014) argues, it should not be surprising that a disproportionate number of post-1965 Latinos identify as white even though they are not treated as white. Pedro Noguera contends this identity assertion connotes an aspirational ideal, recognizing and knowing that "white" is considered the prestige box on a census. On the contrary, Nicholas Vargas' research suggests that Latinos are more likely to categorize themselves as "white" if: (1) there was not a checkbox for "Hispanic/Latina/o" on a survey or the US Census, (2) the Latino respondent was lighter skinned, or (3) the Latino respondent was conservative or in an affluent socioeconomic group. Notwithstanding the arguments presented on Latino racial identities and whether Latinos are actively assuming characteristics of whites and white culture, such self-identification points to the unfortunate reality of colorism that exists in the Caribbean and in the US.

To be clear, the census categories in many of these Caribbean countries define race (i.e., white and black) very differently than the United States. And while these countries' legacies of colonialism still privileges whiteness/lighter skin as being of a higher social and/or economic class, new immigrants both take with them and are socialized during the migration process to maintain these identifications even though they are from a majority black/brown societies. Scholars have found that new immigrants who continue to claim whiteness also do so because of the belief that "being white"/ mixed will provide better access to resources and opportunities. In fact, research has shown that blacks from the Caribbean and specifically those who are darker-skinned black Latinos are more likely to face discrimination (even from other Hispanics) when it comes to attaining better jobs and positions. Other studies, including those by Ruben Rumbaut and Nicholas Vargas, found if a lighter-skinned Latino is perceived as white and/or ambiguously racial, he or she has more opportunities to gain socioeconomic status. Therefore, the tendency for some to distance themselves from or intentionally downplay their blackness contributes to the invisibility of African descendant Caribbean people in the United States.[5]

For those who may self-identify as Afro-Latino (or as Latino with African roots), the popular conception of who is Latino in the United States—physically, culturally, racially perceived as "being nonwhite"—does not often correlate to the reality they see around them. There are efforts, however, among the first generation and more so among the second generation Caribbean population to embrace their African heritage as part of their Caribbean and Latino identity in an effort to reject the "black or Hispanic" dichotomy that has become pervasive in the last 20 years. These groups are engaged in identity movements, located in communities across Columbia, Peru, Belize, Bolivia, Costa Rica, Cuba, the Dominican Republic, and Puerto Rico as well as in the United States. In fact, some of these countries' governments have recently and officially acknowledged African cultural influence and political contributions of this population. For instance, on December 23, 2013 the United Nations General Assembly adopted resolution 68/237 that proclaimed this is the International Decade of People of African Descent (2015–2024).[6] This proclamation recognizes the need to promote and protect the full human rights (economic, social, cultural, civil, and political) and equal participation in aspects of society for over 200 million people of African descent across the Americas. According to Ban Ki-Moon, the U.N Secretary

General, "we must remember that people of African descent are among the most affected by racism. Too often, they face denial of basic rights such as access to quality health services and education." In many ways, these public acknowledgements are an important step toward recognizing the deep roots of race and colorism in society as impacting social relations and essentially, what it means to be "Black and proud" post-Civil Rights.

Implications of "Black" Racial Identity Versus "Anything but Black" Caribbean Ethnic Identity: Intragroup Tensions as Fact or Fiction?

As discussed, American immigration scholars have studied the impact of large-scale immigration to the US, including its effect on the native-born population and their common sentiment that immigrants groups, particularly first generation Asian, Latin American, and Caribbean immigrants, and their American-born children threaten their economic wellbeing and way of life (Card 2001; Crowder et al. 2011; Gans 1979; Gordon 1964; Harris 1999; Iceland 2009; Kasinitz 1992; Kim 2010; Portes and Rumbaut 2006; Waters 1999; Waters et al. 2007). When some of these scholars primarily focused on African American and black immigrant (i.e., African, Latin American, and Caribbean) relations to speculate why these nonwhite immigrants would prefer to downplay their "black heritage," some researchers characterized these relations as hostile and competitive when it comes to housing options, jobs, business and entrepreneurship, and political influence.

On the one hand, this finding is not a far-fetched conclusion; in fact, in most post-industrial and capitalist societies, whenever there are high levels of unemployment and underemployment for its native-born population, the economic situation leads some to promote the myth that new immigrants are taking job opportunities away from the native-born population. In these circumstances, shifts in labor-force dynamics not only lead to competition and hostile interactions between native and foreign-born groups but also countries tend to develop harsh legislative proposals that target their new immigrants. Upon close inspection, however, when it comes to economic opportunities most immigrant and native-born workers do not compete with each other for the same jobs. In fact, many recent US immigrants (particularly those from Central and South America and the Caribbean) tend to compete for and have access to different types of low-skills jobs, which often do not require a high school diploma, GED,[7] and technical skills, or require significant interaction with English-language speakers in major public settings (see Peri 2011). In the case of African Americans and black immigrant groups who may reside in the same or nearby resource-poor or disenfranchised community spaces where unemployment or underemployment is one of several factors that impact well-being, then the myth of the immigrant stealing jobs predominates.

On the other hand, there is also recent research on African American and black immigrant relationships that provides a more contextual, historical account of this interaction in order to demonstrate the complexity of contemporary black intragroup interactions goes beyond mere competition (Bryce-Laporte 1972; Foner 2001; Lorick-Wilmot 2010; Nunnally 2010; Smith 2014; Telles et al. 2011; Vickerman 1999; Waters 1999). I contend it is the complexity of this history of intragroup interactions that influences both MSGCIs' identity assertions and their current conceptions of black community and their participation within it.

This complex history stems back to the first half of the twentieth-century when there was a cohort of voluntary migrants from the Caribbean to the United States. Though US immigration policies such as the National Origin Acts of 1921 and 1924 set restrictive quotas that barred certain racial and ethnic groups from entering its borders, Caribbean immigrants were either subjected to immigration restrictions set by imperial European powers who presided over their countries of origin or encountered political instability and economic conditions in their home countries that constrained their migration to the US, Canada, and Europe in vast numbers. The Caribbean people who successfully immigrated to the US at this time were not only more literate and skilled than their counterparts in their home countries but also were more educated and skilled than the northern European immigrants who entered the country during this time and the extant native-born white population living in the United States. It was this wave of Caribbean immigrants that laid the groundwork for the institutional, social, and political infrastructure of black life in major metropolitan cities along the eastern seaboard, such as New York City, and elsewhere in the nation (Treitler 2013).

Scholars have estimated that between the 1910s and 1930s, almost one third of black professionals (e.g., doctors, dentists, lawyers, writers, artists, and performers) and business people in these major metropolitan cities were either first generation Caribbean immigrants and/or the children of Caribbean immigrants (Foner 2001; Kasinitz 1992; Smith 2014). It is a little known fact that a significant number of the black intellectuals, performers, politicians, and civil rights activists, and contributors to the

Harlem Renaissance and the New Negro Movement of this period were either Caribbean immigrants or second generation Caribbean themselves: James Weldon Johnson, Marcus Garvey, Claude McKay, Eric Derwent Walrond, Wilfred Adolphus Domingo, Arturo Alfonso Schomburg, Hurbert Henry Harrison, Joel Augustus Rogers, William Stanley Braithwaite, Nella Larsen, Cyril Valintine Briggs, and Gladys Bentley, to name a few. But at the time, societal conditions were such that these generations of immigrants were unable to claim a distinct ethno-racial identity in the way we see today. Instead, their racialization as having a shared master status of being "Negro" encouraged African Americans and first and second generation Caribbean immigrants to mobilize and engage in joint activism and cultural production, so as to enhance their collective consciousness and build community to transform how they were perceived and treated by whites (Treitler 2013).

Underscoring this intragroup interaction and solidarity, is the social and political context of the time. Between the late 1870s and the 1890s, the period after slavery and through Reconstruction came to a dramatic halt with great violence and government policy that sanctioned a new period of racial terror and discrimination for the African descended: the era of [white] Redemption and Jim Crow segregation in the rural south. The recent memory of slavery and subjugation was quite vivid for many native-born blacks that the newly instituted system of apartheid via Jim Crow segregation, which sought to strip them of their rights as human beings and as citizens, was one that forged a collective consciousness and prompted the social and political act of black migration to the north—the Great Migration, 1905–1970 (Wilkerson 2010).

The emigration of both native and foreign-born blacks to urban spaces such as New York City, Chicago, and Miami in search of a better life and opportunity from which they came, brought together the opportunity for building a broader conceptualization of a black identity and construction of community. Implicit in this conceptualization and construction of a black collective identity, "is a definition of ideology shaped by the individuals themselves as they become aware of commonalities, establish interpretive frameworks that emphasize these commonalities, and build communities or social networks to reinforce commonalities" (Valocchi 2001:448). Their linked fates due to their black group membership and shared experiences with persistent racism and discrimination contributed to amicable social relations and political coalitions as seen in the Negro Movement, NAACP (the National Association for the Advancement of

Colored People) and other efforts between the 1920s and 1950s. In effect, these coalitions promoted a sense of "blackness" or black racial pride, expression, economic independence, and progressive politics.

At the same time, sharing an ascribed black master status and linked fate does not automatically mean that intragroup solidarity is not without conflict and tension. For instance, the political (and more often) personal debate between African American and Caribbean thinkers and activists such as W.E.B. Du Bois and Marcus Garvey point to the divergent perspectives that existed at the time on black self-sufficiency versus integration with whites when it comes to approaching black/Pan-African liberation and democracy. Such debates elucidated the divide not only between native and foreign-born blacks but also between the working poor and rising middle class blacks; and the darker skinned, former field hands versus the lighter-skinned, college-educated "Talented Tenth." But for the most part, individual opinions and perspectives took a back seat to considerations that benefit the black race (Dawson 1995; Mangum 2008). An important consideration for both native and foreign-born blacks was the desire for social justice that served as a means for overcoming racial discrimination.

By the mid-1960s, however, collaborative activities and political interest between Caribbean descendants and African Americans underwent significant changes. Moore (1984) attributes this to political shifts brought about by the Civil Rights movement; others such as Basch (1992) and Bryce-Laporte (1972) suggest that both the Civil Rights movement and massive post-1965 Caribbean immigration softened US racial barriers and attitudes which resulted in more recent Caribbean immigrants and their children to emphasize ethnic differences. In many ways, the increase in racial-ethnic immigrant diversity at this time transformed the US black narrative and the collective consciousness that we see today. Smith (2014:61) suggest that theories of structural racism help to explain the rise in intragroup tensions by the mid-twentieth century by arguing "minority groups encounter[ed] one another within a larger structure marked by white racial dominance and racial power, and they [needed to] negotiate this structure, which [led] them to perpetuate and maintain the hierarchy of a racialized social system" that for generations African Americans and Caribbean immigrants were collectively fighting against.

Whether it was and remains to be intentional or unintentional, the reification and promotion of negative racial-ethnic stereotypes about native and foreign-born blacks that exists today not only perpetuates animosity and perceived competition between the two groups but also maintains white hegemony. There is one popular stereotype of Caribbean immigrants and their children that suggests they see themselves as hard-working, ambitious, conscious about being black persons but do not share similar political perspectives or approaches as African Americans in the plight for black freedom and equality (see Waters 1999). Interestingly, this stereotype is reminiscent to the sentiments expressed during the W.E.B. Du Bois-Marcus Garvey debate from seven decades ago. As will be revealed, the MSGCIs will describe witnessing for themselves the social distancing strategies some Caribbean immigrants and their children employed in order to avoid being placed at the bottom of the racial hierarchy, which labels African Americans as lazy, poor, and having a lax attitude and criminal mentality. The MSGCIs, however, will share their realization that social distancing strategies dismantle black solidarity, fuel co-ethnic competition, and reinforce white ethnic theories of progress that have served to relegate native-born blacks to the bottom of the social and economic hierarchy. Their realization largely stems from their triple identity consciousness.

Who Are the Second Generation Caribbean Immigrants?
General Demographic Data

On June 5, 2006, President George W. Bush signed a proclamation stating June will be annually recognized as national Caribbean American Heritage Month to celebrate the contributions of Caribbean Americans (both naturalized and US citizens by birth) in the United States. It is true that, as with many racial-ethnic groups in US history, Caribbean Americans have also shaped every aspect of our society—from the arts, entertainment, sports, and sciences, to business, politics, military, and government. There are many influential second generation Caribbean immigrants in the United States people may already know of, including but not limited to Eric Holder, the first black US Attorney General; James Weldon Johnson, the writer of the Black National Anthem; Dr. Patricia Bath, inventor of Laserphaco Probe for cataract treatment and the first black doctor to complete a residency in ophthalmology; Shirley Chisholm, the first black Congresswoman and first black female candidate for President; Colin Powell, the first black Secretary of State; Sir Sidney Poitier, the first black actor to receive the Academy Award for best actor in a leading role; Harry Belafonte, a musician, actor, and civil rights activist; and Roberto Clemente, the first Puerto Rican inducted into the Baseball Hall of Fame—just to name a few. Like the first generation of Caribbean immigrants that came before them, their "offspring" are part of a great national tradition of "descendants of hopeful, striving people who journeyed to our lands in search of a better life…[who] were drawn by a belief in the power of opportunity, a belief that through hard work and sacrifice, they could provide their children with chances they had never known" and have contributed to every aspect of our society (The White House, President Barack H. Obama's 2014 Presidential Proclamation).

Recognizing the positive contributions of first generation Caribbean immigrants and their children is monumental by any government—not only because the legacy of blackness is often denigrated and pathologized as opposed to praised but the sheer contributing number of this population to the US general population is undeniable. Following the immigration reforms of 1965, the number of Caribbean-born in the United States more than tripled from 1960 to 1970, but increased 86% from 1970 to 1980, 54% from 1980 to 1990, 52% from 1990 to 2000, and just 17% from 2000 to 2009. As of 2010, there were 6 million self-identified adult (age >18) members of the Caribbean diaspora residing in the United States. In particular, approximately 3.5 million first generation Caribbean immigrants reside in the United States, accounting for approximately 10% of the country's 38 million immigrants. About 69% of all first generation Caribbean immigrants reside in the metropolitan areas of Miami and Fort Lauderdale in Florida and in the greater New York/New Jersey/Pennsylvania metropolitan areas. There are a notable number of Caribbean immigrants residing in the greater Boston Massachusetts area (approximately 3%) as well as in the greater Hartford, Connecticut area. Of course, these locales are not surprising; due to economic opportunities that influence migrant patterns, the sharing of information via migrant networks and the presence of semi- and more established ethnic enclaves, newcomers will venture to such cities.

Inexplicably, detailed statistics on second generation Caribbean immigrants are a little harder to capture as several demographic and census data center statistics do not collect clear data on this segment of the population as opposed to other second generation immigrants of color (i.e., Asian Americans and some Hispanic/Latino groups). An obvious explanation could be based on the fact that previous data collections relied on stratified samples whose categories for American-born children of Caribbean immigrants may be subsumed under the larger "black and or African American" racial category.

Notwithstanding, researchers are able to approximate that 41% of the 6 million self-identified adult members of the Caribbean diaspora residing in the United States are native-born or US citizens at birth. For the purpose of this book, I will consider the cohort of MSGCIs whose parents migrated to the United States shortly after 1965 immigration reforms. Second generation immigrant births are typically a demographic echo of immigration and the high fertility among first generation immigrants. In this case, their parents' generation had the greatest influx of Caribbean immigrants in the United States and is presumably responsible for the continued US population growth during the latter half of the twentieth century.

From the limited accounting of MSGCI statistics from the Pew Research Center 2013 report and the 2011–2013 US Census Bureau's American Community Survey 3-year estimates are able to generalize certain findings:

- Education: the second generation has more education, reflecting the higher educational attainment in the US compared with the home countries of many immigrants. A greater percentage of second generation immigrants have obtained a level of education beyond a high school diploma and a bachelors' degree. Among second generation black immigrants, (40%) have at least a college degree and only 5% have not completed high school.
- Income: the second generations' higher education levels help explain why they have higher household incomes and a lower share in poverty than first generation immigrants. Second generation immigrants are more likely to achieve higher earnings—$42,000 and above in comparison to first generation immigrants.
- Occupation: compared with foreign-born adults, the second generation is more likely to be in white-collar jobs such as management or office services. They are less likely to be in service, construction, transportation, or maintenance occupations.
- Marital Status: The second generation includes nearly equal shares of adults who are married (40%) and never married (42%), with a smaller share who are separated, widowed, or divorced (18%). The married share is lower than for foreign-born adults (63%) and for all adults (54%). The never-married share is higher than for foreign-born adults (22%) and all adults (28%).
- Homeownership: second generation adults are more likely to own their homes than are immigrant adults and are about as likely as the

overall population to be homeowners. This pattern holds for all age groups. In 2012, the homeownership rate for second generation householders was 64%, compared with 51% for immigrant house-holders and 65% for all householders.

To dig a bit deeper, there are factors, albeit limited, through which scholars attempt to provide a detailed snapshot of who this generation is. Looking specifically to education and educational selectivity as a predictor of life outcomes for migrants' children's social mobility, Caribbean immigration to the United States involved a significant degree of educational selectivity (McCabe 2011; see works by Feliciano 2005; Takenaka and Pren 2010). Caribbean immigrants that chose to migrate to the United States between late the 1960s and late 1970s had significant differences in their educational characteristics compared to those who chose to remain in their countries of origin. Researchers found this especially true for immigrants from English-speaking Caribbean countries. For example, while Jamaican and Trinidadian immigrants were generally more highly educated than their origin-country counterparts, the opposite was true for immigrants from the Dominican Republic.

Moreover, immigrants from English-speaking Caribbean countries arriving during this period were more likely to be highly educated and employed in white-collar occupations than their counterparts who arrived in earlier decades. As the research also suggests, citing specifically the work of Cynthia Feliciano (2005:841), as immigrants' educational selectivity increases, the college attainment of the second generation also increases. In other words, the observable differences in immigrant groups' class positions prior to migration strongly contributes to producing ethnic disparities in educational outcomes among the second generation in the United States. Feliciano's research challenges explanations for ethnic group differences in educational success that favor cultural influences and instead focuses on the social class status of immigrant parent generations both pre- and post migration as influencing their American-born children. This finding is important to gaining insight and understanding the role education plays as a vehicle of social mobility for the MSGCI.

When it comes to examining experiences of the MSGCI, scholars have found exploring political participation among people of color useful in gaining insight on socio-economic status, educational attainment, and other forms of class-conscious behaviors. Mauricia John, in her 2014 study on race, class, and naturalization of Afro-Caribbean immigrants, found the higher the levels of education (and English language acquisition) and higher socio-economic status for first generation Caribbean immigrant parents could lead to an increase in voter registration for their American-born children. She argues that Caribbean immigrants with more economic and social resources are more likely to be actively involved in politics, value and recognize the benefits of civic participation and political incorporation and influence their children to do so.

To extend Mauricia John's analysis, her findings indeed suggest a second generation Caribbean immigrant's family economic situation while growing up, including family structure (e.g., parents' marital status, living with grandparents and/or extended family), homeownership, parents' engagement in political issues, parent(s)' occupational prestige, and/or their mother's[8] employment, would also positively affect voter registration patterns of their generation. This is not to say the second generation Caribbean immigrant's own education, economics, and political ideologies does not influence his or her own civic participation, immigrant incorporation, and subsequent upward social mobility. On the contrary, assimilation theories that focus on immigrant parent and second generation child relationships also suggest that the immigrant parents' socio-economic status are important factors that affect the second generation immigrant's integration into society (see the work of Alejandro Portes and Ruben Rumbaut 2001).

While more specific census data focusing on second generation Caribbean immigrants, and particularly those who identify as black are sparse, researchers Mary C Waters, Philip Kasinitz, and John Mollenkopf in their 2009 book, *Inheriting the City: The Children of Immigrants Come of Age*, found that the second generation adults they interviewed (18–34 years olds) and including those who identified as black (whether of West Indian ancestry or Latina/o) were overwhelmingly fluent in English; were less occupationally segregated than their parents; lived longer with their parents than native-born Americans; worked in white-collar clerical or service jobs in retail and major financial services; and most had achieved "real, if modest, progress over their parents' generation." For Waters, Kasinitz, and Mollenkopf, this second generation is able to have such progress because it can take advantage of civil rights programs, including affirmative action policies, in applying to universities and for jobs in ways the previous generation may not have been as successful or knowledgeable about. At first glance, it would seem the notion of the American Dream is not elusive, given the second generation's slight upward mobility. The authors' findings, however, also point to the persistent impact race, race discrimination, colorism, and economic exclusion has on the second generation and particularly individuals who self identify or are identified as black as in the case of English speaking Caribbean Americans and Dominican Americans.

By observation, contemporary immigration literature often focuses on assimilation, educational outcomes, and ecological factors as impacting first generation immigrants and their subsequent generations' mobility. The literature points to the ways the first generation navigates geographic and linguistic borders, and political and cultural boundaries, which inform their child rearing perspectives and practices and the kinds of opportunities they are able to provide to their US born children. Hence, the educational, economic, political, and socio-cultural factors of the first generation—undoubtedly—shape the race, class, and gender experiences of the second generation too—as the data above revealed briefly. With the data presented thus far, however, it is important not to see the second generation Caribbean immigrant cohort as homogenous either.

HOW RACE IMPACTS THE LIVES OF BLACK, MIDDLE CLASS SECOND GENERATION CARIBBEAN IMMIGRANTS: THE IMPORTANCE OF INTERSECTIONALITY

Fully engaging in a candid discussion on the impact of race in the lives of MSGCI requires resisting the advancement of white supremacist ideas about black people (both native and foreign-born). In particular, we must attend to the divisive frameworks that couch the discussion: achievements, moral, and cultural deficiencies that either lump them into one homogeneous group or emphasize historical and cultural particularities that reinforce the notion of "model minority" success. This kind of anti-black racism or racial resentment ideology asserts the American Dream works for all and especially for blacks if they assume model minority status by "becoming white" (adopting western European cultural and behavioral values) in order to succeed (see Eduardo Bonilla-Silva's *Racism Without Racists*; Anani Dzidzienyo and Suzanne Oboler's *Neither Enemies nor Friends: Latinos, Blacks, Afro-Latinos*). Anti-black racism is then a true outgrowth of the notion of American meritocracy: individualism, hard work, and equality of treatment. Yet, anti-black racism also triggers subtle and insidious racial discourses for black immigrants and their children, including Caribbean immigrant generations. Anti-black discourses suggest in order to have "successful" incorporation into American society black immigrants and their children must rely on ethnic identification as opposed to assimilation, because the latter implies inherent downward social and cultural mobility due to their "black skin." We have seen these perspectives showcased in scores of recent research on Black migration in the United States that examine ethnic identity formation as opposed to racial identities and the ways these immigrants (and their children) negotiate between their black racial identities and choose to assert a "West Indian" identity and/or fully reject any affiliation with African American identities.

Indeed race, as a contextual variable and signifier of social status, is relevant to the second generation Caribbean immigrant as it complicates the social mobility of all people of color in the United States. Anti-black racism is "very much alive and well" when it comes to the persistence of racial and ethnic discrimination, job decentralization and split labor markets, and de facto residential segregation in major metropolitan areas. As such, the second generation Caribbeans' exposure to these affects indeed influences their attitudes, behaviors, negotiations, and practices, and even the extent to which they are numerically counted, civically engaged, and participate in mainstream culture despite their long history of contributions to American society.

Rather, the candid discussion requires an unpacking of ideologies of race and interrogating the intersectional nature skin color, immigrant status, ethnicity, gender, sexuality, and class factors that inform the differential expectations, outcomes, and complexities of identity formation and lived experiences for MSGCIs who are racialized and/or self-identified as black. Doing so pulls the conversation away from the analytical "go-to" culture of poverty explanation or black inferiority lens when looking at the middle class segment of this population and instead looks to how oppressive power structures interact with this generation and their process of meaning making and response to these structures. Central to the intersectionality paradigm (see the works of Kimberle Crenshaw and Patricia Hill Collins) is the need to focus on the unique ways gender, immigrant, class, race, and ethnic factors interact and produce particular sets of experiences and that looking at race alone cannot make visible, the interlocking aspects of power and supremacy in the lives of people of color in the United States as well as those who have unconsciously invested in systems of oppression. Patricia Hill Collins in *Black Feminist Thought* (2000) said it best when she argued:

Although most individuals have little difficulty identifying their own victim-ization within some major system of oppression–whether it be by race, social class, religion, physical ability, sexual orientation, ethnicity, age or gender–they typically fail to see how their thoughts and actions uphold someone else's subordination ... Oppression is filled with such contradictions because these approaches fail to recognize that a matrix of domination contains few pure victims or oppressors. Each individual derives varying amounts of pen-alty and privilege from the multiple systems of oppression, which frame everyone's lives.

Therefore, listening to the stories of this population is an important way to understand and unpack the ideologies of race and its intersectional fac-tors, which will reveal new ways of knowing how this population defines their own reality. In the next chapter, I begin to share MSGCIs' stories and the nuanced complexities of their identity assertions as it relates to race, ethnicity, colorism, gender, and sexuality and class.

NOTES

1. UCLA-Civil Right Project's research, whose projects are often funded and in collaboration with private universities, US Department of Education, US Department of Housing and Urban Development, and the White House Council on Women and Girls. These data makes the correlation between high poverty, crime, unemployment, and housing segregation and apartheid schools and its low expectations for children of color, including the Caribbean immigrant children that attend them.
2. According to the US Census Bureau's American Community Survey 2011 Brief 2011, the term Latin America and the Caribbean includes all countries in Central and South America and the Caribbean. Often *Latin America* or *Latin American* is used as a catchall term to refer to the countries and people from these areas, regardless of racial, ethnic, religious, and linguistic distinctions (English, Spanish, French, Portuguese, and Dutch).
3. According to the US Census Bureau definitions, people born in Puerto Rico and the US Virgin Islands are considered native-born to the United States although distinctions are made between those who are born on the islands versus the mainland United States.
4. Current Population Survey Series and its Supplements, which are spon-sored by both the US Census Bureau and the US Bureau of Labor Statistics, and the Integrated Public Use Microdata Series (IPUMS), which collects and distributes US census data, are two sources of census data center statis-tics that captures a range of demographic data, including immigration and

immigrant generation, fertility, employment, and occupational mobility. The Pew Research Center also pulls data from these same census data sources and supplements.

5. I am reminded of an important quote from Ruben Rumbaut: "If 'race' was an innate, permanent trait of individuals, no such variability would obtain. Instead, these data exemplify how 'race' is constructed socially and historically—and spatially as well." See Ruben Rumbaut's (2009:28). Pigments of Our Imagination: On the Racialization and Racial Identities of 'Hispanics' and 'Latinos.'

6. U.N.'s International Decade for the African Descendant (2015–2024): http://www.un.org/en/events/africandescentdecade/index.shtml

7. GED, also known as a test for general education development, is offered to students who do not complete high school or are unable to meet requirements toward earning a high school diploma.

8. Because of gender roles and division of labor practices of women and their relegation to caring for children and family, women's employment and educational level are often factors used to predict children and family outcomes.

BIBLIOGRAPHY

Basch, L. (1992). The Politics of Caribbeanization: Vincentians and Grenadians in New York. In C. Sutton & E. M. Chaney (Eds.), *Caribbean Life in New York City* (pp. 147–166). New York: Center of Migration Studies.

Brown, A. L., & Donnor, J. K. (2011). The Education of Black Males in a 'Post-racial' World. *Race, Ethnicity, and Education, 14*, 1–6.

Bryce-Laporte, R. (1972). Black Immigrants: The Experience of Invisibility and Inequality. *Journal of Black Studies, 3*, 20–56.

Card, D. (2001). Immigrant Inflows, Native Outflows, and the Local Labor Market Impacts of Higher Immigration. *Journal of Labor Economics, 19*, 22–64.

Colby, S. L., & Ortman, J. M. (2015). *Projections of the Size and Composition of the U.S. Population: 2014 to 2060* (Current Population Reports, No. P25-1143). Washington, DC: U.S. Census Bureau. Retrieved from https://www.census.gov/content/dam/Census/library/publications/2015/demo/p25-1143.pdf

Collins, P. H. (2000). *Black Feminist Thought: Knowledge, Consciousness and the Politics of Empowerment* (2nd ed.). New York/London: Routledge.

Crowder, K., Hall, M., & Tolnay, S. (2011). Neighborhood Immigration and Native Out Migration. *American Sociological Review, 76*(1), 25–47.

Crowley, M. (2008). Post-racial: Even White Supremacists Don't Hate Obama. *The New Republic, 238*(4), 7–8.

Dawson, M. C. (1995). *Behind the Mule: Race and Class in African American Politics*. Princeton: Princeton University Press.

Feagin, J. R. (2006). *Systemic Racism: A Theory of Oppression*. Abingdon: Routledge.

Feliciano, C. (2005). Does Selective Migration Matter? Explaining Ethnic Disparities in Educational Attainment among Immigrants' Children. *International Migration Review, 39*(4), 841–871.

Foner, N. (2001). *Islands in the City: West Indian Migration to New York*. Berkeley: University of California Press.

Gans, H. J. (1979). Symbolic Ethnicity: The Future of Ethnic Groups and Cultures in America. *Ethnic and Racial Studies, 2*, 1–20.

Givhan, R. (2008, March 16). Edging (at Times Clumsily) Toward a Post-racial America. *The Washington Post*, M101. http://www.washingtonpost.com/wp-dyn/content/article/2008/03/14/AR2008031401072.html

Gordon, M. (1964). *Assimilation in American Life: The Role of Race, Religion and National Origins*. New York: Oxford University Press.

Harris, D. R. (1999). 'Property Values Drop When Blacks Move in Because...': Racial and Socioeconomic Determinants of Neighborhood Desirability. *American Sociological Review, 64*, 461–479.

Iceland, J. (2009). *Where We Live Now: Immigration and Race in the U.S.* Berkeley: University of California Press.

Iweala, U. (2008, January 23). Racism Still Matters. *Los Angeles Times*. http://articles.latimes.com/2008/jan/23/opinion/oe-iweala23

Johnson, K. (2003). *Mixed Race America and the Law: A Reader*. New York: New York University Press.

Kasinitz, P. (1992). *Caribbean New York: Black Immigrants and the Politics of Race*. Ithaca: Cornell University Press.

Kim, Nadia Y. (2010). "Campaigning for Obama and the politics of race: The case of California, Texas and beyond." In Donald Cunnigen and Marino A. Bruce (eds.). Race in the Age of Obama (Research in Race and Ethnic Relations), Vol 16: 247–266.

Kochhar, R., & Fry, R. (2014, December 12). *Wealth Inequality Has Widened Along Racial, Ethnic Lines Since End of Great Recession*. Retrieved January 3, 2015, from Pew Research Center's Fact Tank: News In the Numbers: http://www.pewresearch.org/fact-tank/2014/12/12/racial-wealth-gaps-great-recession/

Lorick-Wilmot, Y. (2010). *Creating Black Caribbean Ethnic Identity, Book Series, The New Americans: Recent Immigrant and American Society ed*. El Paso: LFB Scholarly Publishing.

Mangum, M. (2008). Testing Competing Explanations of Black Opinions on Affirmative Action. *Policy Studies Journal, 36*(3), 347–366.

McCabe, K. (2011, April 7). *Caribbean Immigrants in the United States*. Retrieved November 9, 2014, from Migration Policy Institute: http://store.migrationinformation.org/article/caribbean-immigrants-united-states

Moore, C. (1984, August 28). The Caribbean Community and the Quest for Political Power. *Caribbean News*, p. 13.

Noguera, P. (2003). Anything but Black: Bringing Politics Back to the Study of Race. In P. C. Hintzen & J. M. Rahier (Eds.), *Problematizing Blackness: Self Ethnographies by Black Immigrants to the United States* (pp. 193–200). New York: Routledge.

Nunnally, S. C. (2010). Linking Blackness or Ethnic Othering? African Americans' Diasporic Linked Fate with West Indian and African Peoples in the U.S. *Du Bois Review, 7*(2), 335–355.

Peri, G. (2011). *The Impact of Immigration on Native Poverty through Labor Market Competition*. Davis: Center for Poverty Research, University of California.

Portes, A., & Rumbaut, R. (2001). *Legacies: The Story of the Immigrant Second Generation*. Berkeley: University of California Press.

Portes, A., & Rumbaut, R. (2006). *Immigrant America: A Portrait* (3rd ed.). Berkeley: University of California Press.

Rumbaut, R. (2009). Pigments of Our Imagination: On Racialization and Racial Identities of 'Hispanics' and 'Latinos'. In J. A. Cobas, J. Duany, & J. R. Feagin (Eds.), *How the U.S. Racializes Latinos: White Hegemony and Its Consequences* (pp. 15–36). St. Paul: Paradigm Publishing.

Shapiro, T., Meschede, T., & Osoro, S. (2013). *The Roots of the Widening Racial Wealth Gap: Explaining the Black-White Economic Divide*. Waltham: Brandeis University, Institute on Assets and Social Policy.

Smith, C. W. (2014). *Black Mosaic: The Politics of Black Pan-Ethnic Diversity*. New York: New York University Press.

Takenaka, A., & Pren, K. A. (2010). Determinants of Emigration: Comparing Migrants' Selectivity from Peru and Mexico. *The ANNALS of the American Academy of Political and Social Science, 630*(1), 178–193.

Telles, E., Sawyer, M., & Rivera-Salgado, G. (2011). *Just Neighborhoods: Research on African American and Latino Relations in the United States*. New York: Russell Sage Foundation.

Terry, D. (2004, October 24). The Skin Game: Do White Voters Like Barack Obama Because 'He's Not Really Black? *Chicago Tribune*. http://articles.chicagotribune.com/2004-10-24/features/0410240530_1_white-woman-barack-obama-biracial

Treitler, V. B. (2013). *The Ethnic Project: Transforming Racial Fiction into Ethnic Factions*. Stanford: Stanford University Press.

US Department of Justice. (2015). *Investigation of the Ferguson Police Department*. Civil Rights Division. Washington DC: US Department of Justice.

US Department of Justice. (2017). *Justice Department Finds a Pattern of Civil Rights Violations by the Chicago Police Department* (Press Release). Retrived from https://www.justice.gov/opa/pr/justice-department-announcesfindings-investigation-chicago-police-department

Valocchi, S. (2001). Individual Identities, Collective Identities and Organizational Structure. *Sociological Perspectives, 44*(4), 445–467.

Vargas, N. (2014). Latina/o Whitening: Which Latinas/os Self-Classify as White and Report Being Perceived as White by Other Americans. *Dubois Review: Social Science Research on Race, 12*(1).

Vickerman, M. (1999). *Crosscurrents: West Indian Immigrants and Race.* Oxford: Oxford University Press.

Waters, M. C. (1999). *Black Identities: West Indian Immigrant Dreams and American Realities.* New York: Russell Sage Foundation.

Waters, M. C., Ueda, R., & Marrow, H. (2007). *The New Americans: A Guide to Immigration Since 1965.* Cambridge, MA: Harvard University Press.

Wilkerson, I. (2010). *The Warmth of Other Suns: The Epic Story of America's Great Migration.* New York: Vintage Books/ Random House.

Williams, D., Haile, R., Gonzalez, H. M., Neighbors, H., Baser, R., & Jackson, J. S. (2007). The Mental Health of Caribbean Immigrants: Results from the National Survey of American Life. *American Journal of Public Health, 97*(1), 52–59.

CHAPTER 4

Blackness as Experience

*Identities are the names we give to the different ways we are positioned
by, and position ourselves within, the narrative of the past.*

—*Stuart Hall in "Cultural Identity and Diaspora" (1990:435)*

I came of age during the 1980s when there was a rapid convergence
between mass media and social commentary on the contemporary experiences of Black America. This is not to say there were no other times when
television, movies, music, and other mediums within popular culture
reflected an aspect of black culture. But if I needed to pinpoint a specific
period in time, it was the 1980s when my own black consciousness was
first awakened.

Imagine this awakening against the backdrop of "Reaganomics" and
living in New York City at the height of the crack-cocaine epidemic with
its high crime, extreme poverty, and *"Just say no"* slogans on billboards.
This was during the time when anti-drug campaign rhetoric helped to
color the complexion of crime as illustrated in vivid anecdotes, personal-
ized case studies, and journalistic accounts from Peter Jennings and Ted
Koppel. I was exposed to images of blackness that did not differ much
from the evening news. In the early 1980s, I had the opportunity to watch
what was considered at the time to be "wholesome family" television

© The Author(s) 2018
Y.S. Lorick-Wilmot, *Stories of Identity among Black,
Middle Class, Second Generation Caribbeans,*
DOI 10.1007/978-3-319-62208-8_4

shows with social messaging on life in the urban ghetto like *Fat Albert and the Cosby Kids, Sanford and Son, Good Times,* and *What's Happening!!* when they aired in broadcast syndication. In this regard, many of these shows served as a precursor to contemporary African American sitcoms, and their writers and producers wrote their characters in ways that reinforced racist stereotypes of black youth and their families to general audiences.

From the mid-1980s through the early 1990s, I also experienced the shift in popular culture that coincided with a celebration of Afrocentrism as seen in the replication of the silhouette of Queen Nefertiti on t-shirts and the edification of the African black medallion in early hip-hop videos. Anyone with a color analog television with a rabbit ear antenna and turn dial on the front panel also witnessed the surge of diverse, more positive notions of blackness as experienced by the characters depicted on prime-time television shows such as *The Jeffersons, Different Strokes, The Cosby Show,* and *A Different World* each week. Of course I would be remiss not to include the movies that were, dare I say, transformative to both my own black identity formation and the general audience's understanding of the "Black American experience": Julie Nash's *Daughters of the Dust,* Alice Walker's Pulitzer Prize-winning novel-turned film *The Color Purple,* John Landis' all-star comedic film *Coming to America* starring Eddie Murphy, and Spike Lee's culturally significant films such as *School Daze, Do the Right Thing* and impressive film biography, *Malcolm X,* all starring talented black and Latino actors such as Denzel Washington, Ossie Davis, Ruby Dee, Giancarlo Esposito, Rosie Perez, and Delroy Lindo.

Perhaps it was naïve of me to think back then that from these shows and movies I gained insight into the lives of black people in America that did not necessarily have a Caribbean immigrant background like myself. I knew from their storylines that "to be black" is not a monolithic experience. Yet, I also found the interesting similarities between my generation of children of immigrants and the characters I watched on the small and big screens. These characters had parents and grandparents that were also a part of a migrant stream of people—the Great Migration of southern blacks (1916–1970) who journeyed to the north and mid-western United States in search of improved living conditions and economic opportunities for their future generations. The types of obstacles they and their children faced when it came to racism, intra- and interracial race relations as they settled into their new homes and community lives were the basis of some of these storylines.

Some of these television programs and movies (unfortunately not all), as I reflect on them now, were pushing the public discourse and challenging the American consciousness about race, race relations, and more specifically, what it means to be black in America. Putting mass media into sociopolitical context, the United States still experienced major financial crisis, with cuts to several federal programs and aid to the poor and the historically disenfranchised (including blacks) throughout the 1980s. At the time, the United States Supreme Court ruled minority quotas were unconstitutional while supporting affirmative action policies in an attempt to rectify blatant racial discrimination. At the same time, middle and upper middle class African Americans were migrating to the suburbs while their low-income and working class counterparts remained in distressed urban cities impacted by high unemployment, black-on-black crime, and AIDS related deaths. By the early 1990s, racial issues remained a major concern especially with the release of Nelson Mandela and the videotaped beating of Rodney King in Los Angeles. And yet, some movies and television attempted to address these social issues and themes.

Often in a comedic format, "Blackness" was still caricaturized through fictional characters—as in the early 1990s Keenen Ivory Wayan's sketch comedy show *In Living Color's* "Hey Mon." Fans of the show may recall "Hey Mon" stereotypically depicting the "hardest working Jamaican American family" named the Hedley's with each family member working 10 jobs or more and saying "I got to go to work" at the end of each segment. Notwithstanding these types of comedic portrayals and their steady streams of negative racial and gender stereotypes, television programs like *The Cosby Show* and *A Different World* had several storylines that attempted to defy cultivating negative stereotypes about men and women of color as unintelligent, boisterous, law breaking criminals, hypersexual, lazy, and poor. These two programs in particular pointed to experiences, which I always thought, all blacks could identify with in a more positive light: whether these focused on the plight of overcoming poverty to perhaps "moving on up to the East side to a deluxe apartment in the sky," or were aimed to inspire the next generation of black youth to view going to college as being "the chance to make it, if we focus on our goals." For me, shows and movies liked these dared to talk about racism, skin tone, class struggles, black sexuality, and gender issues in ways that revolutionized my emerging sociological imagination.

When it comes to patterns and circumstances that shape intersectional aspects of one's identity, of course mass media was not the only socializing agent in my life. Indeed I recognize the contentions child development researchers raise: the amount and types of exposure to media images and messaging around issues of race and racism are influential on the development and viewing perspectives of youth of color especially during adolescence, which experiences revolve, is identity development (see Berry 1998; Erikson 1999). My experiences with parents and family members, friends and school mates in the social institutions I participated in and the community I lived also served as great learning tools in shaping how I have come to think about race and my own racial and ethnic identity experiences and how these relate to my growing up working class, living an adult middle class lifestyle and being a straight, Christian woman (see also Lee et al. 2003). Was it those times when peers and adults (regardless of race and ethnic background) would say to me *you don't look like a regular black person; you are dark-skinned but have 'good,' wavy long hair … You are exotic looking… You must be mixed with something else like Indian or Chinese…* whenever they paid me a "compliment"? Or maybe it was when I went shopping in a West Village boutique with two white classmates from my prep school and was followed around because the store clerks thought I was the one in the group most likely to shoplift?

Of course not all experiences deemed negative are a necessary part of the ethno-racial and class socialization process. There were many instances I can recall whereby I learned rituals, rules and regulations of my own family, their Caribbean culture and society, the privilege of being black—all within the context of my own American experience that were indeed positive as well as transformative. I recall Saturday morning trips with my Dad to purchase delicious Caribbean baked goods from the popular Vincentian Alan's Bakery on Nostrand Avenue in Brooklyn; participating in the annual Labor Day West Indian Day Parade (Carnival) on Eastern Parkway, which was established by a black Venezualan named Carlos Lezama in 1969[1] and that still continues today; and listening to radio station 1190 AM WLIB which provided constant news updates as to what was happening across the Caribbean. Or perhaps it was traveling to the islands of Grenada and Trinidad with my parents to visit family during Christmas holidays and summer vacations and being called *little Yankee* by friends that I learned the advantages and disadvantages of being American-born with Caribbean parentage? Maybe it was those instances when I traveled to places throughout France, England, and Europe with my parents that I realized that "being black" is experienced differently if you are an American versus a North or West African and Caribbean immigrant traveling to or living in some of these countries?

The experiences we have during our life time, no matter how early, shape who we are as individuals: how we identify ourselves and move in and throughout social life. Cultural theorists and sociologists Anselm Strauss and Stuart Hall, who often examined the concept of identity and what it means for understanding culture and history, contend identity is constructed through discourse and representation that involves the play of power as part of the process of identity development and assertion. In his book, *Readings in Social Psychology* with Alfred Lindesmith, Anselm Strauss asserts identity is flexible and fluid, subject to change notwith-standing a person's efforts for developing strategies for gaining a sense of personal continuity. At its theoretical core, Strauss looks to transforma-tions of identity as a critical part of a person's biography when he says, "changes can be marked by turning points constituted by critical inci-dents. These moments in a biography enable an individual to see the change and make him or her explore and validate new aspects of self" (Lindesmith and Strauss 1969:93).

Similarly for Stuart Hall, identity is a reflection of history in which indi-viduals assume identities at different times, that may be contradictory but that are also continuously shifting as systems of meaning and cultural rep-resentations change (see Ashcroft et al. 2006; Hall 1990, Hall et al. 1996). Hall asserts identity is a matter of becoming as well as of "being;" it belongs to the future as it does to the past when he says,

> Identity, in this sociological conception, bridges the gap between the "inside" and the "outside"—between the personal and the public worlds. The fact that we project "ourselves" into these cultural identities, at the same time, internalizing their meanings and values, making them "part of us" helps to align our subjective feelings with the objective places we occupy in the social and cultural world (in Modernity 1996:597–598)

As such, identities are produced in specific historical experiences (includ-ing institutional sites; see also Lorick-Wilmot 2010) and arguably can emerge as both a product of the marking of difference and exclusion as it is also a marker of constituted unity. A person can be identified as a mem-ber of a racial and ethnic group by institutional sites, policies, by him or herself, and by other people too. But for Hall, identity is a positioning—that is both socio-political and negotiated. The importance Hall's thesis on positioning on this work about MSGCIs is the concept of racial proj-ects: a person or group's positioning is predicated on "simultaneously interpret[ing], represent[ing], or explain[ing] racial dynamics" through cultural representations and social structures (Omi and Winant 1986/2015:56). Employing Hall's conceptualization of "being" for the MSGCIs requires understanding the impacts of racialization—how race and ethnicity serve as an integral (though not only) part of marginalization that shape the social world (e.g., institutions and policies) and their own individual and group identities and mentalities. I asked my participants to tell me their story—a narrative about their own conception of their racial, ethnic, gender, and class identities and the ways these complicated and intersectional identities are constituted in and through each other in everyday social life. What I heard, thought about and felt from hearing the ways individuals' retold of experiences and ways of "knowing" who they are: as a self-identified black person, as a person labeled internally and externally as African American, Latino, man, woman, lesbian, and so on, was very fluid—just as Stuart Hall theorized. Each of my participants had similar as well as divergent tales about how they each "became" who they are and assert themselves to "being."

GEOGRAPHIES AND SOCIAL PLACES AND SPACES OF BEING AND BELONGING

Identity is powerful. Identities are used as labels or descriptors to help individuals categorize themselves or other people; they often give people social context through which to interact with others. Racial and ethnic identity labels, for example, have implicit assumptions and stereotypes, social and political histories, and connotations associated with them and that are imposed on individuals. There is a more personal and fluid component to identity that it is also self-chosen. These self-chosen labels or descriptors are present-day representations of how individuals perceive themselves in this world, sometimes changing as they encounter new experiences, situations, and relationships in a variety of social environments. In this regard, identity is both a form of understanding one's own uniqueness and a form of locating oneself in an internal model of social relationships and along dimensions of social life. The changes or shifts individuals undergo is part of their self-exploration; the talking and thinking about identity as it is revised in a variety of contexts implies a continual rearranging of individuals' selves, renegotiating their interconnections within the context in which they live (Krauss 2006). For the MSGCIs, the identity of "blackness" in particular was considered both multifaceted and nebulous. Not surprisingly, outcomes of racialization for the MSGCI is reflected in the way each individual defined "blackness" over their life course to date and how "blackness" affects how he or she walks, talks, feels, and moves through the physical places and social spaces of their everyday life. An important observation to also consider when reading narratives about their racialization process is in the way their multifaceted meanings of "blackness" remain informed by larger racial structure of subordination that intends to restrict their life chances—both as individuals and as a social group.

Physical Sites of Belonging

As a collective, the MSGCIs in the study were primarily born in states located along or nearby the eastern coast of the United States. Aside from vacations, almost all participants have traveled and lived in various parts of the world. For some, it was work and/or school opportunities that led them to venture beyond their home states to countries in Europe, Africa, and the Caribbean. For others, their travels led them to other parts of the country. But despite where they lived and traveled, one interesting observation I made was in the way each person laid claim and asserted "who they are" racially and ethnically in relationship to where their parents were born, where they grew up geographically, and how these assertions informed the way they move through social, economic, and cultural spaces of interaction.

To understand the relationship between race, ethnicity, and geography is to first engage in the notion there are sites of belonging, where social meanings cohere around specific sites—physical, cultural, and social. Belonging, for the purpose of this research, indicates the various affective meanings individuals attach to places and people and the degree of cognitive dissonance or consonance they associate these meanings across contexts and situations to their own identity (see also Kay Deaux 1996). To quote Baden Offord (2002:4) in his article *Mapping the Rainbow Region: Fields of Belonging and Sites of Confluence,*

> Belonging is the activation of mapping landscape and territory for what is desired, what will bring security, what can be owned, that which will ensure a notion of duration or temporality. Belonging is fraught with irony as it calls for justice within a frame of beguiling and uncanny spatial references.... In other words, do I really belong as a citizen? What are my references for apprehending [my home country]? My sense of place is perpetually called into question through a variety of negotiations I must make.

When MSGCIs link together sites of belonging to geography, their race and ethnic identities are often expressed naturally and in ways that reference their family's country of birth, their own nativity (where he or she was born, to whom he or she was born, where his or her parents were born) as something important to defining who they are as racialized individuals in the United States.

As Robert describes embracing and celebrating ethnic group-based identities and performances that he dubs as "Caribbean," it is critical to recognize Robert's story also points to an awareness that US-born people are socialized into a racialized and racially gendered system that is specific to the US context of implicit associations and meanings about gender, race, and nativity that are imposed by the dominant white male context. Despite constant bombardment and pressure to internalize such racialism, there is the need to challenge these categories in more positive ways.

ROBERT

Robert was born in the early 1970s in the Cambria Heights area in Queens, New York and spent his youth in Brooklyn. He is a Marketing Executive and a Vice President in the division at his company. Robert self-identifies racially as black and ethnically as being a person of Caribbean decent. He is the only child born to his parents who emigrated from St. John's, Antigua. Robert's paternal grandfather was the first to arrive to the United States, specifically Chicago, with Robert's father and paternal grandmother following a few years after. Robert's mother came to the United States on a student visa to attend college in New York City. After a few years in Chicago, Robert's dad and grandparents moved to South Jamaica Queens, New York, where his dad met his mom. After a year and few months of dating, Robert's parents married and moved to an apartment in Cambria Heights where he was born. His parents purchased their first home in the Midwood section of Brooklyn a year before Robert entered high school. After earning a scholarship to study at a university in Massachusetts, Robert went on to earn a graduate degree in Communications and Marketing. He has lived and worked in various cities in the United States and different countries, including England and Germany. Robert is married with four children under 12 years old and currently lives in Montclair, New Jersey.

> For me, being Caribbean is more than eating the foods and listening to music; it is culture. It's pride in the history and expressing it to everyone

who knows you. It is something about being in a place like Brooklyn where it feels and smells like the inside of your house. Like when your grandmother is making that good food. Then sending you to the bodega or the corner store to get that one ingredient from the nosey shopkeeper asking what your grandmother's cooking. That's New York City to me. Kids outside playing when it's hot, a man selling piraguas (shaved ice) to them, the men playing dominoes, talking about baseball or soccer and drinking rum. Or you have merengue or soca music blasting from a double-parked car with the driver's country's flag medallion hanging from the rearview mirror. ...For my parents' generation, it doesn't mean you just leave your culture and way of life behind or let it go once you become a citizen. It's a part of you. You hold onto it and then you teach your kids to see how important and beautiful it is to be black *and* Caribbean. Your neighborhood and the City make it possible to do that. I can't imagine being this proud about my culture and heritage in another part of the country where there aren't public symbols to show the diversity of Caribbean people exist and are appreciated. Yo, it's New York man; when everybody in the same city is from everywhere else, it's easy to be proud and celebrating.

The spatial configurations of Robert's childhood neighborhoods as well as the communities he traversed albeit the West Indian Day Parade on Eastern Parkway, arguably, reflect and reinforce social relations based on race, ethnicity, and even gender, which he viewed as something positive. Robert's description of New York City and its openness to celebrate public symbols of diversity also points to the particular spaces that are established—where lines are drawn and defined—to signal places and spaces in which enclave identities are to be celebrated. Notwithstanding the desire to transform or broaden the meaning related to black racial and ethnic categories into something more positive, I also consider the specificities of physical location as important in the way critical race theory (CRT) examines geography of place as a setting for social action as well and as a place where race and ethnic distinctions become pronounced.

In contrast, Lisa describes how her own racial and ethnic identity process is, in part, shaped by her experiences of growing up in New York and the observations she has made these last several years living in Chicago. In this regard, Lisa's narrative here (as well as other MSGCIs) speaks to the consequences of racist ideologies and discourses of hegemonic whiteness as it relates to racialized identities and the persistence of racial stereotypes which serves to draw distinctions between whites and nonwhites but also distinctions between black ethnics.

LISA

Lisa was born in the mid-1970s and grew up in the Lakeview area of Long Island, New York and is the middle child for her Jamaican father, who is an engineer, and Panamanian mother who is a nurse. Lisa self-identifies as Caribbean American, Black, and more recently as a Black Latino. At the time of the interview, Lisa was in the last few months of her residency program in Chicago and preparing to return to New York City for her medical fellowship at a competitive university hospital. Lisa is married to a self-identified African American elementary school teacher and is a parent to three-year-old fraternal twins.

> When I was growing up I just never thought much about being Jamaican and Panamanian but I guess it's because a lot of people around me identified as West Indian. We'd travel to Jamaica and we would have family from Panama stay with us so I was always surrounded by the culture and values. And there were African Americans in the neighborhood too. If I think about it, it was nice to see the similarities and differences in terms of what it means to be black in the same neighborhood. My parents learned the depth of prejudice, racism, and discrimination at work, from not just white people but from black Americans too. Being from places like Jamaica and Panama—with its own history of U.S. occupation, gives that insight. For a while I wanted to be seen as "just black" because being able to speak Spanish, in my case, can be too hard. Some blacks think *you* think you're better because you are not from the U.S and that people like my parents and me are riding the coattails of African Americans who have struggled for years. But as I have gotten older, married to an African American, and traveled more and now, especially with us making our return trip to New York after living in Chicago, I am appreciative of being more than "just black." Yes, it's wonderful and challenging to be black, but much of who I am is also Caribbean, and is Latino too. I want my kids to feel the normalcy I felt growing up in New York and being able to connect to my people and our rich history.... Yes, there are pockets of Caribbean people in Chicago too but it's a little different here than in the northeast. I'll be honest with you I don't really feel connected in Chicago in the same way. But, maybe it's the nostalgia of home (New York).

For both Robert and Lisa, linking together race and ethnicity to geography is crucial to their own efficacy—an element on one's self-truth. Similarly for other MSGCIs, growing up in major metropolitan areas in the northeast made it easier to learn to embrace and appreciate one's blackness in ways that were more cognitively consonant. Concomitantly, the geography of location (New York City in this example) and the MSGCIs' notion of "blackness" as a racial construct emerge out of physical interconnections between the multitudes of racial-ethnic people and the communities in which they lived, which are themselves racialized spaces—as a result of historical racial and economic segregation, violence, environmental racism, and so on.

In so far as to make the connection between positive conceptions of blackness and physical spaces as Robert observed, *your neighborhood and the City make it possible to do that. I can't imagine being this proud about my culture and heritage in another part of the country where there aren't public symbols to show the diversity of Caribbean people exist and are appreciated,* there are social politics, policies, and structures that shape a person's cultural models about the racial and ethnic group and culture they chose to identify with. It is important to note these cultural models are also rooted in discourses of hegemonic whiteness that serve to reinforce racial identities on the macro and micro-levels of social interaction. As Omi and Winant (1986/2015) have argued on the topic of racial formation, public spheres such as government (local, state, and national) are the primary sites in which concepts of race and racial ideology structure society and that these spheres use a range of "material and symbolic resources to impose categories, classificatory schemes, and modes of social counting and accounting" that frame how individuals subsequently identify with, embrace, assert, and/or reject particular identities (Brubaker and Cooper 2000:16). Depending on the construction of certain racial and ethnic categories (in this case, Caribbean-ness and black identity), the racialization and ethnicization categories produced by city and local governments and its peoples' daily interaction with both bureaucrats and fellow community members, shape the ability of MSGCIs Robert and Lisa, for example, to embrace aspects of these categories and develop positive associations with these identities.

Ruben Rumbaut also makes this compelling point regarding the contextual role between geography of "race" among Caribbean populations in the United States and racial self-identification of Caribbean immigrants (and their children). In his book chapter *Pigments of Our Imagination: On the Racialization and Racial Identities of 'Hispanics' and 'Latinos,* Rumbaut (2009:28) contends, "if 'race' was an innate, permanent trait of individuals, no such variability would obtain. Instead, data exemplify how "race" is constructed socially and historically—and spatially as well."

According to his review of the 2000 US Census, self-reports on Hispanic/ Latino Ethnic Identity, Rumbaut observed Puerto Ricans, for example, were far more likely to self identify as "white" in Florida than in states New York/New Jersey and suggests,

> The more rigid racial boundaries and 'racial frame' developed in the former Confederate states [like] Florida, and the severe stigma historically attached to those marked as non-white there, may shape defensive assertions of whiteness when racial status is ambiguous. [On the other hand], in states like California and New York, the social dynamics have been more open to ethnic options and a rejection of rigid U.S. racial categories (Rumbaut 2009:28–29).

Rumbaut found such assertions most prevalent among the first generation Spanish-speaking Caribbean immigrant population. Interestingly, Rumbaut also made similar observations in his work with Alejandro Portes (Portes and Rumbaut 2001; Rumbaut 2005) via the Children of Immigrants Longitudinal Study (CILS), 1991–2003. For participants living in southern Florida and southern California, they found "striking instance of the malleability of racial constructions, even between parents and children in the same family, residing in the same place" (Rumbaut 2009:35). Rumbaut contends that the second generation of this same cohort of respondents learned to see themselves as members of a racial minority, however, were more likely to racialize their parents' national origins (e.g., "Dominican" as race category as opposed to white, black, or mixed). This notwithstanding, the range of racial categories Portes and Rumbaut's participants in southern California used to self-identify themselves as compared to those in southern Florida were consistent with other findings. Thus, their work illustrates the ways in which racial identities are dependent on the geographical context by which these identities are constructed and have meaning socially and historically.

Social Places and Spaces of "Blackness": Significance of Racialization

In *What is this 'Black' in Black Popular Culture?* Stuart Hall (1993:111) aptly points out that in order "to understand the nuances in black identities, we must recognize the other kinds of difference that place, position, and locate black people." Indeed, geographical context is important to understanding these nuances in black identities that Hall discusses and as previously mentioned by Portes and Rumbaut. I contend that such understanding also requires considering racialization and specifically the concept of differential racialization, particularly in the United States. To clarify, racialization is the process by which race as an ideological construct becomes embodied and performed in socially and culturally visible ways that is then reflected in the social order. People of color are not the only groups racialized; whites are also racialized, however the process is often rendered as invisible or normative when defining social relationships. Hall (1999) discusses the ways social order racializes groups through the US media and its production and dissemination of particular cultural models in the public discourse that are meant to be interpreted according to the ideologies preferred by its creator about particular groups. Similarly, differential racialization is the way in which the dominant racial group in the social order racializes minority groups differently and based on their interests, economic or political needs (see Delgado and Stefancic 2012)—and the intricate sets of attitudes, perspectives, and behaviors that develop as a result of such racialization (and oppression) as a social process.

Asserting one's "blackness" or a black racial identity was of critical importance for many of the MSGCIs, however, the reasons for its importance in each of their individual lives were interestingly nuanced. For some, discovering one's blackness was often through a type of painful awareness: blackness is defined through the lens of deprivation and lack if you are not white; or that blackness is synonymous with "otherness." While I remain leery in my own objectification[2] of the concept of race and/or blackness in my interpretation and analysis of Joachim's story presented here, I am reminded of Frantz Fanon (1967)'s realization of his own blackness as a black man, which he derived from his experiences and encounters with whites. The painful awareness Joachim describes elucidates ascription—the imposition of difference—in which racialization is produced where the individual is able to recognize him or herself by such difference (i.e., skin color, hair texture, and other physiological features), have particular experiences and live with certain consequences of such racial ascription. Joachim explains:

JOACHIM

Joachim was born in the mid-1970s and grew up in Anne Arundel County, Maryland with his Guyanese parents and two brothers. Joachim self identifies as Black, Caribbean Black, and Indian as he closely identifies with both his mother's Indo-Guyanese and father's Afro-Guyanese cultures and traditions. After attending an academically notable public high school in the county, Joachim earned his Bachelor of Arts in sociology at a large Washington, D.C. university and later went on to earn his Master's of Social Work and Master's of Public Health at a large university in Boston, Massachusetts. He has since returned to Maryland to work in the field of Family Therapy and Community Health. Joachim lives near Severna Park, Maryland with his wife and stepchild in order to be closer to his aging parents.

> If everyday you live in this country and say you're black or that you look like a black American, you will experience prejudice and discrimination. Hands down. People will find a way to humiliate you and tell you, you're a trouble-maker; teachers yell at you and the rest of the black boys in class. That kind of humiliation affects people. Makes people feel hopeless and want to reject parts of themselves: that you are not good enough. That's what this country does to black people—the African and Caribbean immigrant too. We are black at the end of the day and we face the same challenge of overcoming the belief that we are not good enough. That's why my folks try keep to themselves. Keep their heads down. You have to protect yourself or else these enemies will eat you alive. I see that in the generation of kids in the neighborhood.

Joachim's narrative reveals a powerful nuance to racial ascription; not only does racial ascription impose an identity upon a person but also makes it difficult, "deprives or prevents [his or her] own assertions of alternative identification and mere possibilities of multiple belonging" (Sen 2006:xii). He goes on to add,

> What was it like for me growing up and hearing negative things about Black people? For one, hearing things like "don't be a jigaboo" was often associated with Black Americans and not necessarily Caribbean people. But I would still think, "wow, that's a new one." I would go to the library, take out books and read a lot. It's not like you really learn so much while in school about black people or, really, people of color. Every year we have one month to learn about the same Black people and that's it. Not discounting these individuals' accomplishments because, of course, the hurdles they had to overcome are in no comparison to what we go through today. For con-temporary, positive images, you had to look to sports athletes. Otherwise, you got the regular images of black people on television: mostly African Americans as welfare queens, crack whores and drug dealers getting arrested

for murder or some other violent crime; or some poor Haitians—since it seems as though every dark-skinned Caribbean person was Haitian—illegally entering the country or spreading disease like AIDS. Which is so foul. If black people did anything positive it happened decades ago without much relevance in contemporary times. But that was black representation when I was a kid. When I got older and watched Cosby I was happy to see something new. Most of my friends felt the same way too although a few of the white kids would say the Cosby black family doesn't really exist.

A prevailing contention among a few MSGCIs, including Joachim, is when societies engage in these types of cultural, social, and political suppression of Africanicity or African roots, its policies and social rhetoric are seen as denigrating positive aspects of African heritage and edifying antiblack racism in the process. Not surprisingly, critical race theorists have also argued racialization and, in effect, racism serve as a normative function in the United States that intentionally attempts to hinder the progress of and perpetually marginalize nonwhites and their communities (Bonilla-Silva 2013; Delgado and Stefanic 2012). Hence, the daily reality of racialization and racism in US society serves to stifle and strip the value of one's identity, language, and culture in ways that are designed to continually exploit and oppress the historically disenfranchised.

Therefore, in thinking about the construction of blackness in these moments of pain or frustration as described by Joachim reveals something powerful in the process of racialization in the United States: blackness had to be learned and only learned in certain moments. And these moments, I assert, are instances in which African descendants in the United States are denied subjectivity—"the right and ability to define their own reality, establish their own identities, name their history" (hooks 1989/2015:42). Instead, these African descendants become objectified—"as objects one's reality is defined by others, one's identity created by others, one's history named only in ways that define one's relationship to those who are subject" (Ibid). Thus, their subjugation as the subaltern "Other" "supports the political economy of domination that characterized slavery, colonialism and neocolonialism" (Collins 2000:71).

But, there is something else that is revealed in these stories: there is more to black identity and the construction of blackness than reactions to anitblack racism as if it is the sole factor in black identity formation. I contend there exist diverse cultural responses and approaches available to people of African descent in the United States that importantly acknowledges the varied responses to experiences that are both apart from and due to black oppression. In fact, several MSGCIs also described growing up and having friends in their neighborhoods who represent a range of black ethnicities that made it possible to view blackness—not from a deficit model—but from a place of pride and connection to a group of people that exist across the world.

Traveling While Black: Blackness as Transnational and Multiple

For a couple of the MSGCIs like Shana, they also grew tired of being constantly reminded of their otherness (not white American) particularly while living in the United States. Some chose to consciously negotiate a hybrid identity of a Caribbean-identified, black, Indian, Latina, American, lesbian—as embodied in Shana's narrative—as a way to combat the social and psychological effects of race and ethnic discrimination that span multiple levels of society in their daily lives. During the discussions, Shana frequently expressed her frustration with being "boxed" in the category of "Other" and the intense process race, ethnic, and gender socialization has had on her self concept and identity, which she is determined to reclaim for herself and define one her own terms.

SHANA

Shana was born and grew up in Brooklyn, New York's Fort Greene area in the early 1980s with her Puerto Rican (mainland born) mom and younger brother. Shana self identifies as mixed, Black and Boricua. Shana's Cuban-born father was in and out of their lives growing up but several of his extended family members stayed in touch and participated in celebrating Shana's milestones (i.e., birthdays, graduations, and holidays). After graduating from one of New York City's premier science high schools, Shana earned her Bachelor's and Master's degrees at a large university in California. While out west, Shana married one of her fellow graduate student male friends but only after two years they divorced due to "irreconcilable differences." In part, they loved each other and are still friends but agreed that Shana's "coming out" as a lesbian woman could not work for their marriage. Shana then went to the United Kingdom and earned her PhD in fine arts. After living in the United Kingdom and traveling to France and Turkey, Shana returned to New York City and has been teaching workshops, producing art, and engaged in community activism. She lives in Bedford-Stuyversant Brooklyn with her partner and cat.

I am not the stereotypical light skinned, feminine, Boricua we see in Jennifer Lopez. I'm the butchy, curly-haired Morena and proud Boricua who celebrates her rich culture and loves her people too. But why do I have to fit into some other oppressive view of myself? A narrow lens that society uses to box me in? Life experience has taught me that I can't live my life fitting into someone else's mold. I define it for myself.

Shana's multiple identities represent an interesting lens in understanding how some MSGCIs define for themselves a new way of being: children of black Caribbean immigrants, black in America and transnational[3] at the same time. Though Shana considers herself to be American (because of her nativity), black (because of her light brown skin, curly hair, and African roots), Latina (specifically Puerto Rican), and lesbian, at the same time she acknowledges a sense of cultural and civic responsibility towards her Caribbean roots and learns to use her resources and energies to give back to her community, both in the United States and in Puerto Rico.

Also, in the way the MSGCIs like Shana talk about their notion of blackness, their triple identity consciousness signals an awareness which frames identity as multiple and contextual. To be clear, this is not to say there are not instances in which the MSGCIs appeal to singular, essentialized notions of blackness when responding or attempting to reject white racism. In this regard, the foreclosure of race as a salient marker of identity within their households and within the communities they live and travel within (especially among other Caribbean descendants) allows the MSGCIs to articulate who they are both in terms of positional and plural states of being. Hence, the MSGCIs also seek to distance themselves or perhaps attempt to transcend the discourses of oppression and black victimhood (or black struggle/suffering/exploitation) that place whites as the eternal oppressor—as framed in postcolonial theories. I contend MSGCI triple identity consciousness appears to push them to consider new ways of being, living, and performing blackness within the context of white supremacy. Here, Shana elaborates on the ways in which she performs blackness through her art and community activism as a function of transcending oppression.

SHANA adds:

I live in the community. I see the need for Puerto Ricans to be active, socially and politically, both stateside and on the island. With our diversity, we are a powerful people. Whether we are voting on issues that affect us on the island or are protesting for or against issues here in the U.S., we need to be involved. That's what I try to do with my art and my activism. I paint beautiful images of our people, that represent our colorful, mixed heritage— Taino, white, and African—working together to uplift each other and overcome, sort of like the famed Nuyorican Juan Sanchez does. He inspires me.... Yes, the art is about expression of culture and history, but education is still the key. The money I raise for programs or when I sell my art, I donate it and my time to organizations in Puerto Rico and here that support young people to get a high school diploma to better themselves for their future.

Traveling to different parts of the United States and abroad to the Caribbean, Africa, and Europe also provided several participants added perspective on what it means to be black in these different parts of the world. By my own observation, I find it interesting there is a vacillation between the foregrounding and backgrounding of blackness for the MSGCIs. Because in many places in the United States blackness is often conferred upon African descendants, and therefore the MSGCIs are socialized to construct a black identity primarily as "the Other," and therefore, marking difference. And still, MSGCIs' travel experiences renders an awareness that they are more than the singular aspect of their identity— blackness—traversing various social situations and social contexts touch on the multiplicity of their gender, religion, and their ethnicity.

NATALIE

Natalie was born in Philadelphia in the early 1970s and lived in the Cedar Park area of West Philadelphia with her parents and two younger sisters. She recalled also spending much of her youth in Bedford-Stuyversant, Brooklyn with her mother's family who arrived from Barbados in the early to mid-1970s. Natalie self identifies as West Indian, Black, American, and, more recently, a woman of the African Diaspora. High school sweethearts in Barbados, Natalie's parents married shortly before arriving to the United States in the late 1960s. Her paternal relatives settled in West Philadelphia a few years prior to her parents' arrival and as such influenced their choice to also settle in the Philadelphia area. Natalie's father was an electrician in Barbados, having skills comparable to a Journeyman even though he was demoted to an Apprentice at his first two jobs; her mother was a nurse and worked in an area clinic. Over the years, Natalie's father went on to become a Master Electrician, after years of additional schooling and training, and worked for a small college in the area, where Natalie and her youngest sister also graduated with their bachelors. Natalie later went on to pursue her

PhD at a large university in Los Angeles, almost 18 months after the 1992 Rodney King uprising. During her graduate studies, she met her husband, another academic, who self-identifies as African American and is from a middle class family from southern California. A few years ago, Natalie and her husband relocated back to the east coast with their three school-aged children to take on professorships.

> It's actually quite fascinating when I think about it; there exists racism outside of the United States. Yes—I know, surprise!!! (Sarcasm). As an American, I see racism to be attributed to their (whites') lack of exposure to Africans in the Diaspora. I say this has been my experience traveling to countries like Denmark and Germany where it is generally racially homogenous. Through the Internet, they are exposed to racial stereotypes and may take it as the gospel truth. But, also these countries do not have the same kind of recent immigration like London or Paris. For me it's pure ignorance and common-sense that these folks lack as opposed to the same kind of blatant superiority complex folks in the United States have and flaunt more casually. When I travel in those places, whether for work or pleasure, I am in the body of an American. Maybe it is in my accent and the way I carry myself. I feel I have this quasi-white privilege because white = American and I must have some of that status too? But the people there tend to be more curious. Curious about my skin and hair and I look at them with my side-eye because you can tell they just want to touch you and feel you, your skin and hair. It's a bit weird. Maybe like a fetish or something. I don't know if I think of it as flattery or not. There was this time when I was in Munich when a young man approached a colleague and I to simply to tell me I was very beautiful. Was he trying to fetishize me? You don't really have that happen in the U.S. I don't want to generalize but it doesn't seem white American men find black women attractive. And if they do, it's like a secret. Now, it's a little different when I am in France or England. It's like I am American BUT I am black. That's when I see how Caribbean or African immigrants are treated. Like crap. And the more recent immigrant you are, the worst you get treated. It's like my American status gives me a slight edge over the racial but at the end of the day, I am near the bottom still.

Natalie's comments about her own racialization when she travels abroad points to the ways group boundaries are defined and bifurcated by race and nationality (being US born). According to Natalie, it seems the more she traveled east in Europe the more curious, exoticized, and perhaps tolerant her blackness seemed to nonblacks whereas in western Europe, Natalie felt the opposite. She felt her presence was viewed suspiciously until nonblacks ascertained that she was foreign—specifically U.S and not an African and Caribbean migrant worker or illegal immigrant in their country. In spite of postcoloniality and racialization, which would suggest Natalie's status of traveling abroad as a woman of color is very much rooted in white male dominant ideology, there is also an ascribed privilege associated with her nationality she experienced that separated her from other non-US born blacks she encountered.

There were other instances MSGCIs described that signaled their awareness of ascribed privileges around their American-ness and ethnicity in relationship to other US-born blacks, children of Caribbean immigrants, and to their immigrant parents' generation. Several MSGCIs, including Eddy, talked about their blackness and the situational contexts in which their ethnic self-identities may be differentially deployed, including in relationship to their American-ness vis-à-vis their parents' culture. In his story, Eddy makes an important point regarding the nature of the ascribed privilege of being US-born black and middle class when traveling to the Caribbean and within Caribbean culture where social class, gender, and religion are the categories used in the social hierarchy.

EDDY

Eddy is a Planning Strategist and works in government. Eddy self identifies as being of mixed race, specifically of Indo-Jamaican and black heritage. Eddy's mother is biracial—of black and Irish Jamaican decent and his father is East Indian Jamaican. Eddy's parents met after they both emigrated from Jamaica to the United States in the mid-1970s to attend a large university in Florida. Eddy was born in the early 1980s in the Tampa, Florida area and spent much of his childhood in East Tampa and Lauderdale Lakes, Fort Launderdale in Florida. When he was a teen, Eddy moved with his parents and younger brother to Prince George's County, Maryland in the mid 1990s where his father took a mechanical engineering job in the Washington, DC area. After attending a mid-sized college in Virginia while majoring in government relations and business, Eddy moved to the West End neighborhood of Washington, D.C., and is currently enrolled in a graduate program at a major university in the area. He lives with his common law wife, who is a data analyst and a child of black Trinidadian immigrants, in a condo they purchased together with their two and one-half year old son.

"Being black" is a state of being that depends on the situation. When I visit family members, I am American. And just like anywhere else in the world people can spot me and know instantly I am American-born. Down in the islands, that's how they identify me: American. I am very conscious of this—even when I was a kid. If you live in the U.S. long enough and have a little something—a car, house, career—then American = rich. Therefore, I must be rich. My parents must be rich too. They try with me but I am no Bank of Nova Scotia! I get it and I give if I can. Many Caribbean islands are beautiful and have all the modern amenities available in the U.S but it's very expensive. For those who can afford these amenities, they are better off than the average. So my being black and American is about social class. It makes sense since it is mostly people of color and social stratification is more along the lines of say, class, gender, and religion. Having African roots is almost a given. In my relatives' and friends' homes in the Caribbean and in the U.S., I am Yankee but Jamaican too; I am also Indian too. The elders talk to me about island politics and culture. They see me identifying as part of them too even though I am born in a different country from them. At work and amongst my colleagues I am Black/African American. It's mostly white American in these environments and for them, black is black—no real difference. Among my friends, I'm black too but I am Jamaican American. That's because they're black but may have Haitian, Cape Verdean, Nigerian or southern backgrounds. So, we bond and share on so many things but our experiences aren't monolithic. My being black depends on the situation and I embrace all parts of it and see them as all equally important in defining who I am in the world.

Eddy and other MSGCIs often made the distinction between having a black identity and the varied black ethnicities they can readily identify. For them, an ethnicity connotes a connection to a specific land or place, a long tradition of history and cultural practice, and of struggle and resilience, that brings people together who share these particular experiences and that of their fore-parents. Here, Lisa defines what ethnicity means to her as it relates to her self-concept around race and identity.

When I think about what it means to be black, it is also about me being Caribbean *and* American or Caribbean American—with the hyphen. I have a connection to the land and culture of my great- and grandparents on both sides of the family. A connection to the people, the culture, the language—everything—which is very different from the connection I have to the U.S. I mean, I am born here but my roots are not as deep as it is for some of my friends who can trace their family history (or at least as far as they can) to certain slave holding families. Take for instance certain traditions my African American friends practice that no one in my family knew existed prior to coming to America. I would be a poser to say that I am an African American when my family history and cultural background is not the same. But I will not correct someone if they assume I identify as African American, since 'African American' means 'black' today. Because I am black in the U.S., I experience similar prejudice other blacks do regardless of their ethnic background. But I will tell you this, when I travel back to Jamaica or anywhere else in the world, no one understands this 'label' African American; I am American, black, and have Caribbean parentage.

As such, the concept of a black identity did not always mean opting to repress aspects of their Caribbean cultural heritage in order to adopt an African American ethnicity (simply because they were born in the United States), per se. There seems a strong desire, too, among the MSGCIs to reject the pressing duality that is often imposed upon the second generation immigrants: that being US-born black is primary and Caribbean immigrant as secondary, particularly when it comes to race discourses. Rather, being a part of a larger black community (a Diaspora of sorts), constituted a racial and cultural solidarity between native-born blacks in America and those from the Caribbean. This sense of global, diaspora thinking about blackness is at the crux of MSGCIs' triple identity consciousness.

During our conversations, Natalie raised an interesting point about one's ability to claim blackness. For her, blacks and whites assume there is a monoracial experience of blackness, of which individuals of multiracial ancestry from the Caribbean cannot claim because they may not have dark skin. Natalie believes that claiming there is a monoracial black experience is, ironically, privileging white supremacy and anti-black attitudes about what blackness means.

NATALIE adds,

I've also experienced occasions where people have tried to deny my right to identify as black, which makes me question this notion of "black privilege." How does privilege manifest in our own lives as people of color? America supports white supremacy in its laws and institutions. America supports a white/ black binary that forces people to box themselves in according to census forms. White supremacy makes black people feel bad about their own blackness—as being only defined by having dark skin, broad noses and coarse hair. And when you are able to claim blackness but have lighter skin or other "more white than black-like" features, it doesn't fit the white/black binary. If it doesn't fit then it is easier to reject or question the person identifying as such. But I live my life everyday being judged; for being too brown and not brown enough by some whites and some blacks too. But for me, it's my blackness that is my beauty and my strength. I am acutely aware of the supremacy around the black body and I reject it. Sometimes I hope others will too.

Natalie was not alone among the MSGCIs to describe instances where she felt her own assertion of "blackness" was questioned as rightful, legitimate or even, appropriate by others. Michelle also reflects on her own blackness and Hispanicity. Interestingly, these instances point to the complications of MSGCIs' identity assertions; they demonstrate the merging together elements of an essentialized blackness with fractures of ethnicity (i.e., Caribbean-ness, Hispanicity) that reveal the entanglements between race, ethnicity, and the impacts of colonialism.

MICHELLE

Born in the mid-1970s in the south Bronx New York to two Dominican parents, Michelle is the youngest of two girls. She self identifies as Latina, Black, and Dominican. Michelle's parents are from the Santiago province in the Dominican Republic. Her father is a business owner who works in the leather textile industry and her mother is an office manager and they both met and married in New York City. During her teen years, Michelle's parents moved to the Baychester area of the Bronx and bought their family's first home. Following in her older sister's footsteps, Michelle attended an all-girls catholic school before heading to a mid-sized liberal arts college in Connecticut to pursue her dream of teaching. During her junior year study abroad to Spain, Michelle met her future husband who is from the greater Malahide area of Dublin, Ireland. After a four-year courtship and graduate school, they later married and moved to the Washington Heights area of Manhattan. Michelle works as an elementary school teacher and lives with her husband and two daughters. At the time of the interview, the couple was expecting their third child.

When I look in the mirror, I see a darker-skinned woman (laugh). Okay, maybe to others, my skin and hair make me more white looking than black and I realize the only benefit of having such features is it has prevented me from feeling the full effects of white racism my sister encounters more often than me because she is very dark in complexion. But for a long time growing up, I was often rejected or not fully embraced by other black people. When I was a teenager, I tried desperately to rub coconut oil into my skin and sit in the sun and literally bake to get browner. The other kids, some of them like me have family from the islands and others from down south, would tease and tell me I will never get dark no matter how much I tried. As an adult, white people are sometimes confused when they see me. I suppose my kids (will) get it too, especially since my husband is a white guy from Ireland. But when people see me, it's like they want to ask: "where are you from?" Or "what's your nationality?" To that I flatly say, "American." [Laugh]. I sometimes feel as though they see me as one of those ambiguously racial people and play that mental game "guess my race" when they are gathered around at a dinner party. I am not white because of my accent. And still, it's like I cannot be black because I speak Spanish too? People always want to question me: "why do you say you are black? It's "in" to be Latino." But I wonder why can't I be all of the above?

Michelle's discussion of hybridity via her Hispanicity points to the politics of race and ethnic identity construction and efforts to synthesize aspects of culture and tradition where there already exists essentialism—the practice of various groups deciding for others and as well as for themselves what is and is not "blackness." For instance, identities are expressed in particular ways as the postcolonial subaltern moves between various social places and spaces. In the context of hybridity, however, the subaltern can experience ambivalence (as Michelle herself described) or the sense that self-identifying as black, being able to speak Spanish, but phenotypically considered by others as "ambiguously racial" is both a blessing and a curse.

Michelle and Natalie's narratives are also illustrative of a deeper issue rooted in the one-drop rule of racial identity that has shaped the development and essentialization of black racial identity in the Americas. In the United States, the one-drop rule[4] intended to divide the populous and classify those with a shared ancestry of African blood as black. On the contrary, in Latin America and across the Caribbean, the one-drop rule intended to support whites colonists' efforts to improve and enhance the race of the Africans and Indigenous people by classifying those with any ancestry of European blood as nonblack and of being mixed race. This nuanced interpretation of the one-drop rule is significant in the study of black identities, and particularly interesting in its application for the MSGCIs who also self-identify as Hispanic or Latino. Whether speaking about their own experiences or learning about blackness from relatives growing up, the MSGCIs talk about the ways blackness or having "black pride" is often buried in "brown pride." Several MSGCIs, including Shana, talked about the ways parents and grandparents may have minimized (but not ignored) their African roots but edified being of mixed race or "Indio." Here, Shana explains:

SHANA

> Yeah, when it comes to culture—food and music, people willingly embrace Africa, otherwise, not so much. When you look at hair texture and shades of skin color, it is obvious that there's some mixing. Like there is a black granny somewhere in the background that people love but are embarrassed to talk about. It's also about being mixed with white or Indian that's better than saying you're mixed with black that I think Latinos make a big deal about. Puerto Ricans love to play up on the fact that we're a mixed race of people. If you have any darkness in your skin color or coarseness in your hair then you must be Taino, with, maybe a little African. My Cuban relatives are similar in this way too but the difference is to say you're black carries the same negative perception as it does here in the United States. But that's Cuban culture and history. Cubans early on were very much influenced by American racial stratification systems that put black people at the bottom. And, who wants to embrace the bottom? They'd rather be mixed with something than be black.

Not surprisingly, as Shana herself pointed out, racialization and particularly the role of racialized systems of inequality shape family structures, family values, and racial socialization of children within families themselves. Applying a critical race theory lens we can see that despite members of Shana's family efforts to embrace the hybridity of African culture and history in their lives, racism is not only an ingrained feature within social institutions like the family but also contributes to family members' internalization and reproduction of racialized stratification systems through social practices. Based on Shana's narrative here, we can make assumptions about the behaviors and practices of some members in her family, the ways in which they engage in racialization, assign racial meanings to particular skin color categories, and produce hierarchies of color privilege while asserting "brown-ness" and Hispanicity. Shana's narrative also shows how colorism in particular, shapes racial and ethnic socialization within families, especially with immigrant parents and elders from countries with racial and color conscious hierarchies as those found throughout the Caribbean and Latin America.

More broadly, we can also begin to glean from these vignettes that participants associate their black identity, both socially and culturally, to the challenges they face—physically, in terms of the color of their skin and the texture of their hair. For a few of the MSGCIs, aspects of their racial and ethnic identities appear to be deployed in social interactions in ways that enable them to negotiate and construct who they are to others. For other MSGCIs, when it comes to color and physical characteristics (stereotypes) and social interaction, these become welded together in the contextual deployment of a black ethno-racial identity that is often marked by the experiences they have in the way others view them and, consequently, treat them. In both instances, the MSGCIs' deployment of a black ethno-racial identity is reflective of the racial socialization fallacy that only nonwhites "have" race and therefore must learn to traverse social environments as nonwhite children of Caribbean immigrants accordingly.

"Blackness" and Colorism: Processing Racialization as Adult Children of Caribbean Immigrants in the United States

Whether an individual's racial identity assertion "I am X" matches the identity other people think and categorizes him or her as "X," "Y," or "XYZ" or not, this process of identity declaration and differentiation is shaped by larger narratives about race and racialization that exists across social institutions, including the family. Embedded within such narratives are meanings associated with skin color, hair texture, accent, and nativity as it relates to both whiteness and blackness, which often suggest who can and cannot claim such identities. Equally significant within such narratives I have found during the course of this research is MSGCIs' agency to define or assert their own meanings as it relates to their conceptualization of blackness; a flexible racialization, in which phenotype especially is not always seen or experienced in the same way across all physical and social spaces of belonging. By my own observation, this is particularly significant for MSGCIs because several of them also recognize (to varying degrees) that they do not always have the privilege of claiming whiteness but have the freedom to identify with African-ness and Indigeneity because of his or her skin tone in ways other MSGCIs are unable to do so. To be clear, both sociological concepts of race and racial-ethnic identity and the concept of colorism (skin tone), as part of the discussion on blackness as experience, are distinct with the latter tied to biology. These concepts, however, are intricately connected to systems of oppression and discrimination that have consequences—both material and ideological in terms of identity formation and assertion for all, including the MSGCIs (see Bonilla-Silva 2006).

Colorism is a mechanism used to assign individuals to a social, economic, and political status that depends on social meanings attached to skin color. It is widely pervasive throughout any society that has experienced white imperialism and colonialism and is practiced by both whites and nonwhites alike. I agree with Margaret Hunter when she wrote in her article *If You're Light, You're Alright: Light Skin Color as Social Capital for Women of Color* (2002:176) that "the connection between racism and colorism is evidenced in the fact that colorism would likely not exist without racism, because colorism rests on the privileging of whiteness in terms of phenotype, aesthetics, and culture." Racism is its larger social process that rests on systematically oppressing, denigrating, and rendering nonwhite groups to second-class citizenship.

Colorism throughout the Americas, including the United States, can easily be traced back to the European colonial project of chattel system of slavery (domestic chattel and productive chattel).[5] A common practice was to force darker-skinned slaves to engage in grueling manual labor in the fields while lighter-skinned slaves were typically designated as cooks or maids and forced to work in close proximity to their slave owners, which often subjected them sexual violence and other abuses. These divisions were necessary to establishing and promoting racial hierarchies that deemed darker-skinned people inferior and of lower status whereas lighter skinned people were more likely to racially mix with Europeans and were considered of a higher status than those darker than them (see also Frantz Fanon's *Black Skin, White Masks*, 1967). This system of white domination continued to reward those who emulated whiteness culturally, physically, ideologically, and economically after emancipation. Unfortunately, this idealized color-caste hierarchy has not only become internalized but vestiges of this history persist over time because it is considered the norm (see also Kimberly Jade Norwood's *Color Matters: Skin Tone Bias and the Myth of a Postracial America*, 2013). Today, lighter skinned people are regarded as having a type of privilege; they are often considered to be more attractive, intelligent, and trustworthy than their darker-skinned counterparts and are found to be more likely to hold prominent positions in the media, business, government, and educational sectors. Hence, this privilege has endemic social and economic effects on overall life chances for those who do not possess such characteristics.

In fact, scores of scholars have found this skin tone social hierarchy often results in reduced educational, residential, economic, and employment opportunities for those who are discriminated against on the basis of skin color by whites and/or co-ethnics. Matthew Harrison and Kecia Thomas (2009) in their article *The Hidden Prejudice in Selection*, for example, found lighter-skinned African American job applicants were more likely to be hired than darker-skinned applicants, even when the resumes of both

light- and dark-skinned applicants were identical. Even during employment negotiations over salary and benefits, Etcoff (2000) found employee
"worth" and value may be tainted by colorism. Others such as Shankar
Vedantam in the *New York Times* op-ed "Shades of Prejudice" (2010)
found that lighter-skinned Latinos in the United States make $5000 more
on average than darker-skinned Latinos and the education test-score gap
between light-skinned and dark-skinned African Americans is nearly as
large as the gap between whites and blacks. Vedantam went on to argue
that colorism is "an unconscious prejudice that isn't focused on a single
group like blacks so much as on *blackness* itself. Our brains, shaped by
culture and history, create intricate caste hierarchies that privilege those
who are physically and culturally whiter and punish those who are darker"
(2010:A31). Looking to social science research on skin color discrimination, it is painfully clear to see how legacies of slavery and racism continue
to influence how post-colonial groups fare in society.

Defining Too Black or Not Black Enough: Skin Tone, Hair, and Stereotypes

Indeed, colorism operates very prominently in MSGCIs' lives. Like racism, colorism—whether as a result of overt or covert discrimination or
bias—has informed their own meanings of blackness at different points in
their lives. In some cases, colorism played an important role in shaping
their ideas around blackness as something beautiful about their own racial
and ethnic identity, where they should live, and who they choose to love.

During my conversations with the MSGCIs, many recounted social
situations where skin tone mattered in defining their blackness. I asked
participants to recall their earliest childhood memory when they consciously thought about skin color and as it related to their racial identity.
Here, Erica—who is the youngest participant interviewed—recalled a
memory in which she first learned the connection between skin tone,
physical attractiveness, and positive life outcomes for dark-skinned girls.

ERICA

Erica was born in the early 1980s and grew up in the Flatbush area of
Brooklyn, New York. She is the third child of four and the only girl born
to her Trinidadian mother and a Grenadian father. Erica self identifies as
West Indian American and more broadly as Black. Erica's parents arrived
to New York City, both on student visas, staying with extended family and

met at a mutual friend's house party. Erica's parents married and had her oldest brother soon after in the late 1970s, which was also around the time Erica's father completed his Associate's degree in accounting. Erica's mother eventually completed her Associate's degree in nursing and went on to become a Registered Nurse by the time her youngest brother was born in the late 1980s. As an undergraduate at a highly ranked college in the mid-West, Erica majored in biochemistry and minored in Spanish. After college, Erica returned to the New York City area and landed a job working as a sales representative for a large company, one of the youngest and highest grossing in her division. Less than a year before our interview, Erica moved to Mount Vernon to be near some of her maternal relatives (grandaunts and second cousins) who had arrived in the United States in the early 1960s. These relatives arranged for Erica to purchase her first home, a two-family home on the south side of Mount Vernon, from another family friend who plans to retire and move to south Florida.

> I remember being like 5 or 6 years old and hearing, "don't play in the sun or else you will get too dark." It was always said in a tone that suggested that getting darker was a bad thing. But I am already dark. Not too dark but dark enough. But what they meant was if you were too dark then you have a dull complexion. Not bright and shiny. Who wants to be dull? Being dull is not being pretty. And, I want to be pretty. Even to this day, I still find myself covering up more, wearing 50+SPF sunscreen in the summer especially. I won't avoid the sun but I won't go searching for it either. But being the only girl, there's lot of emphasis on getting married and "putting away" myself so that I can get a great husband—a man who is successful and can take care of his family.

Not surprising for Erica and the other MSGCIs, physical appearance tends to be an important status characteristic for all women, particularly when it comes to her skin color and hair texture. The relationship between a woman's attractiveness via her skin color and hair texture can determine whether she is marriageable, as Erica mentioned, and/or is able to attain a high occupational status job (see Hunter 1998, 2002). Again, skin color hierarchies with lightness of skin—being fair or bright in color (as opposed to being dark and dull)—is conflated with being "pretty" and reflects deeply held cultural beliefs about white European beauty, sophistication and virtue as superior to all others.

The impacts of the interconnectedness of racism, racialization, and colorism is revealed in the way the MSGCIs internalize colonial values and express their awareness and consciousness about blackness—being too black or not black enough—within the confines of white global beauty ideals and what it means in terms of their self-efficacy and identity as self-identified black men and women. When it comes to dating and mate selection, for example, Maxine Leeds (1994)'s *Young African-American Women and the Language of Beauty* found young black women have a pronounced awareness of skin color, a strong desire to have longer and straighter hair and a cognizance of Black men's preference for light-skinned women. In this regard, beauty, and particularly skin color for women, is considered a type of social capital that can be traded on for advancement within a person's social network (e.g., to "marry up" the hierarchy). Trading on a skin color by being light in complexion and marrying a partner equally as light or white would mean that he or she would have access to more social and economic capital and higher status that could pass on to their children. Again, trading on skin color is simply another indicator of colorism—light or white skin color being an important physical characteristic used as a status resource in social interaction.

With an emphasis on physical appearance and racialized notions of beauty, Susan Bordo (1993) in her book *Unbearable Weight* makes a critical point about women's bombardment with specific Eurocentric images of beauty and its impact on her self-efficacy and identity. Bordo's analysis points to the ways these images, which are often in opposition to natural, chemically unaltered hair and skin, can result in some internalization of images of beauty that reject anything other than the Eurocentric image of beauty as normal. Bordo (1993:254–256) says,

> When we look at the pursuit of beauty as a normalizing discipline it becomes clear that not all body transformations are the same. The general tyranny of fashion—perpetual and elusive, and instructing the female body in a pedagogy of personal inadequacy and lack—is a powerful discipline for the normalization of all women in this culture. But even as we are all normalized to the requirements of appropriate feminine security and preoccupation with appearance, more specific requirements emerge in different cultural and historical contexts and for different groups. When Bo Derek put her hair in cornrows, she was engaging in normalizing feminine practice. But when Oprah admitted on her show that all her life she has desperately longed to

'have hair that swings from side to side,' she revealed the power of racial as well as gender normalization of femininity but to the Caucasian standards of beauty that still dominate on television, in movies, in popular magazines.

Whether an individual has, at one time or another, felt as strongly as Oprah Winfrey has in terms of her own internalization of mainstream notions of femininity, Bordo's point is clear here: these images carry social meanings that serve to reify certain economic and social advantages, which not only perpetuate the race, color, gender divide between groups but also impacts the self efficacy and identity of individuals alike. So, how do the MSGCIs confront and reconcile their own identities and self concept within the context of the historical ideologies of colonialism and internalized racism that would otherwise consider descendants of Africans pathological—for not wanting to use toxic skin bleaching creams as an attempt to achieve lighter skin tones or undergo plastic surgery for narrower noses and lips?

As other MSGCIs like Natalie describe, the infiltration of colorism transcends their Caribbean cultures and families boundaries to the extent that while growing up in the United States, the images and advice they received as children from their immigrant parents' and their friends signaled to them that rewards for whiteness ("having a good life") are real. Here, Natalie describes the normalization of white feminine beauty standards, specifically regarding hair straightening and "having hair that swings from side to side"—an important ideal during her pre-adolescent years. She also speaks to the ways her growing awareness and triple identity consciousness regarding her own notions of blackness gets performed today.

NATALIE explains:

Girl, *fried, dyed and pressed to the side* I used to wear my hair from 13 to about 28 years old. As a little girl my mother would plait my hair and put plenty of ribbons in it. Yes! I hated it. That's how Caribbean women comb their children's hair every day. But Americans got more style. If the black girls had that "good hair" it was easy for them. But many girls got their hair straightened. Black girls would wear their hair up in a high ponytail, or a French braid or two cornbraids. But, me, nope, I had those braids and ribbons. Until one day when I was 13, I protested. I said, "we are not in the islands, we are in America. I need to fit in!" My mom eventually gave in and allowed me to press it. Truth be told, the boys were not looking at me and I wasn't feeling pretty enough. I also remember the conversation becoming more open about how black women should wear their hair. It was okay to wash your hair, oil the scalp and twist the hair into china bumps [Bantu Knots] but you couldn't wear your hair like that in public. My aunts told us we needed to present ourselves properly when working in white America. They would say having both brown skin and too ethnic hairstyles like braids/extensions are considered very threatening to white people. Being conservative in the way you dress and style your hair was key to blending in. So, having a hairstyle with the flip was necessary. The message seemed that you had to be whitened up in order to succeed and anything else was too black or not good enough. It wasn't like my family was saying braids or natural hair was bad but I definitely got the message that having black hair wasn't always considered good enough. I, of course, feel differently now. I wear my hair natural and can appreciate what the good Lord has given me. I guess I've gone back to my roots. I comb my daughter's hair in braids and ribbons too. I'm proud of that and wouldn't change it.

Before proceeding, the timeliness of my conversation with Natalie and other MSGCIs should be noted as well; at the time of these interviews, there is increasing acceptance of natural hairstyling of braids, twists, and locs that are perceived more readily and associated with ideals of black beauty standards. Let me emphasize here, popular acceptance of braids, cornrows, and locs, for example, does not translate into political and social acceptance of "the black body." In fact, the assumption that natural hairstyles are the new norm for beauty standards encourages a false sense of racial progress that reinforce certain stereotypes of what is/should be considered acceptable behavior and practices (including grooming practices) for blacks. Arguably, this assumption can be translated into a "blacks have made it now" narrative that suggests blacks *now* should be considered and treated as equal to whites even though white ideals of beauty, for example, remain the norm.

Natalie's awareness of the privileges of assimilation that are assumed if a woman wears her hair straightened is juxtaposed with her triple identity consciousness that encourages her to embrace aspects of what she has identified as a Caribbean way of hairstyling within the Caribbean American community. Illustrative of Natalie's quote and of her expanding triple identity consciousness is the notion that one's sense of identity (through the markers of hair grooming, for example) have different meanings as the context of relationality changes and the change in context can amend internal awareness of who one is—for themselves and as in the way they are externally perceived as the "black" Other.

There were several other memories MSGCIs recalled as important moments to their developing sense of a black and Caribbean racial and ethnic identity within the context of colorism. In some instances, MSGCIs' awareness of the racialization of hair texture and skin color was expressed in the children's games they played with their friends or in teens' dating choices—as both Shana and Carmen explain.

Here, Shana describes witnessing a friend's experience with skin color discrimination that signaled black and Latino teen males' negative sentiments regarding darker skinned girls' complexions and hair texture.

SHANA

In school, lighter skinned boys never seemed to have an interest in darker skinned girls. And there was no solidarity among darker skinned boys either. They were just as bad. They would make fun of the girls who were dark or would have nappy hair. There was a boy my best friend in high school liked terribly. One day, while hanging out at his friend's house, I heard the boy tell my best friend "I like you but if we were to have sex we couldn't do it in the dark because I wouldn't be able to see you unless you smiled or something." Funny thing, he was a dark-skinned Dominican boy with an even darker complexion than my best friend. It was ironic. She was so upset and we left out of there but not with out her cursing him out first for being ignorant and for assuming they would be having sex. Looking back now, I know it is so dumb but when you are a teenager and you want guys to find you sexually attractive like any other girl, it's hard to hear the self-hate.

Shana's retelling of this type of skin color bias points to the colonial mentality from centuries of colonial subjugation that remains pervasive in the hearts and minds of young people in the post Civil rights era. Her poignant observation also reveals the preference of European values, that lightness or close to whiteness has been and continues to be projected as inherently better than blackness but that such privileging comes with a price: a reflection of white supremacy and devaluation of blackness in teen's dating choices.

Here, Carmen's vignette also points to the pervasiveness of colonial mentality in children's games as she reflects on skin color bias and how children conceive white and black ancestry differently despite the fact that throughout the Americas and as a result of colonization, "sexual relationships between people of different African backgrounds as well as interracial relationships have resulted in even more varied phenotypic combinations" (Abrams 2014:81).

CARMEN

Carmen was born in the late 1970s in the greater Providence, Rhode Island metropolitan area. She is the second of five children born to her Dominican immigrant parents, who arrived in the mid-1960s and met while working in a local manufacturing company. Carmen self identifies as Afro Latina, American, and Dominican. Before entering high school, Carmen and her family moved to Fall River, Massachusetts to be closer to extended family who moved there. After graduating from a catholic high school, Carmen attended a small liberal arts college in Massachusetts, majoring in English with a minor in human development. Shortly after graduation, she landed a job in college admissions as a counselor and has been working in higher education as a college admissions director for several years. At the time of interview, Carmen was a few months away from earning her Master's degree in higher education management. Carmen is married to an Italian American caterer and they live in New Jersey with their four-year old daughter.

CARMEN explains:

> Light skin and long hair is what people pray for, want and think is beautiful. I remember in elementary school, the girls would play a [origami] paper fortune teller game where you would put colors on one side and numbers on the other and count off. And based on the number you land on, you would choose a favorite color. You then unfold the paper and it would reveal a silly fortune. Sometimes you were told which boy in the class you would marry, how many children you would have or what your children would look like. These games could get real tense and emotional especially if a darker skinned girl would get the fortune that she would have a baby with light skin and green eyes. Once my classmate got teased for a fortune and some of the girls told her something like, "well it's only pretend. It's not like you could ever have a baby like that. You are just too dark." Can you believe it? When I think about it, it's like, damn, I can't make this stuff up. But this is the kind of shit you deal with and you carry with you.

Utilizing black feminist thought and critical race theory to understand both Shana's and Carmen's stories, their vignettes offer illustrations in the ways MSGCIs witnessed and experienced scripts regarding intrapersonal relationships and appropriate dating behaviors. Because scripts are the mental structures used to develop attitudes and prescriptions for appropriate dating behaviors to which the MSGCIs have been exposed, they are also responsible for influencing both MSGCIs' self evaluation of his or her status and position in a social situation (i.e., with other co-ethnics) and for others. In this case, the racialized and gender stereotypes that exist about dark skin color and black bodies has a role in shaping beliefs on dating and more importantly, the internalization of these skin color stereotypes on self-efficacy and black identity construction.

Skin color bias is not a gendered phenomenon relegated to the experiences of women only. Men are also are impacted by beauty standards that privilege whiteness but in different ways. According to a few of the MSGCIs, beauty standards for black men is less about their use of skin color as social capital to be used in dating and marriage markets (in the same way women may use it to marry up) but more so related to their masculinity and perceptions about their external successes socially and economically. Robert explains,

ROBERT

I would say guys are affected by color too but are not judged as harshly as women of color are. Girls like the light guys with the curly hair; they call them pretty boys like actors Phillip Michael Thomas from Miami Vice or Michael Ealy. The stereotype is light skinned pretty boys are handsome and successful but not too tough. If you are a dark-skinned brother, then you have to be like those big, dark chocolate mandingo brothas, with a bald head or locs, like I always hear the women refer to guys like Terry Crews and Michael Clarke Duncan or singer Tyrese. Even my aunt used to have a thing for Michael Jordan. Women perhaps look at the big, dark brother as strong, sexual, a little rough around the edges; as a protector. I guess I've never thought about color the same way because I've never had any trouble attracting females either way. And I like all women too—from white, Asian, Spanish girls, dark to light and in between too, though I admit I do have a special place in my heart for dark-skinned women but I married a light-skinned woman. So you see, I don't have a [color] preference like some other guys. But I do see my color playing more of a role in the workplace. Just as people of color have their own color bias, white people do too. I'm a big enough guy but I am not dark, so maybe I am not seen as physically intimidating in the same way. Now, I still will have the white woman clutching her purse a little more tightly if I was walking down the street but that, I would say, is more because she sees a black man approaching her as opposed to the non-dark-skinned black guy approaching her.

Indeed, Robert's vignette acknowledges a double standard exists in dating preferences and scripts for men. Robert's narrative also points to the intersectionality of race and gender within the concept of colorism, particularly when he speaks to the longstanding stereotype about the black male body, particularly dark bodies as "the Black Buck,"—a violent and physical threat to whiteness (and white women)—that is a mainstay in the public imagination. The "Black Buck" stereotype and imagery was popularized during post-Reconstruction in the United States and depicted in racist and misogynist movies such as D.W. Griffith's (1915) *Birth of a Nation* (also known as the Clansman), Richard Fleischer's (1975) blaxploitation *Mandingo* and Quentin Tarantino's (2012) *Django Unchained,* which has helped to further solidify the racialization of black masculinity that is seen today in popular culture, music videos and even within mate selection behaviors. Accordingly, colorism feminizes lighter-skinned men, rendering them more pretty, perhaps suburban and less masculine in comparison to darker-skinned men who are perceived as being strong, masculine, and more urban. Often such scripts on the skin color expectations of black male masculinity among both whites and nonwhites infers that the darker the black man, the more "real" blackness he represents whereas the light skinned black man is inauthentic because his skin represents "the sin of collusion with white society" (Dyson 2016). The idea or notion around "authentic" blackness as it relates to skin color has interesting effects on the self-identity and efficacy of lighter-skinned individuals who are also subjected to skin color bias and colorism, despite the presumed privilege of having a lighter hue.

Skin Color, Ethnicity, and Black Authenticity

The MSGCIs' process of racialization as children of Caribbean immigrants raises an interesting nuance to understanding blackness as experience. As stated previously, racism and colorism both directly and indirectly informed the MSGCIs' conceptions and assertions of their racial and ethnic black identities. Participants discussed the contexts and situations in which they learned to define for themselves "blackness" as something distinct despite being labeled the colonial other. There were several consistencies across the stories told by the MSGCIs themselves; the historical impacts of colonialism have led to the persistence of discrimination and bias experienced by those of African descent throughout the Americas. The interesting nuance to understanding blackness, however, is in the way—despite the diversity that exists intragroup—blackness is perceived as a monolith, particularly when skin color is used to define racial inclusion.

Several MSGCIs talked about the color divide which privileges lighter skin as whiteness while dark skin is considered "authentic black" but low on the color hierarchy and social status. Yet, the interpretation of "dark skin as real blackness" or authentic blackness is considered highly problematic and insulting to those MSGCIs who feel co-ethnics and whites think they are not black enough or authentically black. This sentiment rang strongly among MSGCIs whose light to medium-brown complexions and mixed racial-ethnic backgrounds are assumed to signal their Anglo-assimilation or a lessened race-consciousness and social and political views.

Here, Carmen describes her experiences as a light skinned woman of color subjected to reverse color bias—a belief that because of her mixed racial and ethnic heritage and skin color, she does not identify with nor care about other blacks, thinks she is better than other co-ethnics or wishes she was white.

CARMEN

I'm Black, I'm Latina—Dominican. I have always embraced all parts of my identity. There's also Haitian, Italian, Dutch and who knows what else. When I say I am black, they don't think I am black enough because I have lighter skin and my hair is straight. They think I have it easy or something; they think I am not discriminated against or that people don't mistake me for the housekeeper when I open the door to my own house. Only when they see my mother who is darker than me, then it's different. She is like my "black card." I've tried dating dark-skinned men and there were problems with that too. The men would talk about how much they found me beautiful and exotic until we argued and then they would say some real hurtful stuff, like, "that's why I should get with a *real* black woman." So, again, am I not black enough? One ex-boyfriend said dating him was me trying too hard to be something I'm not. It is very offensive. But I have found other Latinas and especially Dominicans born here (U.S) also carry the stereotypes their parents hold too and deny their own history. I have some relatives that are light skinned too but they are mixed with Haitian somewhere in there. They don't want to accept that or else they would lose their privilege, false privilege with having light skin. No one wants to be dark-skinned because dark means "blackness" and that equals Haitian. That is antihatianismo.

Carmen shares an interesting viewpoint I observed across several MSGCI interviews regarding color conflicts and contradictions, and how these are embedded in a larger context of racial stratification. Skin color becomes a social indicator of status in a way that has impacted both intra-family relations and a person's presentation of self. According to Carmen, some of her own family members, perhaps, have learned that lighter skin affords them membership in a group with Spanish as opposed to African lineage and, as such, received a higher social status. Perhaps this is due to the fact that some of these relatives live in the Fall River area of Massachusetts (with Latinos out-numbering African Americans by double), which provides them with ethno-racial identity options that are similar to color and class categories in the Caribbean and Latin America (see Bonilla-Silva 2009). At the same time, when considered within the process of racialization, MSGCIs that are light or medium brown in complexion and/or of mixed ancestry are assumed to have identities that are centered solely on their immigrant generation; their ethnic authenticity is connected to being foreign-born because they may also be French or Spanish speaking as opposed to having a connection to a English-speaking, native-born African American racial experience. It should be noted, however, that among francophone and hispanophone MSGCIs, regardless of skin color, they seem to activate their triple identity consciousness when it comes to forging and building community with other co-ethnics by utilizing their Spanish/French and English language ability when their skin color status casts doubt on their racial and ethnic identity authenticity.

Several participants also have described the ways Caribbean ethnic identity sometimes complicate how others perceived or viewed their "authentic blackness." Here Eddy discusses predominant skin color stereotypes that people tend to ascribe to Jamaican and Haitian ethnicities that he feels does not fit.

> People have stereotypes about what all Jamaicans look like. I've heard people say, "well Jamaicans are all dark-skinned like Shabba Ranks and Beenie Man" or "Jamaicans are happy and mellow people like Bob Marley, with dreadlocks, and enjoy smoking weed." Then people ask me, "so you must smoke weed too, right? Jamaicans are diverse; some are white, Indian Chinese and black mix. But Jamaicans are not the only ones who have these stereotypes. The worst, I think, is among Haitians. I actually used to date this woman; she's Haitian American. She is light-skinned but people would say to her that she was not a really Haitian because all Haitians are dark,

ugly, terrible dressers and she was not like any of those things. Hearing "you're pretty for a Haitian" or being asked if her parents taught her voodoo was hurtful to her and me too. I couldn't believe the ignorance from people and some of those same people were Haitian too.

The perception of Jamaican and Haitian ethnics as being darker-skinned individuals only, as mentioned by Eddy, exacerbates the idea that they have a low social status both inside and outside of the black community. For the MSGCIs who discussed intra-group conflict when it came to color bias, they were more frustrated by the prevalence of various forms of prejudice perpetrated by other second generation Caribbean immigrants like themselves and more generally from other people of color. Ironically, many seem to expect these biases and prejudice to be directed at them from whites but less so from other people of color. As such, it becomes clear how white imperialism, colonization, and slavery become internalized and has left a lasting imprint on those who self-identify as black and the ways skin color hierarchies inform individuals' initial perception of and experience with blackness.

Discussing colorism, the notion of "authentic black," and the persistence of stereotypes, discrimination, and bias are important components to understanding contemporary race and ethnic relations and how the diverse children of Caribbean immigrants interpret how they "fit" into the larger "American racial project," which assigns significant meaning and status to one's race and ethnic identity. MSGCIs' experiences to date—those deemed positive and negative, played a significant role in the ways they learned about and considered "blackness" in their own identity assertions and as it relates to existing social structures of white racism.

In this chapter, MSGCIs' ethno-racial experiences were framed in multiple ways. Within a geographic context, MSGCIs described themselves in ways that spoke to embracing and challenging culture, values, and behaviors of being both black and of Caribbean descent while living in major cities across the United States. Participants also considered how their American-ness was also related to their blackness especially when they traveled abroad and were visiting family in the Caribbean. In particular, some MSGCIs discussed being "American" and "black" as a duality: being an American by birth but still part of a different society that would never include them because of their race and Caribbean ethnicity. Finally, the MSGCIs also described situations where they had to interpret and internalize meanings of "blackness" as it related to their skin color and hair texture and how these meanings have shaped their own black identity assertions. The challenge is to explore how these meanings of blackness translate in the everyday experiences and interactions MSGCIs have in public and private spaces.

As discussed in the previous chapter, employing Eduardo Bonilla-Silva's (2009) thesis on the three-tier racial hierarchy, which posits this more expansive racial hierarchy model still reinforces whites and honorary whites (Asians and light-skinned Latinos) to the top and blacks (darker-skinned Latinos), suggests there are still questions to be considered. For instance, how does being automatically relegated to a low social status in the racial hierarchy due to one's blackness (racially and/or skin color) be "compensated for" with other high-status characteristics such as social class (i.e., middle class and upper-middle class), education, or immigrant generation? Are these racial/ethnic options possible for this group? What are the costs and benefits of being MSGCI? Further, as it relates to the discussion presented in this chapter particularly—what are the implications of race, ethnicity, colorism, AND social class influencing mate selection, residential choice, and child rearing practices? Interestingly, when I employ the triple identity consciousness framework to understand the MSGCIs' experiences around their notions of "blackness," I contend their awareness and definitions of blackness is not about being anti-white or not white yet being painfully aware of the negative social constructions of blackness that does exist and gets applied to them. In this regard, recognizing the projections of the social world placed on the MSGCIs, and their ability to step outside of these projections to understand the positioning of themselves in relationship to others (both whites and nonwhites) around skin color, hair texture, and nativity as Bonilla-Silva himself examines, and carve out both physical and social spaces to embrace their agency, shows the MSGCIs conscientiously rejecting the coercive effects of these hegemonic forces (see Benjamin 1988).

In the next chapter, I continue to examine what it means to be "Black in America" for this generation by extending the discussion to include a microanalysis of the habitus of blackness and the confluence of middle class-ness for this generation. I present the complex, reflexive process MSGCIs shared of themselves, including how they use cultural capital, how they see themselves as similar to and different from their Caribbean immigrant parents, what their own intentions, values, prejudices are as middle class Blacks and children of immigrants, and how all of these inform and influence their interactions with interpersonal, social and institutional structures, and racialized systems.

NOTES

1. The West Indian-American carnival had its roots in Harlem in the 1920s, when lavish events were held at the Savoy, Renaissance, and Audubon Ballrooms. The carnival left Harlem in 1965 as an increasing number of Caribbean immigrants settled in central Brooklyn. Aside from its economic impact, this Labor Day carnival is an assertion of pan-Caribbean culture, bringing together people from different island nations underneath one umbrella, and demonstrating the power and vibrancy of the peoples of the Caribbean. (http://www.bklynlibrary.org/ourbrooklyn/carnival/; Retrieved May 21, 2011).

2. My leeriness derives from my own consideration of Gaytri Chakravorty Spivak's (1988/2008) essay "Can the Subaltern Speak?" in which she discusses an important viewpoint regarding one's ability to retrieve the subaltern's voice. Spivak urges the researcher like myself to constantly consider or question the lens through which I consider, interpret and perhaps even, translate the narratives shared so that I am not erasing the true voice and subjectivity of the subaltern and objectify it with dominant historiography.

3. In their article, "Transnationalism in Question" by Roger Waldinger and David Fitzgerald describes transnational or transnationalism as having and maintaining connections to various networks or communities that extend beyond loyalties to any particular place of origin or national group. This notion connotes fluidity of identity, belongingness, and membership that exceed boundaries of nation and state.

4. The one-drop rule led to widespread institutionalization of definite racial categories based on "hypo-descent" and gave formal credence to a burgeoning belief that blackness emanated from blood, as seen in miscegenation laws. Refer to Ian Haney-Lopez's (1996) book, *White by Law: The Legal Construction of Race.*

5. There are two basic forms of chattel: domestic chattel, with menial household duties, and productive chattel, working in the fields.

BIBLIOGRAPHY

Abrams, A. C. (2014). *God and Blackness: Race, Gender and Identity in a Middle Class Afrocentric Church.* New York: New York University Press.

Ashcroft, B., Griffiths, G., & Tiffin, H. (2006). *Post-Colonial Studies Reader* (2nd ed.). New York: Routledge/ Taylor and Francis.

Benjamin, J. (1988). *The Bonds of Love: Psychoanalysis, Feminism and the Problem of Domination.* New York: Pantheon Books.

Berry, G. L. (1998). Black Family Life on Television and the Socialization of the African American Child: Images of Marginality. *Journal of Comparative Family Studies, 29,* 233–242.

Bonilla-Silva, E. (2006). *Racism without Racists: Color-blind Racism and the Persistence of Racial Inequality* (2nd ed.). Rowan Littlefield.

Bonilla-Silva, E. (2009). *Racism without Racists: Color-blind Racism and the Persistence of Racial Inequality* (3rd ed.). Rowan Littlefield.

Bonilla-Silva, E. (2013). *Racism without Racists: Color-blind Racism and the Persistence of Racial Inequality* (4th ed.). Rowan Littlefield.

Bordo, S. (1993). *Unbearable Weight: Feminism, Western Culture, and the Body.* Los Angeles: University of California Press.

Brubaker, R., & Cooper, F. (2000). Beyond Identity. *Theory and Society, 29*(1), 1–47.

Collins, P. H. (2000). *Black Feminist Thought: Knowledge, Consciousness and the Politics of Empowerment* (2nd ed.). New York/London: Routledge.

Deaux, K. (1996). Social Identification. In E. T. Higgins & A. W. Kruglanski (Eds.), *Social Psychology: Handbook of Basic Principles* (pp. 777–798). New York: Guildford Press.

Delgado, R., & Stefancic, J. (2012). *Critical Race Theory: An Introduction* (2nd ed.). New York: New York University Press.

Dyson, M. E. (2016, June 1). *Commentary: The Color Line: Stephen Curry's Prominence Resurfaces Issues of Colorism Among Blacks.* Retrieved October 15, 2016, from UnDefeated: http://theundefeated.com/features/light-skinned-vs-dark-skinned/

Erikson, E. (1999). Youth and the Life Cycle. In R. Muss & H. Porton (Eds.), *Adolescent Behavior* (5th ed., pp. 252–259). Boston: McGraw Hill, College.

Etcoff, N. L. (2000). *Survival of the Prettiest: The Science of Beauty.* New York: Anchor books.

Fanon, F. (1967). *Black Skin, White Masks* (C. L. Markmann, Trans.). New York: Grove Weidenfeld Press.

Hall, S. (1990). Cultural Identity and Diaspora. In J. Rutherford (Ed.), *Identity: Community, Culture, Difference* (1st ed., pp. 222–237). London: Lawrence and Wishart.

Hall, S. (1993). What is this "Black" in Black Popular Culture (Rethinking Race). *Social Justice, 20*(1–2), 104–113.

Hall, S. (1999). Encoding, Decoding. In S. During (Ed.), *The Cultural Studies Reader* (pp. 90–103). London: Routledge.

Hall, S., Held, D., Hubert, D., & Thompson, K. (1996). *Modernity: An Introduction to Modern Societies.* Hoboken: Wiley-Blackwell.

Haney-Lopez, I. (1996). *White by Law: The Legal Construction of Race.* New York: New York University Press.

Harrison, M., & Thomas, K. (2009). The Hidden Prejudice in Selection: A Research Investigation on Skin Color Bias. *Journal of Applied Social Psychology, 39*(1), 134–168.

hooks, b. (1989/2015). *Talking Back: Thinking Feminist, Thinking Black* (2nd ed.). New York: Routledge.

Hunter, M. (1998). Colorstruck: Skin Color Stratification in the Lives of African American Women. *Sociological Inquiry, 68*, 517–535.

Hunter, M. (2002). If You're Light, You're Alright: Light Skin Color as Social Capital for Women of Color. *Gender and Society, 16*(2), 175–193.

Krauss, W. (2006). The Narrative Negotiation of Identity and Belonging. *Narrative Inquiry, 16*(1), 103–111.

Leeds, M. (1994). Young African-American Women and the Language of Beauty. In K. Callaghan (Ed.), *Ideals of Feminine Beauty: Philosophical, Social and Cultural Dimensions* (pp. 147–160). London: Greenwood.

Lindesmith, A., & Strauss, A. (1969). *Readings in Social Psychology*. New York: Holt McDougal.

Lorick-Wilmot, Y. (2010). *Creating Black Caribbean Ethnic Identity, Book Series, The New Americans: Recent Immigrant and American Society ed*. El Paso: LFB Scholarly Publishing.

Norwood, K. J. (2013). *Color Matters: Skin Tone Bias and the Myth of a Postracial America*. New York: Routledge.

Offord, B. (2002). Mapping the Rainbow Region: Fields of Belonging and Sites of Confluence. *Transformations, 2*, 1–17.

Omi, M., & Winant, H. (1986/2015). *Racial Formation in the United States*. New York: Routledge.

Portes, A., & Rumbaut, R. (2001). *Legacies: The Story of the Immigrant Second Generation*. Berkeley: University of California Press.

Rumbaut, R. (2005). Sites of Belonging: Acculturation, Discrimination, and Ethnic Identity among Children of Immigrants. In T. S. Weisner (Ed.), *Discovering Successful Pathways in Children's Development: New Methods in the Study of Childhood and Family Life* (pp. 111–163). Chicago: University of Chicago Press.

Rumbaut, R. (2009). Pigments of Our Imagination: On Racialization and Racial Identities of 'Hispanics' and 'Latinos'. In J. A. Cobas, J. Duany, & J. R. Feagin (Eds.), *How the U.S. Racializes Latinos: White Hegemony and Its Consequences* (pp. 15–36). St. Paul: Paradigm Publishing.

Sen, A. (2006). *Identity and Violence: The Illusion of Destiny*. New York: Norton and Company.

Spivak, G. C. (1988/2008). Can the Subaltern Speak? In J. Sharp, *Geographies on PostColonialism*. Thousand Oaks: Sage Publications.

Vedantam, S. (2010, January 19). Shades of Prejudice. *The New York Times*, p. A31.

CHAPTER 5

Habitus of Blackness and the Confluence of Middle Class-ness

In the American Sociological Association's September/October 2015 edition of *Footnotes*, one article highlighted sociologist William Julius Wilson's four-month tenure as the 2015 Klug Chair in American Law and Governance at the John W. Kluge Center, Library of Congress. The author described a public lecture Wilson gave at the Library of Congress in which he revisited the arguments made in his influential 1978 book *The Declining Significance of Race* and the ways race and class continue to both influence Americans' opportunities for success—not just for black people, but for all people of color.

Wilson's *The Declining Significance of Race* was considered a controversial book as many assumed he was arguing race was no longer significant or that racial barriers between blacks and whites had been eliminated. Perhaps the reasoning for this controversy was in the way Wilson compared the contemporary situation of black people in the United States to their situation in the past, and how the diverging experiences of blacks along class lines indicated to him, that race was no longer the primary determinant of life chances for blacks in the way it had been historically. Or perhaps it was the interpretation by conservatives that Wilson's research had a structural bent that led some, including policy makers, to make predictions about individual outcomes and stereotypical conceptions of who defines the black underclass (see also Robert J. Sampson's 2008 article, "Moving to Inequality"). Later, in his 1987 book, *The Truly Disadvantaged* Wilson

© The Author(s) 2018
Y.S. Lorick-Wilmot, *Stories of Identity among Black, Middle Class, Second Generation Caribbeans,*
DOI 10.1007/978-3-319-62208-8_5

considered the controversy of his previous book, and instead focused on social policy. He argued that significant out-migration of black working and middle class families from inner-city neighborhoods in the late 1970s, combined with rising numbers of poor residents due to escalating rates of unemployment, resulted in heavy concentrations of ghetto poverty. Wilson went on to argue that the decline in the number of black working and middle class families in these communities led to the decline in the number of social buffers (i.e., social supports and role models). Social buffers, Wilson argues, have been key to helping racial and ethnic communities minimize the social and economic impacts of long-term unemployment in their communities.

Halfway through the *Footnotes* article, the author makes reference to a June 5, 2015 radio interview Wilson did with Carol Castiel of *Voices of America* where he clarifies the premise of his longstanding arguments in these books regarding the important relevance and intersectional qualities of race and class:

> One would be naïve to say that race is no longer a factor in American life. This talk about a post-racial society is silly.... Race and racism continue to be important factors in American life but we should not reduce every problem facing people of color to race and racism. That's just part of the overall problem...Today, I argue, racial tensions and conflicts have more to do with competition for and access to residential areas, public schools, and municipal political systems than with competition with jobs.

Researchers continue to point to the relevance of race, class inequality, and social policy, as it continues to affect the life outcomes, social mobility, and occupational trajectories of people of color and their children. Indeed, there remains since the Great Recession, a growing economic and social divide between men and women of color who are low-income and working class and those who may be defined as the professional, middle class. Since 2009, poverty rates for blacks and Latinos, for example, have been nearly three times higher than for whites, relative to their population size. At the same time, the United States has also well-documented socioeconomic gains of blacks over a few decades—albeit slow and steady—resulting in the growth of the black middle class. In 2000, the US Census reported approximately "16 percent of blacks 25 years and older have a bachelor's degree or higher; of these, 46 percent live in an owner-occupied housing unit, earn a median income of approximately $32,000 and 25 percent of the black employed are in management, professional and related occupations" (Marsh et al. 2007:741; see also US Census 2000). When these findings are compared to 24% of individuals in the United States as a whole who also earned a bachelor's degree, where of these 66% live in an owner-occupied unit, earned above $42,000 and 34% were in a professional occupation, then it is easily presumed that the black middle class is growing.

To be clear, the growth of the black middle class is not a phenomenon of the last 20 years. Scholars Bart Landry and Kris Marsh in their article *The Evolution of the New Black Middle Class* contend sociologists W.E.B. Du Bois, who famously wrote about "the talented tenth" and "the professional class," and E. Franklin Frazier were one of the first scholars to write explicitly of a black middle class and their growth during the early twentieth century. In fact, Frazier's famous essay "Durham, Capital of the Black Middle Class," in Alain Locke's book *The New Negro* (1925:333) was explicit in the way black middle class was to be defined and perceived as distinct. "No longer can men say that the Negro is lazy and shiftless and a consumer. He has gone to work. He is a producer. He is respectable. He has a middle class." Despite its growth and ability to shape the American social landscape into the twenty-first century, scholars such as Douglas Massey, Kevin Fitzpatrick, Sean-Shong Hwang and David Helms, Mary Pattillo, Melvin Oliver, and Thomas Shapiro, for example, still agree that today's black middle class are not insulated from historical and persistent marginalization, discrimination, and racism, which is a very different experience from that of whites in the middle class. In other words, pathways of upward social class mobility for blacks in the United States are complicated by race and ethnicity in ways that no other groups experience.

As evidenced by these scholars, their important research tells the public a lot about the black middle class in the United States (as more socially mobile and achieving higher educational and residential attainments) and how their experiences figure in to the discussion around persisting structural and income inequality. Interestingly, the sociological research (as of this writing) does not consistently nor clearly examine how these experiences impact black middle class's own self-conception of being the "black middle class" (see also Hunt and Ray 2012; Landry and Marsh 2011). In other words, how does "the black middle class" see themselves as individuals and as a group? What does it mean to be "black middle class" in a society that associates blackness with poverty and dysfunction and associates whiteness with middle class status? How are these self-conceptions especially nuanced if these individuals are also MSGCIs?

What are, if any, the cultural conflicts these blacks experience as black people, as second generation Caribbean immigrants, as middle class, and how they conceive of their own position in American society?

Before considering these questions in relationship to MSGCIs, it is important to correlate these issues with US definitions, logic, and expressions of middle class-ness, which is full of racial meaning. I contend because black racial identity in combination with one's black immigrant status is often equated with poverty, an examination of racialization as it relates to social class becomes imperative in the sociological discussion on black mobility and middle class-ness. The following sections will point to the contemporary racial landscape, which was created and continues to be maintained by systems of racism and white supremacy that are meant to subjugate (educationally, economically, socially, politically, and residentially) people of color while maintaining structures of white privilege and advantage. In this regard, this study on the MSGCIs considers how immigrant generation and racial (blackness) experiences can be informed by social class and the privileges that being middle class and upper middle class can bring.

DEFINING MIDDLE CLASS IN THE UNITED STATES: THEORETICAL CONCEPTUALIZATIONS

It is important to acknowledge the varied sociological meanings and conceptions of social class in terms of who "owns the means of production" and who is "primarily responsible for the means of re/production of goods and materials"[1] as it relates to racial economic division of labor. For the sake of analytic reference, racial economic division of labor is a neo-Marxist concept that refers to the ways capitalism encourages the formation of racial distinctions that are tied to specific occupational categories. Theodore Allen in *The Invention of the White Race, Volume One* (1994:69–70), argues that racial divisions of labor are possible under capitalism because the system itself institutionalizes the association between race (and skin color) and manual labor (means of re/production):

> Where they [whites] find a developed and well-defined hierarchal system of classes the new rulers sought to adapt their pre-existing needs, co-opting amenable elements of the older order into their colonial administration as a buffer and social control stratum order and against the masses of the super-exploited…

Where the conquerors encountered a society with no previously developed significant class differentiation and therefore with no available social handle to serve their rules, they employed a policy tending to the complete elimination of the indigenous population by slaughter and expulsion...In such cases, the colonizers found themselves obliged to seek foreign [African] supplies of commodity-producing labor and were obliged to invent and establish an intermediate social control stratum for each colony by promoting elements of the imported laboring class.

In its application, racialized populations (nonwhites, broadly speaking), particularly during chattel slavery, came to be seen as having low status in the social control stratum. In this social division, people of African descent were defined by their strong bodies and virility and excluded from education and any intellectual labor, often associated with white middle and elite classes. According to Allen (1994), these racial divisions of labor can be observed in societies across the Western hemisphere (throughout the Americas and the Caribbean) where slavery, colonialism, and (neo)imperialism persisted even after slavery was abolished in those same societies.

Class as Race: Middle Class Is Raced as White and Poverty Is Raced as Black

It is the period after slavery where there is an observable difference in the way social class is defined and distinguished across these societies. These differences speak to dimensions of social stratification and mobility that exist in a given society. Take societies in the English-speaking Caribbean, for instance. Until the end of the nineteenth century, countries such as St. Vincent, Grenada, Trinidad, and Jamaica had bifurcated social classes—a white elite/ruling class (land owners) and black laborers (exploited labor force working the land)—that was very similar to the racial divisions in the United States. By the twentieth century, however, as the British presence in the Anglophone Caribbean lessened,[2] colonial rule was amended to involve more Afro-descended people in administrative positions along with Syrian, East Asian, and Chinese merchants also living on the islands.

According to Michael Garfield (M.G.) Smith (1984:29), there emerged a black, 'colored,' and 'creole' middle class that expanded the existing social class structure, although there were distinctions reinforced by differences in education, family structure, religion, language, and color—a residual of longstanding racial economic division of labor. As discussed in the previous chapter, the significance of colorism is an important aspect of racism and racialization throughout the Americas. In some Caribbean countries with majority nonwhite populations, color-social class divisions are not as rigid as they are in the United States, for example. A person's sole reliance on their lighter skin tone does not automatically indicate one's economic status nor does it indicate his or her social position. Henry Louis Gates, Jr.'s *Black in Latin America* (2011) cites the prevailing high rates of poverty among those who are self-identified as black and especially among those who are darker in complexion living in Latin American and Caribbean countries such as Cuba, the Dominican Republic, Mexico, and Brazil, to name a few.

It would appear, according to the works of Fernando Henriques' *Family and Colour in Jamaica* (1953) and Lloyd Braithwaite's *Social Stratification in Trinidad* (1953), that it is possible for a person to transcend their color-class standing, improve their economic wellbeing while achieving upward mobility if certain social conditions are met: achievement of education, adoption of certain cultural values and practices, wealth and land owner-ship, and elite association. A potential explanation for this perceived fluidity in mobility is in the way patterns of race, skin color stratification and income/occupation overlap or as Stuart Hall (1977:171) has suggested, it is a stratification system that is, "over-determined; its public signification is more explicit than in societies where no 'ethnic' index exists [as in European class societies]." Hence, M.G. Smith asserts if we are to examine the dimen-sions of social class and mobility in the Caribbean, especially in societies where black-identified people represent over 80% of the population, there is an additional factor to consider along with color and economics—the coalescing of political ideologies found, "in their participation in voluntary associations, occupational and political organizations for special interests" (1965:237).

I contend David Lowenthal's (1972:92, 138–139) *West Indian Societies* explains it best when he describes social class and the complexity of strati-fication and mobility in the Caribbean as it relates to racialization and racial social hierarchies:

> The range of West Indian stratification do not stem from class distinctions alone, but also from racial and ethnic differences. Racial and ethnic catego-ries overlap in reality and are locally confused with one another, but differ-ent social and cultural consequences tend to flow from each... Compared with South Africa or the United States, the one ideologically and the other

institutionally racialist, the West Indies are in most ways open ...[with] blacks increasingly inherit[ing] his own society...[Although] race and colour are shorthand designations of class, they often overwhelm all other connotations. Colour groupings are blurred and fragmented rather than dichotomised and the attrition of white and light elites facilitates black mobility. The numerical weakness of the elite forces cognizance of pressures from below, and the entire class hierarchy is knit together by [racial] intermixing, acculturation and assimilation.

In contrast to Caribbean notions of mobility, where there is a confluence of race, color, and economic factors that determines one's class position and status, it appears the United States myopically defines social class by a calculated average of occupation, income, and education. For example, using income measures from the US Census Current Population Report (2015) *Income and Poverty in the United States: 2014*, the middle class is considered to be people whose median household income was approximately $53,657. When we disaggregate this data by race and ethnicity and compare across groups, we find Asian Americans had the highest median incomes at $74,297 and whites (non-Hispanic) had median incomes around $60,256 whereas Hispanics/Latinos (any race) and blacks had the lowest median incomes of $42,491 and $35,398 respectively. Most people consider middle class incomes to be closer to $50,000, including the MSGCIs in this study who consider the annual income range of middle class to be $40,000 or more. In fact, the MSGCIs in this study self-identified as middle class but reported having annual household incomes well above the US median household thresholds—ranging between mid $50,000s and $90,000s, with an exception of a few whose annual incomes were slightly under $150,000 per year. Another attribute used to determine a person's class status is education as it directly impacts his or her ability to attain occupations that have greater autonomy and financial compensation. Therefore, most people in the United States perceive having a Bachelor's degree as a key element to ensuring one's access to better occupational opportunities and higher wages, as there is almost a $35,000 wage gap between the median household incomes of those who earned a high school diploma and those who earned a Bachelor's degree.

In reality, the United States has dual conceptions of class: a Marxist conception (a person's position in the marketplace as either owner or laborer), as I mentioned previously, and a Weberian conception of class that speaks to a person's social status (lifestyle dimensions). For theorist Max Weber, when a person has an advantage of being an owner of property, he or she is able to accumulate and possess material resources and access sources of wealth creation—all of which can lead to a particular standard of living. As such, wealth is a key determinant upon which privilege (respect), status or enhanced life chances depends (Gerth and Mills 1958). Weber's emphasis on status and lifestyle is critical to the American ethos of meritocracy and serves as the basis for defining middle class: the belief that success is won from hard work and sacrifice and the ability to accumulate a certain amount of wealth. It is this belief that economists and policy researchers contend is the, "key part of the engine that drives American prosperity. The middle class provides skilled workers consumer purchasing power essential to a strong economy. The quality of life associated with being middle class also fuels aspirations of social mobility" (Shapiro et al. 2007:2).

For those interested in a concise definition of the concept "middle class," be aware that it is the most vaguely defined, of the social classes. According to Shapiro et al. (2007), the concept can be used to describe a relative elite of professionals and managers–also called the upper middle class, who are highly educated, well-paid professionals (high-wage income earners) with considerable work autonomy. Also, the term can be used to describe those in-between the extremes of income and wealth, such as those who are semi-professionals, craftsmen, office staff, and sales employees who often have college degrees and are very loosely supervised (see Gilbert 1998; Thompson and Hickey 2005).

Notwithstanding, there are consistent cultural models that most people in the United States have, when the concept of middle class is evoked in public thinking. Often these cultural models hint to the status and ideal lifestyle dimensions Weber discusses in his theories on class, prestige, power, and status. Weber asserts: the middle class are educated, have incomes that can afford quality housing and healthcare in addition to supporting a reasonable standard of living, has a safety net for its financial security in the future, and has the ability to build intergenerational wealth and are able to pass it on to future generations. There are, of course, additional cultural models that point to family or household structure of the middle class, such as hetero-normative ideals of family (i.e., husband, wife, and children), even though there are steadily increasing numbers of households with members who are "single and living alone," for example.

Race as Class: Who Owns the Means of Production and the Form of Status Property

By combining both Marxist and Weberian conceptions of middle class, defining "middle class" not only focuses on one's education, income level, and purchasing power, but it also assumes having the ability to imitate the "respectable" or status-oriented lifestyle, aesthetics, tastes, and values of others in society who have power and prestige. In the United States, the "others" who have maintained the most institutionalized power are white elites. For the purpose of this book project, it is the absence of a critical race theoretical lens in conventional sociological treatments of socioeconomic standing I find problematic to our discussion of MSGCI mobility. This is not to say that, "race as a category that emerges from capitalist labor relations does not necessarily deny or minimize the importance of racial oppression and injustice or the need to fight against racism directly" as Adolph Reed Jr. suggests in *Race and Class in the Work of Oliver Cromwell Cox* (2001:23). Instead, I contend we need to be critically observant of the racial dynamics of capitalism and its colonial and imperial programs on those of African descent and their mobility over the generations in the United States. Further, I would like to recognize that social class cannot overcome the limits of anti-black racism since it is pervasive anywhere colonial powers existed. To do this, I look to the works of Karyn Lacy, Mary Pattillo, and W.E.B. Du Bois.

In *The Philadelphia Negro* (1899/1996), W.E.B. Du Bois undertook an extensive empirical project to document black family life and "Negro problems" at the turn of the twentieth century in Philadelphia, Pennsylvania. Du Bois' analysis is pivotal for understanding that whites' norms and values, which black slaves were taught to accept but not practice, were held out for blacks in the decades following Emancipation in 1865. While Du Bois is often revered but also criticized for privileging a smaller segment of the black populous (the black middle class) and ignoring the resiliency of poor and working class blacks, his work aptly focuses on persisting racial and social inequality, evident in social structures. In this particular text, Du Bois examined the ways black mobility and improved "respectable" status were often blocked because of blacks' limited access to income, wealth, and enhanced lifestyle opportunities (i.e., homeownership).[3] This remained the case until the passage of The Civil Rights Act of 1964. According to Karyn Lacy in *Blue-Chip Black* (2007:30), this federal policy, which barred discrimination in employment or education on the basis race or gender, was responsible for triggering the growth of the black middle class—"meaning simply that with greater access to both education and white-collar jobs, more blacks gradually achieved a middle class status closely aligned with conventional indicators of class position:" (income, education, and occupation).

Notwithstanding the apparent longstanding inequality that resulted in this race-class stratification system, which both Du Bois and Lacy illustrate in their writings, it is the effects of historically determined indices of status, wealth, and prestige, I contend, are contemporary factors that complicate blacks' middle class position, experience, and performance of middle class-ness in ways that are distinct from their white counterparts. As the Pew Research Center's 2013 article *Black Incomes are Up but Wealth Isn't* suggests, blacks' incomes as a whole increased, since the 1970s but the wealth, status, and prestige gaps are readily observable by race and particularly between blacks and whites. As such, blacks' ability to have wealth to create opportunities and secure a desired status has significant implications for them to establish a particular standard of living and to be able to pass that class status on to their children.

The indices or qualitative measures of class, status, wealth, and prestige are the "respectable," status-oriented lifestyle, aesthetics, tastes, and values and behaviors in which people are held to, and are required to demonstrate their similarities in thinking, lifestyle and identity as a member of their social class (see also Gilbert 1998). We see these influences in almost everything around us and in the choices we make daily "from the clothes we wear, the television shows we watch, the colors we paint our homes, to the names we give our pets" (Thompson and Hickey 2005; see also Kohn 1969/1989). Again, in examining the interconnectedness of race and class social constructs in the United States, be reminded that the "respectable" aesthetics and lifestyle we see daily as the norm perpetuated in the media images, commercials, and television programs intend to signify whiteness—white racial privilege that entitles legitimacy, ownership, and ability to accumulate material wealth and possession. Cheryl Harris (1993) in *Whiteness as Property* argues that middle class-ness becomes raced as white when whites perceive that they have more in common with the bourgeoisie (white elites) than with blacks. She goes on to cite W.E.B. Du Bois' (1935) historical essay on race and class titled *Black Reconstruction in America* in which he was critical of the "contradictions in American society [and] in particular the material force of racism" (Robinson 1977:44).

Harris (1993:1741–1742) quotes Du Bois when he says, "for the evolving white working class, race identification became crucial to the ways that it thought of itself and conceived its interests. There were obvious material benefits, at least in the short term, to the decision of whites to define themselves by their whiteness: their wages far exceeded those of Blacks and were high even in comparison with world standards. Moreover, even when [they] did not collect increased pay as part of white privilege, there were real advantages not paid in direct income but in public and psychological wage." In this regard, whiteness yielded access to resources vital to whites' lifestyle and wellbeing in ways that nonwhites struggled to accumulate because they were legally, politically, and socially denied: freedom to be admitted with all classes of whites, to public functions and parks, to better-funded schools, and to have elected officials and police treat them with respect and leniency (Harris 1993). Therefore, a person's definition of "middle class" and how they choose to perform their "middle class-ness" often hinges on the embeddedness of these symbolic elements of white cultural capital to signal his or her tastes and disposition, as well as the social and institutional arenas in which a person expresses his or her social class position (albeit whiteness) to others.

For the MSGCIs in this study, their definitions of middle class and their performances as high-wage earners speak to the ways they are each engaged in identity projects as it relates to their race, ethnicity, gender, and class status. As such, the MSGCIs' daily interactions with racial social structures, in which whiteness is a construct of middle class-ness for the purpose of racial exclusion, will elucidate how they use their understanding and performance of cultural capital to shift racial perceptions as they traverse social spaces and places (see Harris 1993).

CULTURAL CAPITAL AND HABITUS: PERFORMING MIDDLE CLASS-NESS

Pierre Bourdieu was a French social theorist known to focus on dynamics of power and the ways it is transmitted and maintained within and across generations. As part of his work, Bourdieu extended both Karl Marx's analysis on capital and material assets and philosopher Michel Foucault's premise of power as being ubiquitous, with the ability to influence a person's behavior (see Foucault's 1980 *Power/Knowledge: Selected Interviews and Other Writings, 1972–1977*). Bourdieu introduced critical theoretical concepts such as cultural capital and habitus to explain how power is culturally and symbolically created and performed in social and community/structural contexts. In fact, his most well-known book, *Distinction: A Social Critique of the Judgment of Taste* (1979/1986), considered one of the sixth most important sociological texts in the twentieth century according to the International Sociological Association's Books of the Century, examined how one's taste (cultural capital) and demonstration of his or her aesthetic (habitus) are acts of social positioning and class performance.

Cultural capital refers to the collection of symbolic elements such as skills, tastes (e.g., in movies or music), clothing, mannerisms, material belongings (e.g., luxury car), and credentials (e.g., a degree from a prestigious school and other qualifications) a person obtains as being part of a particular social class. These symbolic elements can be shared with others who also demonstrate similar tastes, mannerisms, and credentials. Sharing these symbolic elements creates a sense of collective identity or community with others that says, "we're the same" or "you're just like me." For Bourdieu, not all forms of cultural capital carry the same cache or social value. For instance, a person who obtained a bachelor's degree from 123 Ivy League University may be considered of "high stock" compared to a person who received a bachelor's degree from ABCD Liberal Arts College or XYZ Community College. This is due to the perceived cultural competence and authority the bachelor's degree symbolizes of a person's skill and ability associated with a certain type of educational institution. In this example, the perceived social value of one's skill, ability, and, even, intelligence is considered (to some) to be greater if one attends an Ivy League school than not. As such, we can presume, theoretically speaking, that the social value associated with certain cultural capital can have gross effects on the social mobility of a person and can "lead to an unconscious acceptance of social differences and hierarchies, to 'a sense of one's place' and to behaviors of self-exclusion" (Bourdieu 1986:141).

For Bourdieu, habitus is the physical embodiment—the knowing, feeling, and demonstration—of cultural capital in various social situations. The knowing, feeling, and being elements of habitus are the result of a person's individual life experiences—the situations where he or she developed a sense of their social place and connection to others that are similar and dissimilar to them. As such, habitus is not static or fixed but created through a social process that is dependent on situation and time. For instance, you may think of yourself as a "regular everyday Joe" among your friends or family since you were a child growing up; you may have behaved and interacted with others in a way you believed personified your "regular everyday Joe" self and that others identified you too—how you talk, the way you walk, and so on. Then, through a course of events or serendipity, you became acutely aware of your "regular everyday Joe" status and identity; perhaps it was a series of interactions with others in a new job or school that you "realized" you had either less or more opportunities than most of the other people. Perhaps it was that you had a set of experiences or resilience strategies that did or did not translate well in this new circumstance. In this regard, it is the habitus of "regular everyday Joe" that you have come to express who you are to the world around you and signify the meaning of "regular everyday Joe" as a social position you occupy, and especially when you are interacting with others.

Bourdieu also links together the concept of habitus to a person's cultural capital and class position. In *Distinction*, Bourdieu argues that a person's aesthetic or "taste" for cultural objects such as art, food, and clothing are shaped by the culturally ingrained habitus. In other words, he suggests that it is assumed that wealthier people automatically have great taste because of their frequent exposure to and early appreciation of certain material items whereas poor people lack "taste" because they have not been able to cultivate the habitus necessary to appreciate certain material goods.

For the MSGCIs in this study, their cultural capital and cultivation of a black habitus is, in many ways, a unique amalgamation of various competing ethno-racial and economic definitions, practices, and performances. At the same time, the definitions the MSGCIs employ and the practices and performances they are engaged in are interestingly similar to other middle class people (both whites and other people of color) but nuanced in several ways. These nuances, I contend, speak to the MSGCIs' desire to earn a considerable income and develop inheritable wealth to afford a middle class lifestyle for themselves as a self-identified black person and their families. At the same time, these nuances also reveal how the MSGCIs are compelled to care for members of their immigrant parents' generation and maintain ties to and a sense of community with both the United States and nations in the Caribbean. When asked to explain what it means to be "black middle class," many MSGCIs described their own self-conceptions and performance of their identities—vis-à-vis cultural capital and habitus—in ways that directly respond to: (1) how they feel society negatively associates blackness with poverty and whiteness with middle class status, and (2) how social class and mobility was discussed and performed in their Caribbean-influenced households when they were growing up.

DEBUNKING MYTHS ABOUT BLACKS
AND THE BLACK MIDDLE CLASS

With respect to discussing blackness and black habitus, the racialization of whites and the construct of whiteness as the norm for defining middle class status facilitate the construct of blackness as its oppositional identity. As the antithetical "other" in this relational social model, foreign- and native-born blacks and other nonwhites alike remain unable to be accepted fully as equal to whites and equally deserving of the norms associated with such identity, including middle class-ness—in the same way twentieth century white ethnic European immigrants and their children were. As such, the hyper-valuation of whiteness automatically denies positive valuation of blackness and black identity. Accordingly, in order to edify and embrace whiteness as middle class-ness, the constant denigration of blackness as poor or poverty-stricken and noncitizen is necessary for the antithetical other to be seen clearly as the identity to avoid. For this self-identified black and immigrant generation, the MSGCIs see this relational model expressed everyday in popular culture as highly problematic, and find it imperative to dispel the accuracy of such models and establish a more positive sense of identity of blackness and black middle class-ness.

Black and Middle Class:
The Black Middle Class is Real and Nuanced

In her book *Negroland: A Memoir*, Margo Jefferson wrote about coming of age in a small region in "Negro America" in the 1950s and 1960s where:

> ...residents were sheltered by a certain amount of privilege and plenty. Children in Negroland were warned that few Negroes enjoyed privilege or plenty and that most whites would be glad to see them returned to indigence, deference and subservience. Children there were taught that most other Negroes ought to be emulating us when too many of them (out of envy or ignorance) went on behaving in ways that encouraged racial prejudice. (Smith 2015:BR12)

One of the interesting aspects of Jefferson's commentary about black middle class-ness, I contend, is in the way she describes the tangled duality evident in being both black and middle class in the United States: the cost and benefits of blackness and privilege of class mobility. Undergirding this duality is the notion that black middle class-ness is seemingly contradictory when juxtaposed with white privilege, when Jefferson says, "in Negroland, nothing highlighted our privilege more than the threat to it. Inside the race [among other blacks], we were the self-designated aristocrats, educated, affluent, accomplished; to Caucasians, we were oddities, underdogs and interlopers" (Jefferson 2015:90). A few lines later she goes on to add, "Caucasian privilege lounged and sauntered, draped itself casually about... Negro privilege had to be circumspect: impeccable but not arrogant; confident yet obliging; dignified, not intrusive" (Jefferson 2015:91). Embedded in this notion of privilege is this idea that there is a social code of behavior which both blacks and whites are to adhere to in relationship to their levels of access to opportunities and institutional resources because of their race. And while the social code of behavior embraces the fact that whiteness is produced and is reproduced by the advantages and privileges that accompanies such an identity, it also buries the significance of social class and social conflict where certain whites are offended by blacks who, in their view, ostentatiously defy the norms of status and privilege automatically conferred to whites—as Jefferson speaks to in her book.

Similar to Jefferson, the MSGCIs in this study also observed the duality between the costs and benefits of blackness and the disparity in privilege afforded to whites and blacks. Some like Ana talked about the similarities between working class and middle class blacks. She observes that despite their differences in socio-economic standing, the racial status of both working and middle class blacks does impact their health, educational outcomes, and life chances in complicated ways.

ANA

Ana was born in the late 1970s and spent much of her youth in south Florida, particularly in the greater Miami area. She is the oldest of four girls born to her Honduran parents; her father ethnically identifies as Garifuna and her mother identifies as Latina. Ana self identifies as mixed, Black, Latina, and Garifuna. Her father is a semi-retired car mechanic and her mother works as an administrative assistant. Prior to migrating, Ana's parents knew of each other in Honduras but met again in church, when they both arrived to the United States in the early 1970s. Growing up, Ana and her sisters attended Catholic schools until college. Ana earned entry to a large university in Massachusetts for her undergraduate degree and graduate degree in dentistry. Currently, Ana works as a pediatric dentist and is a partner in a practice she shares with three other dentists, including her husband whom she married while in dental school. Ana has one child and is expecting her second child in a few months. She and her family live in the greater Atlanta, Georgia area.

ANA explains:

> People are quick to pit middle class blacks against working class blacks. You hear it all of the time. I think it is the idea of exceptionalism that exists in our culture. That poor black people are lazy and that middle class blacks are sellouts and stuck up. You know part of that bootstrap theory of, hey, they [middle class blacks] got themselves together and made better choices why couldn't you and your people [working class blacks] do the same? Right? Looking at economics only does not paint the full picture. I would say that economics hides the way race still matters. Take health disparities. Yes, poor and working class blacks and Latinos have higher rates of chronic conditions compared to their white counterparts but overall the medical field is not culturally competent in the way they treat all people of color. Middle class blacks have to work harder and figure out ways to sound more educated about their health care and be more prepared to ask questions and advocate for themselves but they are not treated the same way white middle class people are.

Ana's comment highlights an important nuance to understanding how the pathways of upward mobility and social class status are complicated by race and ethnicity. For her, popular discourses tend to demonize and label working class blacks as deviant for not being as "successful" when compared to their middle class counterparts. It is no surprise this type of zero-sum framework blames working class people's failures on their lack of drive, ambition, and morals. Compounding this belief, is the idea that upward mobility will rid working class groups of the endemic social ills that impact their lives. As Ana astutely points out here, preexisting race-based cultural models about black intelligence and ambition still impact middle class blacks despite their economic mobility. As a dentist, she observes how race perceptions influence how both social class groups of blacks are treated within the medical field as patients, but how the black middle class attempts to remediate such treatment by relying on other soft skills and experiences to self advocate, but sometimes without much more success than their working class counterparts. Persistent marginalization, discrimination, and racism is still alive and well for middle class blacks.

Am I My Brother's Keeper? The Divide Between Black Working Class v. Middle Class

Others made observations about black middle class-ness on television and the ways blacks had to be confident but not, "too proud that they've made it." Participants expressed similar sentiments Margo Jefferson describes in her book, that the black middle classes' "negro privilege" should still adhere to social codes of behaviors and those who defy such codes are often perceived as being arrogant, aggressive, and hard to work with, in professional settings and often face significant social and economic consequences (e.g., alienation, ostracization, and sometimes underemployment) as a result. Similarly, Karyn Lacy (2007:27) argues there is frustration, even disappointment, among the black middle class, "in whites' stubborn refusal to consider their group apart from the uncultured (black) lower classes; White people draw the line at the wrong point and put all of us in the same class." When thinking and talking about black mobility among the middle class, there is an important complexity that begs to be considered here if examining the intersectionality of race and class within the US social hierarchy. I argue the frustration both participants made about the public perceptions' of the black middle class and those Lacy describes in her book speaks to the way the black middle class is often perceived as teetering along the dichotomous lines of black-white class divisions. Let me elaborate more here.

There indeed exists a longstanding generalization that middle class blacks consciously and proudly choose to distance themselves from their working class and lower class counterparts. There are some who may have received certain social "rewards" and privileges for engaging in distancing strategies, such as choosing not to reside in predominately low income and working class neighborhoods or attend its schools, choosing to affiliate with or join class-focused affinity groups and associations, and/or passing for white, for example. And with such strategic effort made on their part, these individuals may also become frustrated by whites who do not make the distinction between blacks across class groupings solely because of skin color. Perhaps for some, this frustration is based on the notion that upward mobility is associated with hard work, self-improvement, and achievement, and any denial of having earned the right to have a well-appointed life is considered a rejection and a contradiction of the American Dream ethos. For others, their frustration lay with the middle class' enduring association with the "Old Negro" trope, which existed since slavery, Reconstruction and through Jim Crow, and is exemplified in caricatures that most people should be familiar with today, such as Sambos and Mammies (see Gates 1988; Jarrett 2006). Thus, the sensitivity to the intersectional relationship between blackness and middle class-ness, as Langston Hughes also discusses in his autobiography, is rooted in the experience of blacks seeing "their race laughed at and caricatured so often…" and wanting to "…put their best foot forward, their politely polished and cultural foot, and only that foot" to which that becomes the goal (qtd. in Robert M. Dowling 2008:114).

The black middle class' efforts to distance themselves from this trope are ironically but unsurprisingly modeled after a set of social values and habits that, at its crux, intends to reject all those perceived as lesser than in the racial and social hierarchy from really achieving such levels. Du Bois in his analysis of the black middle class, to which he popularized the term the "Talented Tenth" (see evidence of this in Evelyn Brooks Higginbotham's *Righteous Discontent: The Women's Movement in the Black Baptist Church, 1880–1920*), suggest that they experience "double consciousness." In his book *Souls of Black Folk* (1903), Du Bois argues that blacks (and especially the middle class) have an acute awareness or knowing that most Americans [read: white] perceive them as unwelcomed pretenders trying to escape their lower racial and social status despite their own best efforts of self-improvement. The "double consciousness" or the ability to see one's self through the eyes of others as Du Bois theorizes is, however, perceived as an "inferiority complex" or a pathological struggle by E. Franklin Frazier in his book *The Black Bourgeoisie: The Rise of the New Black Middle Class in the United States* (1957). In effect, Frazier and writers like him (see Langston Hughes' 1926 essay "The Negro Artist and the Racial Mountain") consider such efforts for self-improvement and achievement to be about blacks' need for recognition in an idealized white society in the name of racial uplift. Instead, folks like Hughes encouraged avoiding the climb of the racial mountain of standardization and embracing the unique and positive aspects of a black identity—both its beauty and ugliness. Hughes (1926/2002) elaborates, "We younger Negro artists who create now intend to express our individual dark-skinned selves without fear or shame. If white people are pleased, we are glad. If they are not, it doesn't matter. We know we are beautiful…"

Notwithstanding the ongoing debate between proponents of both perspectives—double consciousness and black inferiority complex and the rationale undergirding black middle class frustrations regarding public perceptions—a complex cultural narrative also emerges. The black middle class are used as tools of oppression and symbols in popular discourse to punish low-income and working class blacks as well as other people of color who do not "measure up" or mirror certain aspects of white US culture and codes of acceptance, while also being accused of imitating white standards of being that will never fully embrace or see them as being anything else but interlopers. Millicent further elaborates on these complex points.

MILLICENT

Millicent, born in the late 1960s in East Flatbush, New York, is the third child born to her parents. Millicent self-identifies ethnically as Chinese Trinidadian and West Indian, and racially as Black. Her mother emigrated from Trinidad to the United States in her early twenties and her father immigrated to the United States from St. Vincent a few years earlier. Millicent's parents met while working in the same hospital during their night shifts. They married two years later. Millicent attended public schools throughout high school and earned a scholarship to a university in Florida. She relocated to Fort Lauderdale to pursue her nurse practitioner's degree and licensure. While working at the same hospital, Millicent met her future husband, a recent widower. After a brief courtship, they married and have three children together plus two stepchildren from her husband's previous marriage.

At one point during our conversation, I asked Millicent to elaborate on what it means to be black and experience upward mobility. She cited to particular consumer practices that signal a person's socioeconomic status, but also immediately linked how a person, especially a black person, is expected to "perform" upward mobility in ways that are different from expectations placed upon whites across all social classes.

> [Laughing] I call it the "safe" black person: the 'not too aggressive' and "in your face" kind of black person. The non-confrontational black person that is almost de-raced—is that a word?? [laugh]. It's like you can't call too much attention to yourself and be fucking proud that you sacrificed and stressed but accomplished and achieved awesomeness. It's too hard because you have to watch your back and tread lightly not to offend anyone. *We* have to present in a way that does not offend. You have to speak well but not be arrogant because you have an advanced degree. Dress nice and have expensive clothes but be humble and gracious—almost thankful to be wearing them [the expensive clothes]. As if someone gave them to you, like charity.

> You can drive a nice car but not too nice. I have had white co-workers and supervisors say, "Oh, so that's your car? We must be paying you too much." Can you imagine? I work hard for my shit. No one gives it to me for free but it's almost like I don't deserve it but only they do. Shit. When they walk in with their scrubs and designer hand bags on their arms, no one says [with a sarcastic tone] "how can you afford that Chanel or Louis Vuitton on your nurse's salary—we must pay you too much." If you show up in an Audi or BMW, it's like you have to have the low end model of the luxury car and still it can't look too nice—maybe a used one with a ding or scratch on it. It's like they expect us black people to always be the same, poor, living in the ghetto, on drugs and welfare. That is simply not true. Not all working class people are even like that. But regardless, black people are supposed to know their place, whether you are successful like them [whites] or not.

When Millicent makes reference to the "safe black" person as performing upward mobility, she elucidates the racialization of blackness as the signifier inferiority and deviance, and for those who perform in ways contrary to this, stereotypic perception or race narrative are the exception to the rule. In effect, the "safe black" person becomes an interloper in white privilege and behavioral codes. Despite the racial exceptionalism applied to the "safe black" as unique, Millicent's triple identity consciousness assists her as she explains how racialization persists to the degree that the even "safe black" person cannot overcome daily reminders of social and structural discrimination. The sentiment of frustration Millicent expressed stems from the perceived bias received from her white colleagues and their stereotyped assumptions and schemas about blacks and the finite (low expectations) roles they should play in certain interracial and class-based settings.

Class Origins, Immigrant Generation, and Current Class Experiences

To understand the intersectional impacts of race and ethnicity and social class for the MSGCIs, we must consider how race and ethnic identification also carry social class meanings for children of immigrants in ways that influence their own definitions and responses to race ascription (Waters 1999). As the MSGCI experiences mobility, I argue race and ethnicity do not trump social class (as is presumed in the immigrant model minority trope); instead, I contend that MSGCI social class origins, their childhood home and community lives, and other adult experiences to date demonstrate a vital part of how they understand their race, ethnic, and class identities as interrelated and mutually reinforcing.

Indeed a handful of the MSGCIs were raised in middle class households growing up, despite the assumption that a majority of contemporary immigrants, and particularly black immigrants, who come to the United States are working class or poor. An interesting nuance to consider when reading these MSGCI vignettes, however, is that several of them grew up differently from people like Jefferson in *Negroland,* who was raised in a household where her father was a physician and mother a socialite. In the following section, several MSGCIs in the study recount instances during their childhood and adolescence where they grew up working class or lower-middle class—a different economic class position from how they live today as adults, and how these experiences have shaped their current understanding about social class and race.

Defining Middle Class: Mindset, Cultural Capital, Social Values, and Stereotypes

When describing their childhood home life, some of the MSGCIs' stories were often about their immigrant parents' values around social mobility and the importance of "becoming" middle class. Some spoke about the limitations placed upon them (and their parents) because of their race, ethnic, and immigrant origins but not necessarily the middle class origins. Others discussed their hopes to "break free" from these limitations and/ or their efforts to rise above the conditions of their childhoods. Indeed, all MSGCIs recognized and discussed the subtle social lines that are drawn between working class and middle class, in the way each person conceptualized being a child of Caribbean immigrants and self-identifying as black middle class as an adult.

When asked to define "middle class" and to explain her own self-conceptions of middle class-ness, Claudette took a brief moment to reflect on her response. It soon became clear to me that Claudette's anecdotes were very much informed by her academic and professional training, which emphasizes the necessary connections between society, organizations, communities, and individuals as it relates to a person's overall well-being and lifelong success.

CLAUDETTE

Claudette was born in the late 1970s in New York City and is one of five children born to a Haitian immigrant father and African American mother, with ties to South Carolina. Claudette self identifies as Black, Native American, African American, Caribbean, and Afro-Caribbean. Her father and paternal grandparents migrated to the United States from Haiti in the early 1970s while other paternal relatives also migrated to other parts of the Caribbean and Latin America. Several years later, Claudette's parents met and married and remained in the New York City area until their divorce in the 1990s. Having one immigrant parent and one native-born parent, it was important to Claudette that she learned several languages (English, Spanish, and French) in addition to learning about her Haitian and African American culture and histories. After high school, Claudette left New York City to attend a premier liberal arts college in Connecticut and shortly after, she went on to pursue her graduate studies at a large research university in Georgia. Working as a public health research professional and registered nurse with a focus on health disparities and infectious diseases, Claudette has traveled to and lived in West Africa, the Caribbean as well as various parts of the United States. At the time of interview, Claudette was living in the greater Miami, Florida area with one of her younger siblings and pursuing her PhD.

Here, **CLAUDETTE** reflects:

For me, being middle class is having a certain level of education, beyond high school, having a place to live and not worrying about losing your place. It's not struggling to make ends meet. And that is all relative because you may have folks who are low income but are not worried or not necessarily consciously thinking about making ends meet in the same way as someone else who may be making six figures. I remember during my youth and before my one of my younger sisters was born, about the time when my parents were looking to buy a home on Long Island (New York). I am not sure what happened to the house. I think it was in a neighborhood where they didn't want black people to live. But something terrible happened to the deal and the house was never built. So there was a period where we didn't have a place to live. We lived with relatives (grandparents on both sides) for a short time, then we were living out of a hotel and commuting to school and work—I was in the 5th grade. At the time, I remember thinking it wasn't like we were thinking, "oh my God, we are homeless. What's going to happen?" Not like that kind of fear. Both my parents were working. I know my mom continued working as a nurse and she was 7–8 months pregnant. I am not sure if that was the kind of experience they were creating so that we [the kids] wouldn't be nervous or if they [my parents] really felt "hey, this way is the way things are. Things happen and you just keep moving, forward." Then we moved to Brooklyn in temporary housing and I remember there was a period of several months where I remember being chronically late to school and getting yelled at by teachers for that. But then we were able to move into a condo my parents bought in Brooklyn. But it's funny to think back now that there were several months where it was like we were actually *homeless* and eating food prepared on a hot plate. Then a couple of months later we were in a condo in Brooklyn—my parents, *homeowners*.

Claudette immediately reflected on the ways she saw this childhood experience with housing instability as important in helping her understand social mobility and class for blacks, and specifically black immigrants and their families. The theme of "difference in mindset" emerged in her discussion of disposable income, financial literacy, and homeownership, as she described distinctions between being working versus middle class.

Here, **CLAUDETTE** elaborates:

Most of the polls and the politicians always put a number on it but [income] should not be the only marker of defining middle class because you have some people who have a high level of education but are not making so much. I think the things that help distinguish the middle and upper class from other classes is that you have to have a ceiling of what you spend. There is definitely more conscientiousness for the working class and lower middle class about priorities on what you spend, how much you spend, and where you spend but also an understanding that there is a ceiling. With the middle class, you are a little bit more educated about money—investments, 401Ks, etcetera. That is not to say that low-income people are not savvy or literate about money. In fact, many are very good at trying to figure out how to spend and save on limited funds and resources. But I think the difference between them and the middle class is whether you feel you are in dire need of something: that you are not going a day without eating, you are not threatened that your water or utilities are going to get shut off. It speaks to vulnerability of your situation including the physical vulnerability of yourself. Education is key to understanding those limits and what you can do in managing your money and wellbeing. And when I think about Caribbean people specifically, or more broadly black immigrants, I think many come with a [higher] level of optimism in comparison to middle class whites and black Americans. The attitude and mindset behind your experiences of being lower class or middle class shapes and frames the experiences you have later on. You see these middle class Caribbean neighborhoods in Brooklyn—Flatbush, Crown Heights? You see homeownership. Homeownership is interesting when it comes to the middle class since you have literature out there that supports the connection between owning your home and one's ability to climb up the ladder. Some of these people may not be highly educated but may work in construction in order to buy a home. But the mindset, the optimism is not pronounced in the same way for blacks who are poor or working class. But like I said, I think about my earlier situation growing up and then look [at] my parents and how they became homeowners.

For other MSGCIs, the concept of social class was also discussed as a mindset or a framework of thinking, which a person embodies in their everyday life—attitude and self-perception. For instance, Brenda was very explicit in talking about the ways she sometimes considers her own social class and mobility as still being working class as opposed to being "truly" middle class. For her, there are stereotypes and characteristics that exist among those who do identify as middle class, which she feels she does not wholly embody.

BRENDA

Brenda was born in the late 1970s in Danbury, Connecticut and is the youngest of four girls. She self identifies racially and ethnically as black, Caribbean, West Indian, and Jamaican. Her mom and dad emigrated from Jamaica in the late 1960s and early 1970s, respectively. Brenda's mom worked in social services and her father worked in agriculture when they met through mutual friends and later married. While in grade school, Brenda and her family moved to Boston, Massachusetts and lived in the Roxbury and Dorchester neighborhoods. Throughout her childhood, Brenda and her sisters enjoyed spending summers and holidays with her Jamaican maternal grandparents and extended family in Hartford, Connecticut. After high school, Brenda earned both a Bachelor's and Master's degree in Public Administration at a large private university in the greater Boston area. She has worked in the health care and social services industry for several years and currently works at a large nonprofit in Connecticut. Brenda currently lives in Hartford, Connecticut, nearby her maternal family members.

Explaining what black middle class is and how Brenda views her own class status proved to be a complicated topic in our discussion. The "complexity" is rooted in the ways Brenda conceived of and defined middle class as different from her own daily performance of middle class. She elaborates more:

BRENDA

What does it mean to be middle class?? Girl, I don't know. I've always been poor! [laughing] When I think about being middle class, I think it is being in a financial situation where you have a better chance at opportunity. Some of it is about perception of having a certain level of material things like a single family home or a condo. Having a degree, at least a BA or higher. You also could be seen as middle class but are still struggling to pay your bills and provide for your family. No, I don't think I really identify as middle class because I am poor. I think people would perceive me as middle class but I do not perceive myself as middle class because I feel there is so much to improve on—to strive for and achieve. I'm not in a place where I would like to see myself financially, with the house and so on so I am working class because of that. See, the middle class has this cushion. And the working class is this in-between poor and middle class. The poor are on public assistance and if you are not on public assistance, then you are utilizing some form of support or services to help you survive. The middle class is someone who has the degree and is already in the process of building some kind of wealth whether that is through some kind of real estate or more than a $75,000/ year job. Where the working class is anything below $75,000. I know what the statistics say but in reality, you need to earn this much income to really do the things like build wealth to be middle class. I know there are people who may earn $35,000 but also own real estate. But for me, I don't own a home and other things that I would consider helping me build that kind of wealth in a way that makes me feel like I am fully middle class.

Despite having incomes that are at or above the US median household income level, and undergraduate and graduate degrees, some MSGCIs like Brenda feel they have not quite "made it yet" due to their own perceived lack of material markers of cultural capital and material belongings (e.g., owning a home and amassing a certain amount of wealth). As such, the lack of these acquired material belongings informs their self-perception of their social positioning and acts of class performance (habitus). Concomitantly, there was also the perception among these MSGCIs that one's mindset and Caribbean ethos helps them achieve cultural capital they require to feel and identify with being middle class.

BRENDA elaborates:

I also think being middle class can be attributed to the concept or attitude of always trying to stay a step ahead. This attitude is always going to be with you. As a black person you are always striving to do better and to be able to stay in that state and never been seen by others as being below that. Strive to be beyond that. Whites have the same idea about trying to stay a step ahead but it's not the same kind of focus around race though. Black people always have to be mindful of their race. I mean, it is always in the back of our minds, like: am I going to get this opportunity based on my merits or will I be denied because I am black? Then trying to figure out how to navigate the situation when dealing with other groups and cultures. That underlying racism black people face all of the time versus when a white person thinks about striving. To strive, whites don't have the underlying race or racism they have to deal with. Whites' struggle is often being in the right place at the right time and not having to worry about their race as a hindrance. In terms of being West Indian, I think culture and the perception of the culture plays a role too. Like, for example, I will give you the stereotype of being Jamaican: "A Jamaican got like 20 jobs" [said in a Jamaican accent]. So, being Jamaican with like 20 jobs is about having the work ethic instilled in you so that you can work hard, provide for your family and strive. This is part of the motivation too to strive ahead.

Participants' narratives also revealed the complex dimensions of social class, as an aspect of their ethnic identity experience. Participants often reflected on the advice or lessons their parents shared with them around managing racism and prejudice. Several described growing up working-class but were reared to have "middle class values," a distancing strategy some considered intended to help them manage the internalization of discrimination, especially since many blacks and Caribbean immigrants they knew growing up disproportionately experienced a similar working class economic condition.

Here, **NATALIE** illustrates this point:

I would say we were working class but that was everybody else in the neighborhood too. The men hung outside the corner store, drinking and playing cards or dominoes or something. You had the mom with what seemed like ten kids but it was really like three boys or something [laugh] outside all of the time making a bunch of noise. Then you had the old lady like a Mrs. Johnson who was the community matriarch—at least to some. Now, come to think of it, it all seems a bit stereotypical, like our neighbors were the characters from Good Times or something. We were a bunch a black people scraping to get by—West Indian, Caribbean, American, whatever. We all lived where we could afford. It just so happened we were altogether unable to afford anywhere else [laugh]. And, so, yes, it was tough for my family, financially too, but I think what was different about us living in our neighborhood,

I think, was the way my mom always talked about growing up differently in the islands. How her family actually had money. They were not rich-rich but had enough disposable income to invest in things that folks in my neighborhood could not. She was educated in private schools, studied nursing, and was able to travel to a few other countries in the Caribbean. She would tell us how important education was to making it. Through education, we would climb up and experience 'success.' Unfortunately, it really did not seem like some of my friends' folks pressed education in the same way. But again, I guess if there's a choice to pay for food or the light bill versus Malikah's math tutor, the answer would be clear, you know.

As such, education, income, and occupation coupled with racial characteristics play a role in the production of a racial-ethnic identity. The correlation scholars make between race and ethnic identity and social class suggests that the higher one's social class, the more incorporated an individual is into that society. Yet, many participants found that this sort of incorporation really meant that the more education they attained and the more money they earned, they were more likely to come into contact—and sometimes conflict—with whites and the stress of discrimination that such conflict sometimes brings.

For Isaac, being a child of Afro-Caribbean immigrants, specifically Haitian immigrants, and to be able to achieve middle class-ness is of personal significance to him. His self-identification as an upwardly mobile black middle class man is very much connected to his middle class Haitian immigrant upbringing and his parents' middle class values and aspirations.

ISAAC

Both of Isaac's parents migrated to Boston in the early 1970s and soon married after their arrival. He grew up learning and speaking English, Haitian Creole, and some Spanish—as his maternal grandparents hail from the Dominican Republic and lived in Cuba and Puerto Rico prior to their migration to the United States in the early 1970s. After graduating from high school, Isaac attended a prominent historically black college (HBCU) in Georgia and later returned to Boston to complete his law degree. Isaac works in urban planning and government administration and has traveled to and lived in several countries, including those in the Caribbean, Africa, and Europe, working with nonprofits and nongovernmental organizations that are focused on uplifting and improving the life chances of those of African descent.

Here, Isaac talks about the emphasis his parents placed on social mobility, particularly around being a model of civic responsibility in the black community and in the world, and how he saw their lessons informing his own thinking about social class.

ISAAC says,

To be middle class means that you have a sense of aspiration around mobility. You are in a place where you have certain values around education, work ethic, values around the potential and opportunity, to move forward. These are not just Haitian immigrant values, but definitely one's emphasized a lot amongst Haitians. So when I think about these values for myself today, it is to use the talents God has given me to make it a better world if you will. For people like me whose parents had the means to come to this country for University from Haiti, for example, or even for those whose family came to the north during the Great Migration, and these blacks worked in factors or whatever…we have to shoulder some personal responsibility too. Now, I get it; it is easier to say that when you had some tools of middle class mobility given to you from your parents, like: "you better get your ass up and read" or being able to have conversations in multiple spaces and places with different kinds of people. It's getting used to that so that you can learn how to function in this society that judges us black people.

But when I think about the American Dream, we've been sold a bill of goods [scoffs] that black people weren't successful or can only be rappers, athletes or professional criminals. When I was back at [HBCU], I would go to my friends' beautiful homes and find out their parents are professionals and it was like going to the "Cosby kids'" house. If I had stayed with my previous conception I would have been like: "oh, these people [black students at HBCU] are tremendously impressive" as if they were an anomaly. I needed that exposure to open my mind up. Success is about modeling. And in this country you need to see that. It is not directly shown but you need to be around it and see it to understand the possibilities that exist to be successful and that you can achieve it too. The key is to see yourself as a citizen of the world and not a part of just some little tribe. We need to see ourselves as still connected to a place like Haiti or wherever and carrying a legacy, so as to not to forget where we come from and what we are blessed with: the capacity to give back.

A common thread across these narratives is an emphasis on having a particular mindset and values—a combination of the Caribbean ethos of hard work and the importance of striving toward and/or maintaining middle class-ness. The MSGCIs' stories also point to the anti-black stereotypes that negatively associate blackness with poverty and whiteness with middle class status and the ways their Caribbean immigrant parents explicitly and implicitly attempted to instill the importance of rejecting these stereotypes. I contend this observation is worth exploring further in terms of what it means in the adoption, expression, and assertion of black racial and ethnic identities for the MSGCIs. In other words, does their emphasis on a Caribbean ethos mean an outright rejection of African Americans and the perceived monolith of a black experience in the United States?

RACE, SOCIAL CLASS MOBILITY, IMMIGRANT GENERATION, AND THE BLACK HABITUS

In contemporary sociological research on Caribbean immigrants and their children in the United States, such as Mary C. Waters' *Black Identities* and Phillip Kasinitz, John Mollenkopf, Mary C. Waters, and Jennifer Holdaway's *Inheriting the City,* there still remains the analytical position that the second generation and especially those who were raised in working-class households, will engage in one of two ethnic strategies (immigrant advantage versus native disadvantage). These authors have argued the second generation will either participate in ethnic distancing from their parents' culture, which means they are more likely to adopt African American ethnic identities and become a part of the "black underclass," or adopt ethnic and immigrant identities more readily, which shields them from "oppositional African American" identities. As a result, these children of Caribbean immigrants, and especially those who join the American middle class, are assumed to reject the cultural identities and values of lower-class African Americans and choose to assimilate into the white middle class or form their own middle class ethnic community.

Employing a critical race theoretical lens, I contend these segmented assimilation perspectives not only reify anti-black sentiments that tend to pit native-born and foreign-born blacks against one another, but also do not fully grapple with the nuanced experience of social, structural, and cultural integration. For the MSGCIs like Isaac, some were exposed to and learned to appreciate and embrace as they got older both their immigrant history and culture and the social benefits local African American history, culture, and organizations provided in the community as they grew up. Here, Isaac tells a story about his decision to apply to a particular historically black college and university (HBCU) and how this experience and others like it made him acutely aware of his blackness—both his American nativity and Caribbean ethnicity.

ISAAC

When I applied to [HBCU], I was in a predominately white high school and I did all of those honors and AP classes, I actually wondered: am I really exceptional or is it something else? Why was I one of only a few black kids in these classes? Unlike friends at other high schools, I had the opportunity to study the American South and it was amazing. I mean, the history; that's when I learned about HBCUs and Dr. Martin Luther King, Jr., and doing a lot of reading and learning more about black nationalism and black empowerment and thinking yes! Then when I was a junior and looking to colleges, mostly in the Boston area, the headmaster, who was a black man said, "you know [Isaac], you can go to any of those schools. I got my PhD from Boston University and you can go there too. These schools are fine and a safe choice. But, with your leadership qualities, you should really consider a place like [HBCU]." A few folks in the network between my parents and the headmaster suggested that I meet this professor over at Harvard Business School (HBS) who also attended [HBCU] for undergrad. In the meeting, he started pulling out Harvard grad info, and cited the number of black men at HBS and the Kennedy School who attended [HBCU]. Then he said to me, "you go can go to these schools and you may find that you are not really all that exceptional." And I thought, wow. Ok. I want to be around another cohort of blacks, black men also middle class and striving and I didn't see that around me. When I got to [HBCU] for my freshman year, they sit you down in an auditorium and ask "raise your hands if you went to a predominately white high school? How many of you were class president? Did AP and Honors classes? Valedictorian at graduation?" You'd see all of these hands going up. Then they said, "you all are here to learn, you all are exceptional with similar backgrounds and do not let someone tell you: oh, you go to a black school so then you must all be the same anymore than they would say that at a predominately white school that all the white kids are all the same." At [HBCU] you had some kids who would say my Dad is a diplomat, or my Dad is from Nigeria or that my parents are from Venezuela and I speak Spanish. And so I realized that as much as we were all considered "black," there was diversity and approaches in the universe that existed. And I am glad I went to [HBCU]; I made great friends at [HBCU] that I am still connected to today. And I think about where I could have gone and met a whole bunch of folks--black folks that were doing it, striving, and succeeding, and I am not sure if I would have been able to see it in this great number anywhere else.

Indicative of Isaac's story presented here, the MSGCIs often relished, seeing firsthand, the parallels between the African American and black immigrant experience in the United States and their confrontation with anti-black stereotypes and notions of black exceptionalism. To be clear, this is not to say that perceived black intra-racial group stereotypes and tensions do not exist. In fact, a few MSGCIs did share instances where they were either exposed to an array of negative opinions voiced by their own parents about African Americans or the belief that whites tend to respond more favorably to foreign-born blacks. Here, Daniel describes a time he felt police racially profiled him as he drove through a predominantly white upper middle class neighborhood in the Greater Boston area with his infirmed Haitian immigrant uncle, who "helped" de-escalate the situation with police.

DANIEL

Born in the late 1960s in Brooklyn, New York, Daniel grew up in the neighborhood of Mattapan in Boston, Massachusetts with his two younger siblings and Haitian-born parents, both working in the healthcare field. His parents were part of the cohort of middle class Haitian migrants that came to the United States, fleeing Francois Duvalier's tyranny, and initially settling in New York while other family members migrated to Montreal. Daniel self-identifies as Black, Haitian, and of Caribbean descent. Daniel went on to college and graduate school to earn his JD and MBA at a large university in Pennsylvania. Immediately following his law school graduation, Daniel married and had two children (one son and daughter) to his then wife, a Guyanese-American from Atlanta, Georgia. After several years of living in Georgia and southern California as a practicing attorney, Daniel and his family returned to Boston. Currently, Daniel is undergoing a divorce and living in Massachusetts.

Racial profiling, and particularly black men's (and women's) treatment by police officers, is an issue that struck a cord for Daniel during our conversations. He talked about being frustrated by the negative treatment (e.g., the questioning, harassment, and physical abuse) black men receive, at the hands of police because it is assumed blacks are more likely to sell drugs, commit violent crimes and larceny. Though Daniel admitted that he was at one time naïve to believe such negative treatment by police would lessen once he moved out of urban areas and away from "stereotypical blacks"--African Americans. Daniel had thought being Haitian American, moving to the suburbs and able to afford a middle class lifestyle would create enough distance from having these negative perceptions applied to him. But in the story Daniel shares below, having his Haitian immigrant uncle, whose thick accent "should have" signaled to the police officers that Daniel was "a good and different type of black," also confirmed to Daniel that any difference between being an immigrant generation versus African American does not really matter if you are only seen as and defined by your racial master status—black, regardless of your socioeconomic situation.

DANIEL explains:

> My uncle was visiting from Haiti. Before his trip, I told him I wanted to buy some property and he thought it a great idea to drive through one of the neighborhoods to get a "feel" for the place. We went out on a Sunday afternoon to do that together. I slowly drove passed a parked patrol car and did not think anything of it before the car came up behind us and the officer told me to pull over. The officer gets my license and registration and starts asking the 'regular' questions like 'what are you doing around here?' 'Are you the true owner of this car?' So, my uncle in his thick accent says, 'what is this? We are driving a fancy car in a nice neighborhood. We do nothing wrong. We are good people.' The officer looked away from my elderly uncle and told me that he is going to run my information. That is when I said to the officer, 'yes, go run it.' Boy, that is when the situation escalated. Two other patrol cars arrived on the scene. The police detained us for over an hour. I was angry and humiliated. My uncle had to do a lot of explaining on my behalf. Fortunately, one of the other officers (who happened to be black) convinced the first officer to let us go on. When the first officer did so, the black officer walked over to me and leaned in my car as I got back in it to give me some 'advice.' He said, 'you should mind yourself when you are driving through certain neighborhoods and especially when you are by yourself. You will not always have your uncle to get you out of situations.' I decided not to buy property in a neighborhood or any other for that matter if I could not, as a black man, drive through it without problems from the police or anyone else.

Hearing stories like these remind me that it is important to analytically consider transcending the persisting dichotomous conception of black identity and social class. Isaac and other MSGCIs like him share similarities with other upwardly mobile African Americans: that their middle class social status does not always translate to full social inclusion. Understanding this, I argue, helps the listener to appreciate the minimizing social boundaries that exist between themselves, whites, and other ethnic groups.

Further, these stories bring the sociological analysis one step closer to reconsidering the social dynamics and complexities of ethnic identity among black identified middle class groups and the ethnic and racial climate of an increasingly diverse United States.

Significance of Cultural Capital in Black Intra-group Relations and Black Mobility

Several MSGCIs told stories about becoming adults and the conscious effort put forth to deny or reject the stereotype of the "black underclass" and anti-black sentiments regarding black mobility. A few MSGCIs, like Erica, admitted to putting a lot of effort in rejecting such stereotypes because they lack their parents' accents (particularly for Anglophone participants) and believe society is likely to identify them as African American. Erica clarifies:

> I'm going to be clear with you. It's not that there is a problem with being considered African American. There's good and bad in every group of people in the world. And although it should not be, I think it is my responsibility to show white people—my colleagues or otherwise, that not *all* black people—West Indians or Nigerians or blacks from Mississippi, sometimes I say it outright—"not every black person lives in the ghetto or is poor just like not every white person is rich." Other times I try to talk about my personal experiences when growing up and doing some traveling with my family. They would be surprised to know I had some insight into traveling that was not work related. So I would be like, "see, black people do have passports and actually use them for leisure."

Employing Darlene Clark Hine's thesis of culture of dissemblance, this effort or conscious act of rejecting stereotypes is seen as important and necessary for some of the MSGCIs, but has been found to be exhausting, inhibiting, and taxing on their self-esteem and self-efficacy. MSGCIs' efforts to discard general stereotypes of black poverty have led to ironic incidences of what Derrick describes as misplaced emphasis on conspicuous consumption.

DERRICK

Derrick is a hospital administrator. He is married and a father of a toddler girl of almost three years and they live in the greater Durham, North Carolina area. Derrick self-identifies as Latino and Black. Derrick was born in the early 1980s in the Riverside community of Patterson New Jersey and spent much of his youth in New Jersey with his mother and stepfather who is of Mexican and African American heritage. His mother and biological father are Costa Rican-born, though he does not know much about his biological father's upbringing. Derrick's biological father is from the Guanacaste province in the northwestern part of Costa Rica, of mixed heritage (Amerindian and African decent). His maternal grandparents were both born and lived most of their lives in the greater Puerto Limon province, until they migrated to San Jose around the time Derrick's mother was born. In San Jose, Derrick's mother and biological father met, but his mother's family did not approve of the relationship. They sent Derrick's mother to New Jersey to unite with her maternal side of the family and to finish school. It was during her travels that Derrick's mother discovered she was pregnant with him. In Riverside, Derrick was raised by his immigrant grandaunts, uncle, cousins, and mother who always maintained ties to family in Costa Rica and those who ventured to other parts of the English-speaking Caribbean. Several years later, Derrick's mother met his stepfather while working in a bank. Derrick's mother and stepfather recently relocated from New Jersey to Houston Texas to be closer to his stepfather's ailing mother.

Here, Derrick explains the complex struggle of managing what he considers to be diverging expectations between what society [read: white] has for people of African descent and the expectations people of color have of themselves:

DERRICK

Much of the advice and teachings you get is to defy the cultural norms or I should say stereotypes of what it means to be black. My parents wanted me to focus on assimilating to a certain degree. Not to forget your roots and culture or pretend to be white, but prove that we are deserving of the things and lifestyle we are choosing to work hard for. My mom came from a country where if you wanted to pursue certain careers you left for more opportunities. Folks, who already come from some kind of money, or get scholarships or support from family and the church, travel to the U.S, Canada and even to the U.K for these opportunities. I think my generation's Caribbean immigrant parents instill that drive in you to appreciate the sacrifices they made to come to this country so you can carry the torch, so to speak. But what does that look like? That's making sure you are happy; that you are not in a situation where you are trapped or feel that your family is in physical danger everyday. Going to an excellent school and having a prestigious career.

Enjoying the arts and culture, knowing how to entertain and go to restaurants, surrounding yourself with the "right" people that can build up your network. Living in a nice house, in a nice neighborhood, with a beautiful family, and doing all of the things that you are supposed to do when you succeed. So when, and I think about my parents specifically and what they used to tell me you dress to impress; tailor shirts and suits. That's part of being perceived as successful in many professions in this country. But then you find yourself buying all of these material things, always proving to be the exception to the rule. But it also creates more debt and more problems because you are constantly trying to prove something. For some people, they are always wondering, is this enough or will this be enough? Will I be accepted now? It's never really enough. And, I know because I've done a little of this myself. And it seems that every time I think I have proven myself and met the benchmark, showing others I have achieved some professional and economic success, it's like the mark moves further away. That's a lot of work and can be exhausting, stressful and even harmful, mentally. Never measuring up.

While Derrick raises an important perspective on conspicuous consumption as an act of cultural dissemblance, I believe it raises an equally important observation about race, social class mobility, and black immigrant assimilation across generations. Evoking tenets of Ajit Maan's theory on *Internarrative Identity* (2010) and Frantz Fanon's (1967/2008) *Black Skin, White Masks*, where he examines the multiple masks colonial subjects must wear to escape the alienating facets of colonialism, I contend Derrick's and other MSGCIs' stories, too, unveil the complexities ingrained in the relationship between the "dominant" and the "dominated" in US society.

It is my observation that Derrick and others describe their "double consciousness" (see Du Bois' *Souls of Black Folk*, 1903/1990) and the pressure of shifting from mask to mask via their conspicuous consumption, for example, as both a survival tactic and necessary for succeeding in the US middle class. Yet, as Fanon theorized, there is a psychology of colonialism that continues to impact the ways blacks define and express their self-image today. Fanon argued racism, at its core, inculcates insecurity and "epidermalization of inferiority," where people of African descent are required not only to be black but must be black in relationship to whites (1967/2008). And if social mobility is the focus, then he saw this as black people emulating their oppressors, in an idealized way. It is in this psychological space of cultural dissemblance and epidermalization of inferiority that intersects with Du Bois' notion of double consciousness. Du Bois (1903/1990:5) in his chapter "Of Our Spiritual Strivings" says:

> ...it is a peculiar sensation, this double consciousness, this sense of always looking at one's self through the eyes of others... one ever feels his two-ness, am American, a Negro; two souls, two thoughts, two un-reconciled strivings; two warring ideals in one dark body whose dogged strength alone keeps it from being torn asunder.

Looking to both Du Bois and Fanon, it would lead me to speculate that the prejudices, pressures, and social expectations to follow certain rules or codes of behavior of what is considered to be "acceptable American society" (read: white) for several of the MSGCIs are not only stressful financially, but also elicit self-questioning that is psychologically costly too: "how do I balance being a child of a Caribbean immigrant, black, American, and middle class?" "How do I blend in, stand apart from and 'keep it real,' or be somewhere in the middle?" As such, it appears that many of the MSGCIs' efforts are focused on creating his or her best forward-facing self or front-stage persona, so that there is an appearance of success; at the same time, struggling not to reject his or her true self as efforts to strive for upward mobility are made.

Notwithstanding my mention of a few MSGCIs whose immigrant parents thought it was in their "best interest" to distance themselves from American-born blacks (assumed the "black underclass"), this second generation has a strong interest in connecting with other blacks, both native and foreign-born (of all classes), while still maintaining certain ethnic, gender, class distinctions they were taught to value, as children growing up.

PERFORMING CLASS: CULTURAL CAPITAL, MSGCI MOBILITY, AND CARIBBEAN PARENT INFLUENCES

One of the ways the second generation's interest in connecting with other blacks seemingly differs from their parents' is based on the lessons they learned about race, gender, and class while growing up. It is no surprise that family influences, and specifically parent influences, are one of the most important factors in children's socialization process. Researchers have found these influences are often informed by goals and values closely associated with parents' occupation, income, conception of their class status, and parenting style and practices. Studies have pointed to concerns about parents' mental health, abilities, goals, values, and attitudes that could impede and or improve children's life chances (Mayer 1997, 2010). For the MSGCIs, they reflected on their immigrant parents' strong emphasis on investing in their development, despite their parents' economic constraints or ability to spend time in stimulating activities with them. Income is considered an important factor since it enables parents to purchase materials, experiences, and services to building the human capital of their children. These can include math tutors, after school programs and cultural activities (e.g., girl/boys scouts, music lessons, and fête des quinze ans or quinceañera dance lessons), and striving to live in safe neighborhood environments with other blacks and ethnic groups (McNeal 1999).

Since education and better employment options were the motivating factors for their parents' own migration, MSGCIs understood their parents' reasons for emphasizing education, specifically higher education, since it was associated with future economic success. The MSGCIs also found their parents' economic sacrifice to invest in goods and services as necessary "add-ons" that helped enhance their overall wellbeing and navigation of the social world around them.

ROBERT elaborates:

> I think immigrants pay close attention to the messages they get about society and how things are supposed to be. I think for my parents they learned being black and middle class is fundamentally different to being white and middle class. Its class *and* race…and hearing co-workers talk about what they're doing for their kids and maybe thinking "my son has to do this too." I think they saw the importance of ensuring the next generation achieves success is not only through building wealth or educational achievement but adhering to certain values. Like living in the "right" neighborhoods, attending the theater and having children participate in the "right" activities with the "right" children. It is interesting but being middle class and doing the "right" things means doing the things that white people see and value as important. Ok, let me put it another way—it's not about trying to be white but it's learning how to play the game and win. As an adult, I appreciate why my parents tried to show me how this kind of knowledge is important to getting ahead. There were times money was hard but my parents tried to make sure I also went to [the local youth center] for after school or to play sports, or was active in church and did church-sponsored activities with other kids that stayed out of trouble. When I was 11 or 12 one of my aunts took me to Radio City and I saw the Christmas show with the Rockettes. These activities opened my mind about the possibilities that existed beyond my neighborhood in Cambria, where we lived at the time. They emphasized that by being black, people are going to judge you negatively and that you have to somehow prove you're not a thug or crack head. You have to be

proud that you are black in America and to stay positive. Learning all of this really solidified for me when we moved to Midwood and I was in high school there and there was a mix of Jews, other American born kids like me with West Indian parents and other black Americans.

In addition to income and access to material goods, MSGCIs cited their parents' parenting style (e.g., authoritarian versus permissive), attitudes, goals, and beliefs as equally important factors in shaping how they think about their own ethnic and class identities. Parenting style and practices are the attitudes and dispositions that are expressed directly from the parent to the child through gestures, tone, explicit talk, and other performances of parental duties. According to Nancy Darling and Laurence Steinberg (1993) and Judith Smetana and Susan Chuang (2001:178), "parenting beliefs illuminate the values and socialization goals that parents hold...and are significant components of the socialization process and determine both parenting style and particular parenting practices." Researchers have also found each socioeconomic class is thought to value particular qualities their children should possess and that their socialization goals should achieve. For instance, middle class families tend to emphasize improving and enhancing intrinsic qualities—being autonomous, an independent thinker and having personal initiative. They also value keeping family issues and particularly family troubles private in order to preserve an image of "keeping it together." On the other hand, working class parents tend to emphasize extrinsic qualities—being disciplined and having strong respect for authority (see Hoff-Ginsberg and Tardif 1995; Luthar and Latendresse 2005; Wolfe and Iris Fodor 1996).

Several MSGCIs described their parents' parenting style to be a combination of the two, however certain distinctions were highlighted. For instance, they saw their parents' value of independence as important to building self-esteem but were not sure if being independent is "enough" when it comes to being self-efficacious as an adult. Equally important to their parents is the value of interdependence, such as helping siblings and family in the United States and in the Caribbean, a characteristic MSGCIs believed is prevalent within both Caribbean and African American culture. Interestingly, the MSGCIs parents' varied in their views of their children's individuality, particularly when it came to self-expression. MSGCIs perceived their Caribbean parents' reticence for embracing their children's self-expression to be based on the perception that American parenting styles tend to be more relaxed and unstructured, thus leading children to be disrespectful (e.g., talking back, being rude) and unambitious. This perspective resonated with many MSGCIs when they recalled periods in their adolescence when parents emphasized studying and going to church as opposed to socializing with neighborhood youth (mostly African Americans and Latinos) perceived to get into trouble (e.g., selling drugs, dropping out of school, and/or becoming teen parents). While MSGCIs disagreed with their parents' negative perceptions about their friendships with some African American youth (these friends will "bring you down"), they also thought their parents viewed setting firm limits were necessary to protect them from physical and social dangers that existed in their neighborhoods and to help keep them on track for upward mobility.

LISA makes this point:

> When you are a teenager, you want to try to fit in. Go to the cool spots, dress in the latest fashion, hang out with friends. Maybe experiment, lash out at your parents—rebel. It's a normal part of social development. But when you have Caribbean immigrant parents, they can be so overbearing. I was a good girl and never got into any trouble at school but they got more controlling as I got older. My mom especially would "lecture" a lot to me and my younger sister while my brother got away with so much more. They were always focused on whether we were hanging out with boys and having sex, or drinking 40s and smoking weed since my friends from the neighborhood were doing that. I get it but to have stereotypes about my friends who were black American was not fair. But it's hard to say if they were judging my friends solely because they were black American or because some of them were actually involved in this stuff. But I don't know, I can, though, appreciate the lesson—"your friends or people you associate with are important if you want to go somewhere and do better."

As such, their parents setting and maintaining parental authority was considered to help the MSGCIs learn formal rules of society (e.g., decorum, respect). At the same time, some MSGCIs found this stringent approach not necessarily helpful in developing competency, "because you are always focused on 'am I doing the right thing' and not always feeling sure of yourself even though you are supposed to be confident too," as Natalie mentioned in our conversations.

To engage with Pierre Bourdieu's theories on class and cultural capital, I contend, it is in the "Caribbean parenting style" and practices along with parents' income and conception of social class that influences MSGCIs' makings and performances of class identity—habitus (see work of Lehmann 2009). Across all MSGCIs' stories, there carried a thematic thread of immigrant social mobility. Whether their parents had "humble beginnings" or were upper class, educated or had comparable to a high school diploma prior to migrating, MSGCIs' parents impressed upon them their own values lessons around success and "making it" in a country where success is a means to enhanced life chances.

To say MSGCIs completely embraced or rejected these initial lessons about blackness and being middle class would be a misstep analytically. In essence, MSGCIs' triple identity consciousness is revealed in the stories they told; their stories pointed to their realization of the complex contradictions and limitations these lessons placed upon them and the ways they tried to navigate a social environment that played by a "different set of rules" than the ones they were told existed back in their parents' home country. For instance, some MSGCIs described feeling unprepared to navigate certain educational, professional, or other social spaces their parents had yet to travel through.

MSGCIs' triple identity consciousness displayed in these stories also demonstrates a complete awakening that there exists a particular mindset and cultural capital that intends to divide racial-ethnic and class groups socially, economically, and politically and how they are subjected to the trappings of a stratification system which judges them based on how well they can accept the deviancy of its system and participate in it or not. They described ways in which their parents' teachings and advice did not provide them with all of the "know how" to navigate undergraduate norms and expectations, for example, which sometimes led to feelings of uncertainty and insecurity.

In light of the perceived disadvantages related to their parents' immigrant cultural capital, these MSGCIs felt they had to learn quickly and "in real time" how to adapt to these new expectations and demonstrate middle class belongingness in the form of high achievement, a focus on social acceptance, and career success. There was consensus among these MSGCIs that there are particular value orientations associated with being immigrant and being raised in working class or lower-middle class households, such as appreciating hard work (and maybe working 20 jobs if necessary as Brenda mentioned earlier), being independent, taking responsibility, and having grit and discipline. At the same time, there was a simple acknowledgement that "striving"—as presumed to be a positive mindset and activity to engage in for one's upward mobility—is interestingly considered an important but deliberate design of anti-black racism that intends to create competition between black low-income and working class and the black middle class by rewarding or praising one group for working hard and the other for being lazy.

By observation, MSGCIs often draw on this awareness as well as the value orientations learned from their parents' parenting style and practices as part of their own middle class habitus. In the next chapter, the MSGCIs describe how these value orientations as well as their parents' emphasis on middle class cultural capital helped to shape their conceptions about their own social position in American society, by race, ethnicity, and gender, and the lessons they hope to impress upon their children.

Notes

1. This is in reference to Karl Marx's theory of classes as written in *The Communist Manifesto with Friedrich Engels* (1848): "The history of all hitherto existing society is the history of class struggle. Freeman and slave, patrician and plebeian, lord and serf, guild-master and journeyman, in a word, oppressor and oppressed, stood in constant opposition to one another, and carried on an uninterrupted, now hidden, now open fight, a fight that each time ended, either in a revolutionary reconstitution of society at large, or in the common ruin of the contending classes."

2. M.G. Smith in the book *Culture, Race and Class in the Commonwealth Caribbean* (1984:3) made reference to the mid-1930s, where "there were mass protests and disturbances across the English-speaking Caribbean, in places as Barbados, Guyana, Jamaica and Trinidad." For him and scholars of his generation, "these disturbances signaled the end of 'Crown Colony government' and initiated the hesitant British reorientations, first towards colonial reform, and then towards decolonization, thereby introducing the contemporary period of formally independent Commonwealth Caribbean mini-states that introduced an expanding class system."

3. For Du Bois ([1899] 1996) in *The Philadelphia Negro*, homeownership was understood as an important element of achieving the American Dream— one that was accepted and respected by the larger, white society.

Bibliography

Allen, T. W. (1994). *The Invention of the White Race, Volume One: Racial Oppression and Social Control*. London: Verso.

Bourdieu, P. (1979/1986). *Distinction: A Social Critique of the Judgment of Taste* (R. Nice, Trans.). London, UK: Routledge.

Braithwaite, L. (1953). Social Stratification in Trinidad. *Social and Economic Studies, 2*(2 & 3), 5–175.

Darling, N., & Steinberg, L. (1993). Parenting Styles as Context: An Integrative Model. *Psychological Bulletin, 113*, 486–496.

Du Bois, W. (1899/1996). *The Philadelphia Negro: A Social Study* (with introduction by Elijah Anderson ed.). Philadelphia, PA: University of Pennsylvania Press.

Du Bois, W. (1903/1990). *Souls of Black Folk*. New York: Vintage Books.

Du Bois, W. (1935). *Black Reconstruction in America: An Essay Toward a History of the Part which Black Folk Played in the Attempt to Reconstruct Democracy in America, 1860–1880*. New York: Harcourt, Brace and Company..

Fanon, F. (1967). *Black Skin, White Masks* (C. L. Markmann, Trans.). New York: Grove Weidenfeld Press.

Frazier, E. F. (1925). Durham, Capital of the Black Middle Class. In A. Locke (Ed.), *The New Negro: Voice of the Harlem Renaissance* (p. 333). New York: Albert and Charles Boni.

Frazier, E. F. (1957). *The Black Bourgeoisie: The Rise of the New Black Middle Class in the United States*. New York: Free Press.

Gates, J. H. (1988). The Trope of a New Negro and the Reconstruction of the Image of the Black. *Representation, 24* (Special Issue: America Reconstructed, 1840–1940), 129–155.

Gates, H. L., Jr. (2011). *Black in Latin America*. New York: New York University Press.

Gerth, H. H., & Mills, C. W. (1958). *From Max Weber: Essays in Sociology*. New York: Oxford University Press.

Gilbert, D. (1998). *The American Class Structure*. New York: Wadsworth Publishing.

Hall, S. (1977). Pluralism, Race and Class in Caribbean Society. In *Race and Class in Post-Colonial Society: A Study of Ethnic Group Relations in the English Speaking Caribbean, Bolivia, Chile, and Mexico* (pp. 150–182). Paris: UNESCO.

Harris, C. I. (1993). Whiteness as Property. *Harvard Law Review, 106*(8), 1707–1791.

Hoff-Ginsberg, E., & Tardif, T. (1995). Socioeconomic Status and Parenting. In M. H. Bornstein (Ed.), *Handbook of Parenting: Biology and Ecology of Parenting* (Vol. 2, pp. 161–188). Mahwah: Erlbaum.

Hunt, M. O., & Ray, R. (2012). Social Class Identification Among Black Americans: Trends and Determinants, 1974–2010. *American Behavioral Scientists, 56*(11), 1462–1480.

Jarrett, G. A. (2006). New Negro Politics. *American Literary History, 18*(4/ Winter), 836–846.

Jefferson, M. (2015). *Negroland: A Memoir*. New York: Pantheon.

Kohn, M. (1969/1989). *Class and Conformity: A Study in Values (with a Reassessment)* (2nd ed.). Chicago: University of Chicago Press.

Lacy, K. R. (2007). *Blue Chip Black: Race, Class and Status in the New Black Middle Class*. Berkeley: University of California Press.

Landry, B., & Marsh, K. (2011). The Evolution of the New Black Middle Class. *American Review of Sociology, 37*, 373–394.

Langston Hughes. (1926/2002). The Negro Artist and the Racial Mountain. In C. C. De Santis (Ed.), *The Collected Works of Langston Hughes: Essays on Art, Race, Politics and World Affairs* (Vol. 9). Columbia: University of Missouri Press.

Lehmann, W. (2009). Becoming Middle Class: How Working Class University Students Draw and Transgress Moral Class Boundaries. *Sociology, 43*(4), 631–647.

Lowenthal, D. (1972). *West Indian Societies*. London: Oxford University Press.

Luthar, S. S., & Latendresse, S. J. (2005). Children of the Affluent: Challenges to Well-Being. *Current Directions in Psychological Science, 14*(1), 49–53.

Maan, A. K. (2010). *Internarrative Identity* (2nd ed.). Lanham: University Press of America.

Marsh, K., Darity, W. A., Cohen, P. N., Casper, L., & Salters, D. (2007). The Emerging Black Middle Class: Single and Living Alone. *Social Forces, 86*(2), 735–762.

Marx, K., & Engels, F. (1848/1992). *The Communist Manifesto* (Reprint ed.). New York: Bantam Classics.

Mayer, S. (1997). *What Money Can't Buy: Family Income and Children's Life Chances*. Cambridge: Harvard University Press.

Mayer, S. (2010). Revisiting an Old Question: How Much Does Parental Income Affect Child Outcomes? *Focus, 27*(2/Winter), 21–26.

McNeal, R. B. (1999). Parental Involvement as Social Capital: Differential Effectiveness on Science Achievement, Truancy and Dropping Out. *Social Forces, 75*(1), 117–144.

Reed, A. J. (2001, February). Race and Class in the Work of Oliver Cromwell Cox. *Monthly Review: An Independent Socialist Magazine, 52*(9).

Robinson, C. (1977). A Critique of W.E.B Du Bois Black Reconstruction. *The Black Scholar, 8*(7 (The Black South)), 44–50.

Sampson, R. J. (2008). Moving to Inequality: Neighborhood Effects and Experiments Meet Social Structure. *American Journal of Sociology, 114*, 189–231.

Shapiro, T., Wheary, J., & Draut, T. (2007). *By A Thread: The New Experience of America's Middle Class*. Dēmos: Brandeis University, The Institute on Assets and Social Policy.

Smetana, J., & Chuang, S. (2001). Middle Class African American Parents' Conception of Parenting in Early Adolescence. *Journal of Research on Adolescence, 11*(2), 177–198.

Smith, M. G. (1965). *Stratification in Grenada*. Berkeley: University of California Press.

Smith, M. G. (1984). *Culture, Race and Class in the Commonwealth Caribbean*. Kingston: University of the West Indies.

Smith, T. K. (2015, September 15). *Sunday Book Review: Margo Jefferson's Negroland, A Memoir*. Retrieved September 22, 2015, from *The New York Times*: http://www.nytimes.com/2015/09/20/books/review/margo-jeffersons-negroland-a-memoir.html?_r=0

Thompson, W., & Hickey, J. (2005). *Society in Focus*. Boston: Pearson.

United States Department of Justice. (2015). *Investigation of the Ferguson Police Department*. Civil Rights Division. Washington DC: US Department of Justice.

Waters, M. C. (1999). *Black Identities: West Indian Immigrant Dreams and American Realities*. New York: Russell Sage Foundation.

Wolfe, J. L., & Fodor, I. G. (1996). The Poverty of Privilege: Therapy with Women of the "Upper Classes.". *Women & Therapy, 18*, 73–89.

CHAPTER 6

From Lessons Learned to Real-life Performances of Cultural Capital and Habitus

Cultural capital is acquired through a variety of sources. Thus far, I have examined how the MSGCIs' cultural capital and cultivation of a black habitus is, in many ways, a unique amalgamation of various ethno-racial and economic definitions, values, and practices they learned from their parents. In particular, their stories point to the ways social class and mobility were discussed and performed in their Caribbean immigrant parents' households. Lessons learned from their parents and families helped to shape their desires to earn a considerable income and develop inheritable wealth to afford a middle class lifestyle for themselves as adults and for their future generations. The key to understanding how these MSGCIs perform or signal their ethno-racial identity and class status to others, however, is to also explore the ways that being American-born and raised also influences them to "move through the world" and navigate social spaces differently than their immigrant parents. This chapter will continue to explore the role of cultural capital and black habitus by examining the specific practices and performances MSGCIs are engaged in that are similar to other middle class people in the United States (both whites and other people of color) but nuanced by their Caribbean ethnicity, gender, and middle class identity.

© The Author(s) 2018
Y.S. Lorick-Wilmot, *Stories of Identity among Black,
Middle Class, Second Generation Caribbeans,*
DOI 10.1007/978-3-319-62208-8_6

GENDER ROLES AND SEXUALITY

When discussing the lessons learned from their parents and how these helped to inform their own identity assertions and experiences, the MSGCIs also talked about the role of gender and gender role expectations. Scholars often look to socialization theories to explain the process individuals come to assert the gendered aspect of their overall identity. Similar to race and class identities, the accumulation of gender identity is considered a process that occurs over time and through experience, and is prescribed by a culture and communicated through verbal and nonverbal messages from the social environment, including the media. As such, individuals are not passive in their conception and development of gender and gender roles. In fact, individuals are social actors that are not only shaped by their environment but also interact with and have the ability to influence the environment around them (Freeman and Mathison 2009; West and Zimmerman 1987). Individuals interpret meanings associated with particular traditional gender role stereotypes, take into account their own sense of authenticity or preferences and consider any potential consequences (perceived positive and negative) of rejecting or conforming to such stereotypes when making decisions about how to express their gender identity.

There are particular traditional gender role stereotypes and expectations MSGCIs felt compelled to adhere to as children of Caribbean immigrants but felt these often contradicted with their understanding of American notions of gender and sexuality. Several MSGCIs believed the more educated and "exposed" a person is to different ways of living, the more likely he or she is open to nontraditional gender roles, marriage and child rearing, or gender equity. Dennis Gilbert (1998/2014:117) in *The American Class Structure in the Age of Growing Inequality,* who focused on sex-role socialization by social class, found "college life, generally a prologue to upper-middle class careers, delays marriage and encourages informal, relatively egalitarian association between men and women" of the middle and upper-middle classes. He argues high rates of social and geographic mobility is a typical characteristic of this class, and when it comes to heterosexual relationships specifically, the men and women must rely on each other to provide support and companionship as their professional trajectories of two-person careers take them away from their kin networks, which they would rely on for child care and other family supports.

Of course the irony is, as we see in other books such as anthropologist Wednesday Martin's (2015) memoir *Primates of Park Avenue* about white Upper East Side mothers in New York City, these interactions still replicate traditional western gendered interactions and social class ideals, with the expectation that wives are to be, "gracious, charming hostesses and social creatures, supporting their husbands' careers and motivating their achievements" (Kanter 1977:108; see also Gilbert 1998/2014). Exposed to these understandings about gender role socialization both in American culture and those of their parents' Caribbean culture, the MSGCIs told stories that pointed to gender-specific lessons and advice about what it means to be a woman or man, when dating or in relationships, and when it comes to parenting and family life. This was an interesting theme to come up in conversation because of the ways in which the MSGCIs seemed to grapple with the relevance and utility of the advice received and lessons parents' taught as they experienced upward social mobility in adulthood.

Gender Role Conceptualizations in the Caribbean and the United States: Influences of Chattel Slavery and Colonialism on Women's Roles and the Institution of Family

Not surprisingly, there are similarities in the way gender roles are conceptualized in the United States and the Caribbean. As is the case for many countries in the Caribbean and throughout the Americas—who were colonized by the British, French, Spanish, or the Dutch, they adopted the laws, policies, culture, and social practices of their colonizers and embedded them within their cultural ethos and national narrative post-emancipation. The social rules that governed the power dynamics between men and women in these societies were informed by their colonizers' value in Enlightenment philosophy. Generally speaking, men held the majority of power, both in public and private spheres of social life, whereas women were considered second-class citizens and relegated to the private sphere (e.g., home life and child rearing). Utilizing a multicultural and Afrocentric framework to understand gender and gender dynamics, there is an important role race and history play in this discussion.

The ideals and practices of white colonialists impacted the structure, function, and behaviors of Afro-descendants in the Americas as a result of the institution of chattel slavery. Africans and Afro-descendants were often represented and observed through a European, patriarchal ideological perspective that ensured the institutionalization of male dominance and subordination of women, while also emphasizing the ideal of white female frailty and dependence. As such, Africans and Afro-descendants were forced to conform to rigid, Eurocentric racial and gender hierarchies that not only relegated those of darker hues, lesser means of power and authority, and women to the bottom, but aided in the domination of black family structure and gender roles. For example, white Christian missionaries within Caribbean colonies indoctrinated Africans with Christianity and used religion as a tool for social control. These Christian missionaries also used religion to help sanction slave marital unions to mirror European nuclear family patterns and gender roles. This was a shift away from traditional polygamous family patterns that had existed and were practiced in certain West African communities for centuries. Unless there were legislative policies set forth that outlawed the separation of slave marital unions across the Americas, most blacks lived in and relied on matrifocal kinship ties for survival, since slaveholders can sell mothers, husbands, and children at will.

As is well-documented, black men and women were subjected to and endured the horrors and degradation of slavery across the Americas, historians also point to the plantation system as not being gender blind. The double jeopardy of race and gender defined black women's low social status and economic role within the system. Their low social status during slavery was directly connected to their duties in the plantocracy: black women's perceived "ideal suitability" for field and domestic labor, "immoral and animalistic nature," high sex drive, and capacity for childrearing and household duties. Because of their race and gender, black women were often subjected to rape or forced to perform sexual labor at the hands of slave masters and mistresses. When it came to performing economic duties, black women were also assigned menial and hard labor tasks, while their male counterparts could be assigned tasks that required learning new skills and/or having relative autonomy. This rigid gender segmentation continued in circumstances where black women represented over 60% of the slave population on plantations with shortages of black men to perform more "complex" labor. I would be remiss not to mention there were Spanish-speaking Caribbean societies in the late sixteenth and early seventeenth centuries where free African and Afro-descended women strategically ascended from this low status and maintained an intermediate social and economic positions for its era (see the work of Wheat 2010). But because of the race–gender divide, these women were still blocked from the full privileges enjoyed by other males (persons of color or otherwise), such as equal pay for equal work, opportunities for educational advancement and the ability to vote.

Since the period from emancipation and when these Caribbean nations achieved sovereignty from their colonizers to more contemporary times, there have been dramatic shifts in the conceptualizations of gender roles across the Caribbean's cultural landscape. This shift can be attributed to several factors. Of these include Caribbean women's suffrage and the expansion of a women's movement across the Caribbean region. Scholars such as Rhoda Reddockand Bridget Brereton have examined the ideologies and conditions that led Afro-descended women to challenge sexual division of labor and the legitimacy of women and women's experiences in the workplace that still exists today: equal pay for equal work, increased women's visibility, women's right to vote and education, and campaigns against violence against women and girls. Other factors that led to shifts in the conceptualization of gender roles can be attributed to changing economic factors, including out-migration of both men and women in search of employment, gender liberation movements in the United States and Europe, and overall changes in global discourses around gender equity.

Notwithstanding these shifts, traditional (read: patriarchal) attitudes around gender roles and sexuality remain an integral part of the ideological discourse and expression in Caribbean culture that gets passed down through generations and across class groups. The mainstay of such discourse is directly connected to the intersectional role capitalism and colonial ideology plays in gender role dynamics. Here, Rhoda Reddock (2008:4) cites to Bridget Brereton's book chapter "The Promise of Emancipation" to emphasize the connection between capitalism, policy, and colonial ideology:

> Antislavery activists, clergymen, officials and British policymakers all shared a basic assumption: ex-slaves should model their domestic lives on the middle class western family. Husbands should be the head of the family, the main breadwinner, responsible for family and endowed with authority over wives and children; wives should be dependent and domestic. Of course, lifelong monogamy based on Christian marriage should be the norm. (Brereton 1999:102)

Contrary to a popular misconception that capitalism (and later, globalization) would provide a Caribbean woman—Afro-descended and Indo-Caribbean, the opportunity to participate in an economic system so that she may work outside of the household to create and develop wealth, both plantocracy and capitalism are economic systems focused on owners and factors of production. These two systems also rely on ideologies and policies that ensure women's dependency: women are still paid less than men, not seen as legitimate workers and primarily tasked with household duties (see Reddock 1994, 2008). Hence, the system of capitalism easily perpetuates contemporary gender role conceptualizations and practices that were established during chattel slavery and throughout the colonial period that we still see today. Therefore it was not surprising to learn home life was considered an important space through which MSGCIs learned about gender roles, specifically when it comes to division of labor in the household, and how things are "supposed to be" between men and women. Again, the social space and place of "home life" as a socializing mechanism is reflective of the ubiquitous influence patriarchal and colonial ideologies had during the period of slavery and continues to have on Afro-descendants today.

Gender-Specific Roles and Sexuality Within MSGCI Families: Balancing Caribbean Tradition and Expectations with Western Feminism

When asked about home life growing up, Brenda described some of her family's Jamaican cultural rituals and traditions. She also shared the gendered aspects of these traditions, such as who is responsible for completing certain tasks, and the subtle and not-so subtle messages she interpreted about the expectations that are set for her and her own family life:

BRENDA

Sunday dinners are a must and have to happen by 3 o'clock. And everyone has to be there. That's what I thought when I was growing up. I don't think it is necessarily a Jamaican thing if I think about it in retrospect. Because there are Nigerians and other black families that I know that have set Sunday dinner times too. But our food is very traditional West Indian though: curry chicken or jerk chicken, rice and peas, are staples. Those are things that are instilled in me. But this also goes to show how things are done in the household. One thing I can now appreciate learning was when my Aunts and my older sisters cook, they make sure the men are served first. And that's kind of nice. [My older sister] serves her husband because we saw our grandmother serve our father. It's not necessarily a "West Indian only" thing but

I definitely pick that up as part of the Caribbean culture. This allows the men to be focused on work at all times. The concept of a man working, with a big emphasis on being a provider and hard worker is huge in the West Indian culture.

Many of the messages MSGCIs received about gender and specifically about female sexuality and womanhood fit into aspects of the Freudian Madonna-Whore trope, which emphasizes the Madonna as the figure all women should aspire to be—socially virtuous and an object of worship—as opposed to the Whore figure, who is promiscuous and lacks morality. In fact, the MSGCIs were able to recite, to some extent, several aspects of this trope that suggested Caribbean women needed to be a combination of the two: a Caribbean woman should be able to "keep a good house" (e.g., cook a fresh meal daily and clean), care for the children, be attractive and wear the latest fashions, support her man in all that he does, and be able to sexually satisfy him. Of course such aspects are entirely conceived as hetero-normative but a ubiquitous trope or cultural model among those in same sex unions. The MSGCIs also mentioned women are expected to be educated (as it is valued highly socially and economically) and that her having an opinion and being smart (because she will make smart children) is okay but she should not talk back or have too much mouth. In other words, she cannot be *a loud "market woman" who carries on and makes a huge ruckus. She has to play her role*—as Eddy mentioned in his interviews, because it would emasculate her male partner and render him powerless in the relationship.

This dichotomy is a social trap that leads women to think of themselves as and feel inadequate for not measuring up to these contradictory beliefs. Further, the Madonna-Whore trope ignores the true and fluid complexity of womanhood—that women can be all of these things, some of these things and also none of these things at the same time if and when they choose to be. Yet, some of the MSGCIs expressed feeling conflicted between what they learned in school about US feminism and sexual liberation, which is perceived to be more in line with the Whore figure, and what they were taught at home, which was to value the Madonna figure—a mainstay in Caribbean culture with strong Christianity roots. Here, Erica describes that neither traditional Caribbean ideals of the "Madonna" nor American ideas of sexual liberation fit her life because these perspectives were too limiting and did not seem to fit.

ERICA adds:

Some of my earliest memories of my grandaunt are of her telling me how to be a demure girl—a good girl. One who keeps her virtue, takes care of home, and who turns a blind eye to a misbehaving husband—unless the affair becomes public or too embarrassing. That's what these women do, in the islands. What's good for the goose isn't good for the gander, I suppose. I do think it is important for a woman not to be "running around," putting shame on her family name but I also don't think that hooking up with a bunch of random men is okay either. What does that prove?

There were other MSGCI women who sought to reconcile this mismatch by reinterpreting these expectations and reorganizing them into new rituals that fit better within the social context that they lived. An example of this is Michelle's reflection on her experiences as a dark-skinned, black Dominican woman from the South Bronx, finding the right balance between Caribbean cultural/gender traditions and American feminism to define what it means to be a strong and empowered black woman:

MICHELLE

My teen years, especially, [were] full of pain and stress. For a long time I thought my mom's and 'buela's [grandmother's] ideas were old fashioned and "old world." But now, I've come to appreciate what they've been saying to me all of these years because I have seen some of it come to pass. But, I've also had different experiences from them because: I was born and educated here, I married a white guy from Ireland and not the lighter-skinned son of a prominent Dominican businessman from Santiago they wanted me to, and now, work as a 6th grade teacher. I guess I have the vantage point of a three-sided coin, maybe. You know, I have my family's ideas, America's ideas, but importantly my own ideas. Together I have a tool belt of strategies I use to help me navigate through many life situations.

Michelle's triple identity consciousness compels her to consider the importance of an amalgamation of ideals—Caribbean family tradition and expectations with American feminism she has learned and in many regards, in order to function within its daily rhetoric and implication on her life. This is significant to note because it clearly demonstrates MSGCI fluidity and hybridity of their personhood across multitude situations that is neither considered an "either"/"or" of adopting Caribbean versus US traditions and mentalities but points to possibilities for MSGCIs to create new traditions and expectations that may borrow from other traditions and expectations.

Masculinity and Male Sexuality and Its Significance for Gender Role Expectations and Child Rearing among MSGCI Men

Masculinity and male sexuality was also a topic mentioned among several of the male MSGCIs. Whether there was a focus on male sexual prowess and performance as Daniel describes or on the importance of being a responsible father, the viewpoints these MSGCIs were taught exemplified traditional gender roles about "being a man." Here, Daniel elaborates on the gender/cultural expectations that helped to define manhood for him: a breadwinner, a professional, heterosexual, a father, hard-working man, and a "man of sacrifice":

DANIEL

We never talked about homosexuality; that topic would not be broached. It is a hush-hush topic. You may have heard rumors about 'so and so' but no one talked about it. My dad, back then, ignored it. It's only now, after being in this country for years he may mention it because of some pop culture reference. But it's the culture. It's as if "real men" are not gay because men are the "givers" and not the "receivers." Real men provide for their families. Real men are defined by their sexual conquests and prowess or how many children they have. That is what I was exposed to as a child and as I got older, I would overhear the stories my mom's friends told and began to realize men who could not keep their woman satisfied or provide for their family were dogged out! But my dad was a considered a good man and a good role model—hard working and always sacrificing for the family. I knew these qualities were ones I aspired to have too. But, I was also a bit of a 'playa' too. I had my ladies. What--? They love me, what can I say? [laugh].

Ironically for Daniel, although he admitted to but did not want to talk much about his teen son's recent "coming out" as gay, it has been a huge adjustment for him to think about masculinity as it relates to homosexuality and his own son being different from him as a teenaged "playa." I chose not to push Daniel to further discuss his son's sexual identity as it was obvious to me—both as a listener and observer, he was not ready to engage with me on the issue just yet. Upon reflection, I am able to observe, however, the strong connection between male sexuality and patriarchy within Caribbean culture and how Daniel, who perceives himself as both a loving father and a man who strongly identifies with notions and expressions of hyper-masculinity, must begin to consider his own parental child-rearing practices with his son. In the same way that MSGCI women described persisting tropes that frame cultural definitions of femininity and womanhood, MSGCI men—including Daniel—are equally exposed to messaging and cultural models that condemn homosexuality (for both men and women) as a social norm and legally in some Caribbean nations and create a hierarchy that values heterosexuality. According to the work of scholars Errol Lamont Fields et al. (2015) and Kamala Kempadoo (2009), European patriarchal gender ideologies emphasize heteronormativity and especially masculinity as necessary to the assertion of power and authority, where "manly men" are dominant and able to subordinate other men and, of course, women too.

Much of the conversation among MSGCI men on the topic of manhood also centered on presenting a positive image of "black fatherhood." To the MSGCIs, being a good man also means being a good father: being present and involved in their children's lives as a role model to them. They emphasized the importance of showing their children, by example, that they can be successful black men in society, who are doing positive things, and are resilient in dealing with racism, including covert discrimination and racial profiling. In many ways, their emphasis on black male resilience can be perceived as a way for these black men to challenge the predominant stereotype and cultural narrative—neglectful and irresponsible absent black father who is frequently under- or unemployed or incarcerated. Rejecting this narrative is important to the MSGCI men because they want to show their children and the wider community that black men—both African American and those who are Caribbean identified—are strong, powerful, and able to overcome obstacles and social pressures, and protect their children.

Many of the men described building positive relationships with other black men and men of color, mentoring black male youth (Caribbean, Latino, and African American identified) living in low-income and working class neighborhoods, and increasing their presence in local communities as a way to show *you don't need to play basketball or football to get out of the 'hood; going to college and grad school and pursuing a career can be profitable and cool too*, as Robert explained to me. When it comes to their own children, the MSGCIs also talked about making better attempts at volunteering at their children's school and extracurricular activities if time allowed, and showing their own children that they care and love them regardless if they are in a relationship with their mother or not. For some, being "caring" means balancing being an authoritarian figure while also saying "I love you" to their children more often than their own fathers told them, but not too much for fear their male children might become "soft" and ill-equipped to handle harsh and real world realities black men face. This point particularly resonated with Joachim as he said jokingly, *that's why they [boys] have their mothers to do all that.* All the MSGCI men talked about the importance of providing new opportunities and sharing positive experiences with their children. Through these experiences vis-à-vis trips, expensive camps, and educational programs, the MSGCIs are focused on helping their children be confident, have self-esteem, and learn to think and express their emotions effectively—a kind of emotional intelligence seen as an important skill to master in predominately white spaces, and especially in social and work situations and when managing encounters with law enforcement.

While being a "strong father" aligns well with prevailing social values and cultural beliefs around masculinity, the MSGCIs' race-gender performance can also be viewed as a type of cultural capital. At first glance, we observe MSGCIs using their middle class incomes more readily to purchase opportunities and experiences for their children very much in the same way their Caribbean immigrant parents attempted to do for them but with less access to fiscal resources. However, in revisiting Bourdieu's theory on cultural capital, we also observe the MSGCIs actively engage in developing within their families and passing down to their children particular values, skills, and knowledge as a way to raise the status of black fatherhood and masculinity as a whole. An important component of raced gender work the MSGCI men are engaged in is perceived as necessary emotional work to help their children develop a more positive sense of self and identity.

JOACHIM elaborates:

The men in my family are strong, confident and educated. They speak up for themselves. They have presence. That's how we were raised to be. But I see for that generation, the older men grew up in a [Caribbean] society where it is majority people of color. You can look everywhere and see someone who looks like you. Yes, there is classism and discrimination too but it's different from here. I want our child and any other kids we have down the line to be confident like that. But it's hard in this country where there are so many messages that tell you otherwise. Where people treat you otherwise. I know what is out there and it can get in you, under your skin, if you are not right in the mind. Get discouraged, demoralized, feel the need to get involved in drugs and thug life, running the streets. I need to prepare [my child] for this world to be different from those images. I would have failed as a parent and as a black man if I didn't.

MSGCI men often spoke with vigor about the need to be "father-protector" in their children's lives—children whom they see as having a far more privileged life than the one many of them grew up with—to protect them and teach their sons (and also their daughters) how to minimize the mental, emotional, and physical effects of these assaults that their middle class lifestyle may render them unprepared to manage discriminatory situations.

FAMILY SOCIALIZATION ON MATE SELECTION AND MARRIAGE: HOMOSEXUALITY, HOMOGAMY/ ENDOGAMY, EXOGAMY, WOMEN'S WORK, AND RELIGION

Notwithstanding socio-cultural influences on a person's identity and conception of self and their role in the social world as taught through the institution of family, family socialization remains an important feature in an individual's identity development—particularly when it comes to sexual identity, and eventually when it comes to forging romantic relations. The family socialization process also reveals a host of expectations and rules that intend to guide its members on how to choose mates according to particular traits and characteristics deemed appropriate for future progeny.

Homosexuality and Caribbean Culture

When I asked the MSGCIs to elaborate on division of labor in their parents' or family home and how family members got along, interestingly, the conversation shifted to mate selection, dating, and marriage, and in some cases, divorce. Marriage, in particular, is considered to be an important event for women and the MSGCIs felt there was a huge cultural emphasis on it. Most of them felt that women are supposed to aspire to marriage and learning "the basics" of home economics was intended to groom them for hetero-normative family life. Shana briefly talks about being a lesbian and how her family has since responded to her relationships:

SHANA

At first it took a little bit for them to get over the fact we got divorced, they didn't get it. Especially because [my ex-husband] wasn't cheating on me or beating me. We got married young and still had a lot of growing up to do. I came out, and, understandably, he was mad and hurt. We went to talk to a therapist at one of the local community centers and he admitted that he suspected I was gay but felt heartbroken that he married his best friend and it didn't work out. It was sad to hear that and it took a lot of time and healing but we are friends still and he has since moved on. They [my family] just don't get it. But I am lesbian, been gay for years and I love [my partner]. And it's not like there aren't gay people in Puerto Rico but many of the older folks think that being a lesbian is an American, white thing that you do. That I "do lesbian sex" and that I must not have had good sex with [my ex-husband] which is why I must be gay. [laughs]. I mean they are cool with [my partner] and they love her too but some of them are still stuck on, "okay so when are you going to stop playing around, marry again and have some babies?" And I am like, "I can go and do all that with a woman!" I love my family and they love me and accept me but not all the time they *really* understand what it means to be a woman loving another woman and creating a happy home with her.

Similar to Daniel's conversation around hyper-masculinity and patriarchal ideologies, Shana's discussion about her family not "really" understanding what it means to be a lesbian points to the deeply rooted religious beliefs around gender and female sexuality that were brought to the Americas by European colonialists to the Caribbean.[1] Shana's family's view that she "does lesbian sex" and will eventually come to her "senses" to marry a man and have children with him is indicative of existing religious and cultural understandings as to what is morally and socially acceptable as well as what is legally permissible.

Currently, several nations across the Caribbean have anti-sodomy (buggery) laws as well as other policies that make same-sex activities illegal. Interestingly, there is particular emphasis on activities among men who have sex with men (MSM) and barely any mention of criminalizing same-sex unions between women. Arguably, the lesser focus on lesbian relationships is not only attributed to religion and individuals' interpretation and endorsement of religious expressions of heterosexism and homophobia, but also correlates to patriarchy's view of femininity as connected to male homosexuality and its reliance on heteronormativity. To be clear, the Caribbean collective religious and cultural effort to endorse homophobia, heteronormativity and patriarchy should not be perceived as occurring more often in this culture or broadly among those who self-identify as black. On the contrary, in her book *Talking Back: Thinking Feminist, Thinking Black* (2015:122), bell hooks wrote the perception of blatant homophobia in black communities is simply because "there is a tendency for individuals in black community to verbally express in an outspoken way antigay sentiments" and not that other cultures or groups are less homophobic in comparison.

In an oversimplified way, patriarchy is concerned with men exerting and maintaining power over others. The activity of sex and the performance of sexuality becomes a tool for exerting control as well as male sexual expressions and identity that emphasizes sexual prowess with women. Accordingly, heteronormative ideals of masculinity among MSMs trouble hegemonic constructions of sex and gender because MSMs are viewed as being feminized because they are willing to be dominated by other men (Kempadoo 2009; White and Carr 2005). In contrast, women in same-sex relationships do not threaten the norms of patriarchy in the same way—not only because of women's perceived lower status in the social system but also women's sexual behavior and expressions of erotic desire are socially seen and are often codified in law as sexual practice, differently from gender role and expectations (see work of Wekker 2006). In this regard, for Shana, the view among some members of her family that she "does lesbian sex" confirms the existence of the aforementioned viewpoint that Shana's sexual desire and sexual activity with another woman is less about being in a mutually loving relationship and more about her sexual practice. Accordingly, it is then thought that Shana's sexual practice is not related to, nor should it detract from, her ability to conform to religious and heteronormative, patriarchal gender ideals of marriage and motherhood for women in Caribbean society.

With that said, it is also worth noting the persistence of racist structures of whiteness, as it relates to class and sexuality. For instance, you may recall Shana saying, *many of the older folks think that being a lesbian is an American, white thing that you do.* Shana's interpretation of her family's perspective on homosexuality suggests that being gay is synonymous with American, whiteness, and middle class-ness. In his chapter essay "How Gay Stays White and What Kind of White it Says," Allan Bérubé (2011) spoke to this perspective and argued a majority of people indeed perceive LGBT people as homogenous, white, and wealthy. He described the various whitening practices (e.g., making race analogies, mirroring the whiteness of men who run powerful institutions, excluding people of color, and selling gay as white to raise money and gain economic power) reproduced in people's actions and in the media that perpetuate the stereotype "that gay must equal white—a universal and representative (and male and economically secure), and assumes white (and male and middle class) as default categories" (Bérubé 2011:214–215). According to certain members of her family, this stereotype assumes Shana experiences a certain level of privilege as a lesbian because she may be able to avoid the social stigma of her homosexuality more easily in the United States as opposed to in the Caribbean. Unfortunately, a consequence to the stereotype or assumption that homosexuality is a "white thing you that you do" ultimately silences and contributes to the invisibility of LGBTQ community, including individuals like Shana who self identifies as American, black, Latina (specifically Puerto Rican), lesbian, and middle class.

Homogamy/Endogamy and Exogamy: Family Attitudes, Skin Color, and Identity Assertions

When it came to discussing mate selection, it was a topic often raised when MSGCIs considered whether their parents were explicit about them dating and/or marrying a person with Caribbean ancestry. Among the MSGCIs in this study, almost half of the sample is either married to a self-identified African American or white person where as one third are married to a person of Caribbean descent (either first or second generation immigrant) with the remaining participants being single and dating people of various ethnic and racial backgrounds. Brenda discusses dating and marriage as a topic among her Jamaican parents and relatives:

BRENDA

I think for my parents, they are more so focused on us bringing home someone who is respectful. It's never been "you need to bring home a Jamaican boy." But at the same time it is also somewhat implied. I see it with my aunts and cousins; they will date or have married someone who is Jamaican. They don't say you have to date a Jamaican but you get the "oh, so you are dating him?" if you don't. Now, marriage as a topic is not really a huge thing. Both sets of my grandparents had strong, long relationships but as an adult only now do I hear and can appreciate the kinds of problems their marriage had to deal with. Perhaps it's a generation thing because my parents' generation—my mom got married to my dad but separated. Then I have a couple of aunts who never got married. After them is my generation and this idea of marriage for life was not instilled in us that you *had* to be married. But I probably think it would be different if folks stayed in Jamaica. Getting married is more emphasized there.

For the most part, like Brenda, MSGCIs felt their parents were more explicit about the personality characteristics they were expected to choose in a potential mate, such as: believes in God, is family oriented, attractive, respectful and loving, hard-working, ambitious, smart and educated, and can provide a good lifestyle and home life.

And while the MSGCIs felt their parents implied they should date or marry a person with Caribbean ancestry, a few MSGCI women talked about the explicit ways family members have commented on a previous partner's ethno-racial characteristics from skin color and hair texture to language and country stereotypes as important to their mate selection process, a reflection of their own identity assertion and how a decision regarding one's mate would have on their children's generation. Michelle explains an explicit emphasis on a partner's skin color and hair:

MICHELLE

In Spanish we have a saying, "mejorar la raza"—it means to better the race or improve the race by mixing with people who are light skinned or have curly hair but no one that really looks too black because black is considered ugly and low status. Now in my family, I got those old school aunts in their 70s and 80s who are little dark-skinned and have curly hair but push this stuff about "pelo malo" [bad hair]. You also have to choose a boyfriend or husband that has "good hair" and is not dark so your kids aren't considered black and ugly, like it's a curse or something. It's sad because it goes on for generations and people don't realize it's racist. I happened to marry a person who is white and we fell in love. My aunts were so happy that I married him because of the way my kids look, but he stole my heart [smiles]. But isn't that what it's all about? Having someone who loves you and your crazy-ass family, who respects you and supports you? But people judge me too. Other Latinas look at me and when I am out with my husband, who really looks white, they are either like, "oh, you did well" or are sarcastic, "you got yourself a white guy and now you can move up in the world. Aren't you lucky?" You just have to ignore it.

While skin color and hair texture were discussed among most MSGCIs at various points during our conversations, Michelle and other MSGCIs who self identified as Afro-Latino and/or Latino presented a nuanced discussion on skin color and hair texture when it came to mate selection. The discussion focused on the cultural dimension of ethnoracial characteristics that are reflective of the colonial racial projects encouraged by the Spanish and Portuguese colonizers of their parents' native countries. Informed by the colonial caste system of slavery throughout the Americas, which insists a racist paradigm that attributes cultural and genetic superiority and inferiority values to individuals based on phenotype, characteristics such as skin color and hair texture were often the most salient features used to categorize people to groups. Different from British and French colonizers, Iberian colonizers encouraged the process and policy of absorption—the mixing between Africans, indigenous Indian groups, and Europeans intended to create a society, where those of African and indigenous descent would disappear as a distinct group (Wade 1997; see also Montalvo and Codina 2001). Undergirding this process of absorption or *blanquea-miento/branqueamento* (whitening) is the belief that darker skin and kinkier hair texture are African traits that contaminates rather than improves the race. Therefore, the practice of "marrying lighter" to produce offspring with light skin or that can pass for white becomes an avenue to escape oppression and elevate one's familial social position and lifestyle (Montalvo and Codina 2001; see also Hughes and Hertel 1990).

For MSGCIs like Michelle, who described dating and marrying a white person out of love and common interest, there is an assumption that she made a conscious racial choice to a seek mate that was light skinned or white in order to downplay her ethnic origins and pass her (and her spouse's) collective whiteness on to their children. This assumption was made clear when Michelle reflected on the negative comments she received from other Latinos—*you got yourself a white guy and now you can move up in the world. Aren't you lucky*—which suggest her life and those of her children will be enhanced because of the "social legacy of preference for and greater value given to lighter skin colors [that exists] among Hispanic populations" (Stephen and Fernández 2012:80). Another interesting point Michelle raises here is related to the idea that beauty and attractiveness is connected to cultural beliefs on the degrees of relative blackness: a strong preference for partners with lighter, tanned skin complexions as opposed to darker ones. Researchers Montoya (2008), Masi De Casanova (2004), and Twine (1998), for example have found skin color and hair texture's influence on attractiveness perceptions exist within families. According to their research, social valuations of darker skin color and kinkier hair textures (*pelo malo*) become problematic to one's social capital and ability to "marry up," and are seen when family members are encouraged to hide their African heritage and even hide their African-looking relatives in order to highlight more mestizo (European-indigenous mixtures) and/or European traits (Stephen and Fernández 2012).

As you may recall, Shana also makes this connection when she says, *there is [always] a black granny somewhere in the background that people love but are embarrassed to talk about.*

Here, Claudette shares the explicit advice she and her siblings received about dating and how her parents' experiences informed the lessons they taught her about dating and adult relationships. In particular, Claudette discusses various generalizations and stereotypes she was exposed to that were intended to signal which black ethnic group was most acceptable to date and marry.

CLAUDETTE explains:

One of the things my mom says "you have to marry an African American" and I am like "Mom, please. No." [laugh]. I think this was based on her experience being married to my dad [laugh].Ironically, even before my father, my mom dated Caribbean men. For my mom, it wasn't planned for her to marry my dad because he was Caribbean. She thought it was good to diversify and choose to mix with Africans or Caribbean people not just with African Americans. Now, I remember that my father said "don't marry a Haitian," [laughs] "because they're sexist."My stepmother is Jamaican and she makes it a point to tell us that she didn't date Jamaican men. And for a while I was dating someone, he was Garifuna, and my father was head-over-heels and thought this boyfriend was the "greatest thing since sliced bread." My dad and stepmother liked him because he was black Latino and from Honduras and was able to speak Spanish, so they were able to speak Spanish together. I think [my dad] liked this boyfriend because he was foreign-born. I do get the sense that [my dad] feels Caribbean people are a bit more progressive. When it comes to dating, I mentioned to him [my dad] that most of my friends are bicultural like me and are from a medley of different places. He said that was to be expected particularly at this age and experiences and I should be able to mingle and so forth. I guess what you have here is the adoption of the first generation black immigrant, adopting what it means to be black here [U.S] and then you have these folks that have been here for a long time and their views start to vary in terms of roles in society and how progressive they are going to be toward certain issues.

Other MSGCIs also observed the longer families remain in the United States and with every new generation, the more open or less stringent their immigrant relatives seem to be about their dating and mate selections, especially for those in heterosexual unions. Of course there are generalizations that are still made regarding a mate's ethnic background, skin color, and hair texture. Yet, the presumption—one that Claudette and others make—is that the longer each immigrant generation remains in their "new" country, the more likely they are to adopt more inclusive attitudes around mate selection.

Marriage and Women's Work

When asked about inter-generational attitudes about endogamy and exogamy as it relates to cultural views on gender and gender roles, most MSGCIs observed an attitude shift regarding gender roles for men and women and marriage becoming more egalitarian, which is a contrast from traditional family life in the Caribbean. But as Natalie points out here, this notion of egalitarian gender roles applies when it comes to women's employment outside of the home, but not necessarily a shift in values regarded as most important and related to cultural behaviors, practices, and family relationships.

NATALIE explains:

Of course there are many more opportunities women have today than there was when I was growing up. Yes, they [parents] tell you to work hard: "you can do and be anything—even president." But you somehow can't do as well as your husband though, or earn more than him. You have to let him be the man and you be the woman. I've had to take the back seat to [his] career so that he can pursue his goals but I think I am okay with doing that because it makes most sense financially. Though it changed the dynamics in the relationship, I don't feel oppressed because of the choice I made.

Claudette reflected on her African American mom's employment outside of the home and how that impacted her own parents' marriage, which eventually led to divorce.

CLAUDETTE adds:

I think there are cultural nuances that put a strain on [my parents'] relationship. For example, on my mother's side, my African American grandfather and grandmother are very much into the idea that the man is the provider. My mother was making more money than my father and that was looked down upon. My maternal grandfather was old school. He was a [Veteran]. You take of your family, you provide and that is what you do. It wasn't that [my father] was not a good provider but that there was a differential between my parents income, and for my maternal grandfather, you are just supposed to make more money than your wife. I think for my dad, being a Caribbean—a Haitian man, this also really bothered him too. As a woman, you cannot emasculate your man.

As expressed by Claudette, the persistence of patriarchy in both Caribbean and African American cultures (and subsequently in marriage) establishes men as the head of household with the women expected to be by his side and care for his children. Even with the social, economic, and legislative strides made to improve the status of women in the United States, for example, these MSGCIs are acutely aware of both the pressure and need for women to contribute to their households economically and maintain their own professional identity while not emasculating their male partners. But the value of masculinity and the man's role as head of household in the Caribbean family serves to promote and emphasize the viewpoint that traditional, male headed, heterosexual unions, and legal marriages are the cornerstone for successful family units—a perspective that several Caribbean countries' support via their national development strategies, policies, and programs. Not surprisingly, when we also look to MSGCIs and reflect on the significance of socioeconomic determinants in family patterns and gender roles, the middle classes generally appear to adopt European male-headed and nuclear family structures, which we can see its genesis in slavery. In *The Sociology of Slavery* (1967), sociologist Orlando Patterson explains that legal marriage was considered a practice associated with wealthy proprietors within the plantocracy and became associated with privilege and nobility and rarely of the slave or subordinate whites. Over time, with the influx of Asian immigrants and the emancipation of Africans across the Caribbean, patriarchal family types continued to prevail and its value passed on to subsequent generations even if social attitudes are less rigidly adhered to.

When talking about the choice and/or sacrifice to work outside of the home, MSGCI women talked about the pressures of being professional women of color. They detailed instances where they felt they needed to work harder and longer hours than their white colleagues (male or female) in order to prove their economic and intellectual worth, especially when they pursued white-collar professions. At the same time, these women also talked about their feelings of guilt and selfishness. They wondered whether those choices were the best options for their marriages and their children, especially at times when their personal relationships were on the brink of divorce or when their children were in trouble.

LISA, for example, recalls:

By my mid-twenties I knew I needed to make good on my parents' dreams. They worked hard and encountered a lot of hardships to make a better life for my siblings and me. But now I understand that that type of success comes with a price. On TV, you see these high-powered white women that have it all—thinking you can have it too: the nice house, fantastic career, good marriages and well-adjusted children. But as a black woman, white feminism doesn't speak to my experience. I still have to be the good wife and mother, and be able to build the children up to be strong and proud—'cause hiring help can't teach my children why it is important for them to understand their Jamaican and Panamanian immigrant roots but also know my [American] history too. At the same time, husbands need their wives and children need their mothers.

While there is multiethnic and linguistic diversity among the MSGCIs, there are observable similarities in their notions, understandings of and specific beliefs in family structure and composition, mate selection and gender role segmentation. For Lisa, Claudette, and Natalie, the explicit and implicit lessons learned from their parents and family members had a strong influence on their own conceptions of what family is, the gendered roles its members play, and the values it should endorse and pass on to the next generation. As discussed earlier, the observations these women have made about their parents' generation and about their own experiences reveal the powerful but nuanced way in which patriarchy continues to play out in family life for this second generation.

Religion, Marriage, and Culture

Religion also plays an important role in social life—and particularly in married life. In many cultures, religion is significant in reinforcing traditional gender roles and especially when it comes to marriage and family structure. Many MSGCIs view religion as a stabilizing agent that families rely on in crisis and when preserving tradition. While the majority of MSGCIs identified as Christian (including Catholic), Eddy, for example, talked about growing up Christian, but recognizes his dad's Hindu roots as playing a role in shaping how he views marriage and family obligations. According to Eddy, marriage and enduring family bonds are considered to be at the center of East Indian culture. Eddy's mother, who is of black and Irish descent, left the Mandeville area of Jamaica to continue her teacher training. His father left Claredon, a predominantly East Indian parish in

Jamaica, to pursue mechanical engineering. His parents met in the library, where his mother worked in the evenings part-time as a reference desk clerk. According to family folklore, Eddy's father and mother were part of the same, small community of Jamaican immigrant students at the University and had a lot in common in terms of culture and other interests. Eddy did share that his father's family was not initially enthused at the match since his mother was not East Indian and unfamiliar with certain Hindu cultural practices (e.g., celebration of Diwali[2]) the family maintained, since converting to Christianity sometime during the early part of the twentieth century.

According to Nevadomsky (1982), maintaining the Hindu tradition of arranged, caste-based marriages (also known as caste endogamy) among people of East Indian descent in the Caribbean changed over time, in large part because the interracial living conditions among blacks, whites and other groups often interrupted Hindu caste rituals. Further, the strength of social and cultural influences of Christianity in the Caribbean as well as the fact that several Caribbean countries, such as Trinidad and Tobago and Guyana did not legally sanction Hindu marriages, contributed to many East Indian descendant families to embrace Christian norms. To be clear, the adoption of Christian norms and practices did not mean East Indians completely abandoned Hindu cultural rituals and traditions that existed in India. For many East Indian descendants across the Caribbean, the independence of India in 1947 served to revive Indian culture in which co-ethnics see merit in its "old" practices and traditions and emphasize the importance of passing such rituals, norms, and traditions to future generations. For Eddy, his father's family (and extended family) embraced the tradition of syncretism of Christian and Hindu culture and marriage values. Here, Eddy describes the impact his father's observance of certain Hindu cultural practices has on his own interaction with his in-laws, wife, and son:

EDDY

I know from my father's side, though they are [Christian] they still try to hold on to their Hindu Indian culture. It's a mash-up of religion and culture… when it comes to family, Hindus are clear about family obligations. Children are seen as long-term investments. They are supposed to bring honor to the family and contribute to the family. Some may think it's being a show-off when your child does well in school, but it is supposed to reflect well on you as the parent too. That's why, among Indians, there is a focus on being doctors, engineers and the sort. It shows to others that my son or daughter is smart and successful and therefore I am successful. My mom is not Hindu but she believes the same thing too. And her parenting is the same. I suppose that is what worked for them in their marriage. She took care of the house and [the kids] even though she worked part-time but my father made sure we were serious about school and studying. I definitely see this way rubbing off on me and how I am with my wife and son. My wife's parents are Trinidadian, so she gets it. In Trinidad, there are more people like my dad but more of them seem to practice Hindu culture. So, she gets it about Indian [descendants in the Caribbean]. I am teaching our son about Diwali, the music, and all the things I had growing up. On weekends, we spend time with my parents. My wife is interested in having her parents come live with us in a few years. We may need to look into buying somewhere close to my parents if her parents are going to live with us too. Plus, if we need some cash toward a down payment, I know our families will be glad to pitch in because it's how we look out for one another.

When I asked Eddy, specifically, about his marital status, he shared there exists some tension between his family and his common law wife's because they have yet to officially "walk down the aisle." Here, Eddy elaborates on the rite of passage of marriage in Hinduism and Christian relationships:

EDDY

So [my wife] and I are both Christian, her parents are Anglican. My dad's family is Church of God like most of the people in Clarendon. All sides of the family think we are living in sin and should get married. But my parents or really my grandparents want us to do a joint type Hindu-Christian wedding or ceremony even though we don't practice the religious aspects of Hinduism. My wife doesn't want to upset her parents but I am not sure if she is feeling a Hindu ceremony; she wants a church wedding. We've seen other people—some friends and colleagues do some variation on cultural weddings and ceremonies but she's like "I'm not converting so why bother." So, we just haven't agreed and I guess over the years, we've just lived out our lives as a married couple—common law, without the actual religious ceremony part. My son has my last name and our lives are legal in the way common law marriages function but I don't know. I wouldn't mind a Hindu ceremony or something symbolic that acknowledges that part of my family's side but I figure I am not going to push it. Both sides bring it up and say passive-aggressive stuff like, "wouldn't it be nice if...." but you can't live your life for other people. You do what makes sense for you...

Across their stories, including Eddy's above, the MSGCIs often mentioned the importance of "doing what makes sense to you" as they each grappled with whether culturally prescribed religious and gender roles fit their lives as adults. This is an important feature of MSGCI triple identity consciousness; it is their realization that the values, expectations, and traditions they were taught or exposed to as children inform how they conceive of the ways to choose to apply these lessons to the life they are living as adults. It is quite a natural but methodical process that is grounded in an awareness of competing forces that confront their desires of a life they envision for themselves and how they choose to perform it.

In terms of the identity development and the MSGCIs' narratives about their own racial and ethnic identity process, there is an additional layer in which we must consider, when examining identity performances: the MSGCIs' knowledge and understanding of their self (or self concept) in terms of their physical and social attributes and the identity politics that are associated with particular self concepts. In this regard, MSGCI ethnic identity is another aspect of their identity where MSGCIs felt the need to find a safe medium between what their parents' Caribbean culture tells them, what US society tells them, and how they feel most authentic about themselves. While identity formation and assertion is a continuous process, the MSGCIs referred to the period of their pre- and mid-adolescence as the impetus of their attempts to understand their ethnicity.

IDENTITY AND THE IMPORTANCE OF AUTHENTICITY: SYMBOLIC EXPRESSIONS OF CARIBBEAN ETHNICITY

As discussed previously about racialization, MSGCIs perceived their race to be, at times, a fixed aspect of their identity due to other people's perceptions of them—from their physical features (e.g., having dark skin and natural, curled hair/locs) to behaviors that are linked to contemporary cultural understandings associated with meanings of blackness, such as attending a black church, using popular black vernacular and living in, or in close proximity to black/minority neighborhoods. As I continued to dig deeper into our conversations about being children of Caribbean immigrants, I found MSGCIs described instances where their identification with and performance of their ethnicity, specifically their Caribbean ethnicity, affords them a level of identity fluidity, which they view as both natural as well as necessary to their overall well being. In other words, their ability to combine elements of a black cultural identity and their

Caribbean ethnicity across various situations and groups of people, spoke a little more authentically to how the MSGCIs self-identify racially, culturally, and ethnically.

I asked the MSGCIs to recall, if possible, their earliest memories or instances, where being black and of Caribbean parentage was significant to them and if any, what dilemmas were faced. Often memories of such instances took place when they were either older children or in their teens. Indeed, at the forefront of their Caribbean ethnic identity assertions were specific cultural practices, such as learning to prepare and eat certain foods and delicacies, speaking their parents' native language or dialect, listening to certain music (e.g., reggae, calypso and soca, compas, twoubadou, salsa, merengue, and bachata), and visiting relatives still living in their parents' home countries, that indicated how the MSGCIs view their ethnic selves. For the most part, their commitment to continuing these cultural practices is seen as important to the MSGCIs, because it allows them to demonstrate their authenticity and connection to their Caribbean heritage. There were, however, interesting distinctions related to the emergence and pronouncement of these ethnic performances, which varied across different social and institutional contexts.

In school settings, the MSGCIs' black racial identity was often pronounced. At their schools, which were in most cases predominantly black, MSGCIs' teachers and school administrators often presumed the majority students were "just black" with the exception of those who were multiracial or "ambiguously racial," and/or can speak Spanish or Haitian Creole. MSGCIs found there was significant emphasis on students learning and celebrating aspects of African American history and culture in the United States, even though there were students of diverse ethnic backgrounds, including African American, Asian, Caribbean, and African immigrant ancestry within the school community. For the MSGCIs who were bilingual or spoke other dialects, they recalled instances when teachers dedicated classroom time to embrace other cultures, such as in Spanish, music or art classes but often its occurrences were limited, because classroom time was dedicated to English language literacy. These observations were of no real surprise to me since I had found in previous research for my book, *Creating Black Caribbean Ethnic Identities* (2010), institutions such as community-based organizations, health centers, and schools influence its clients or members' maintenance of particular racial and ethnic identities through its culture, climate, and programming services. Within these institutions, people internalize the norms and values of the culture and overall society, including their understanding of race and identity. For these MSGCIs, they participated in a school community whose culture and climate emphasized an African American experience to facilitate assimilation and acculturation of its racially identified black students.

Informal social settings within schools or neighborhoods, however, are sites MSGCIs found to be distinct from institutions where ethnicity and class performances would emerge. Many MSGCIs spent their childhoods and teen years in urban areas, which were often perceived to be ethnically, socially, and to some extent economically divided between those who were *really poor and on welfare, working class, and those who seemed to have enough,* quoting Millicent. Because there was often a shared perception that most of the youth in their neighborhoods were also other people of color, ethnicity, and class mattered in complex and intersecting ways.

It is commonly understood and talked about in any popular parenting magazine available online and in print that older children and especially adolescents (ages 13 to 18) look to social bonds and relationships with their peers to help them define who they are as individuals. Essentially, youth use a social identity to construct a personal identity. Because there are so many physiological, biological, and emotional things happening during this phase of brain and physical development as well as their changing roles in family, gaining acceptance from peers becomes paramount. Much of youth time and effort is spent expressing their "right" music tastes and speech, dressing well, owning desirable possessions (e.g., the latest Michael Jordan sneakers), and appearing confident. And equally as important is in the way the youth talk to their peers about themselves and the things they are interested in so as to fit in and/or feel they are popular among their peers and the broader social network. An interesting nuance is the concept of popularity for the MSGCIs. The concept of popularity is often perceived as being able to discern and conform to the mainstream, however, being "popular" for many of the MSGCIs during their adolescence reflected a combination of 1980s and 1990s hip hop aesthetic and urban culture (signifying a low-income or working class African American experience), with some influences of mainstream (meaning white American) status symbols. It is in their patterns of vernacular, music, and dress choices, which are not only seen as race and gender signifiers, as Julie Bettie argued in her book, *Women Without Class: Girls, Race and Identity* (2003/2014), but also serve as key social class performances associated with life expectations. In effect, it is this social context where MSGCIs developed and combined symbolic elements of their racial and ethnic identities of being both black US-born and of Caribbean ethnicity.

Among their friends in the neighborhood, several MSGCIs were fluid in their command of Standard American English and urban slang, Creole, Spanglish, and/or Patois. This allowed MSGCIs to signal their racial authenticity with African American youth and ethnic authenticity with other second generation Caribbean immigrants and participate in environments where social value is placed on being non-black middle class. Here, Carmen talks about using popular culture and fashion as symbols of her identity to become a "chameleon," adapting and blending into her different social environments, between family and friends:

CARMEN

I did well in school and was kind of a nerd. I learned the "King's English" pretty well. Because if we were to make it out here, with the white people, we had to learn how to put sentences together. But with my girls, I needed to show I was down ...yeah, they teased me about sounding white because you almost have to downplay the Spanish accent if you want to sound "proper" [mimicking a British accent]. So I had to change it up with them. It was Hip Hop. I wore the doorknockers [earrings] and the Carhartt jacket and jeans. My friends wore the Calvin Klein stuff, Cross Colours, maybe an 8Ball leather jacket. Timberlands were a must. I knew all the R&B, the latest rap lyrics and dance steps and had seen the latest movies. When I got around my family and my cousins, it was different too. To them rap music was a bunch of noise and cursing. They really didn't get the clothes. The women in my family didn't like the baggy style... [With] the Dominican kids and some of the other kids from like Puerto Rico, even some of my cousins, we listened to bachata and merengue like Villalona, and played that music in the house and at parties on the weekends. Us younger people listened to like Menudo, Brenda Starr or house music, and merengue like Los Hermanos Rosario and reggae artists like Shabba Ranks, but then you had like El General, which was the Spanish version of Shabba Ranks. That combined my world music—it was Spanish, it was reggae and rap put together. We also watched Spanish channels and novelas in the house with my aunts and grandmother. I spoke Spanish and Spanglish, really with my cousins, at home too. I learned to be like a chameleon and adapt to the crowd.

Being seen as "Americanized" and speaking "proper" English and not in the dialect of their parents' immigrant society had some drawbacks for the MSGCIs when it came to fitting in or expressing their Caribbean ethnicity. Brenda describes the assumptions other second generation Caribbeans have made about her and her lack of a strong Jamaican accent.

BRENDA

I was 13 when we moved to Connecticut and I was submerged in this West Indian-Jamaican-Caribbean culture. I could be in an environment with my American-born cousins and their friends and I'd start singing a song and they are like, "how do you know that song?" And I am like "just because I am Americanized, doesn't mean I don't know my culture." Then it becomes, "do you know how to speak Jamaican patois?" Yeah, it's all of that. [Laugh]. For quite some time, the Jamaican guys—even if they are first generation American-born like me, felt the need to speak proper because they thought I spoke well and that I didn't understand patois. And I would ask, "why would you think I wouldn't understand?" And it's because they may not have heard me speak patois so they assume that I wouldn't understand them. Now that I've moved back to this area, everything is in patois because they know I can understand and speak it back to them. I guess I come off more as an "American," someone who is black American, like African American, than American with Caribbean parents. And I am like, "what are you talking about? My parents, both of them are from Jamaica." West Indian people have a way of talking, like sucking teeth in a particular way or the way you say, "uh" or "Ay" that sounds like a typical West Indian person.

As teens, several MSGCIs saw value in learning both African American and Caribbean cultural codes of behavior and interaction. Not only did it seem emotionally important to them to *know how to connect with all of my people,* as Carmen subsequently mentioned, but it was also seen as a necessary tactic for knowing *how to appear like one of them,* in order to escape conflict situations with other teens, as Derrick mentioned in our conversations. As they grew older, MSGCIs became more fluid and comfortable with being able to culturally straddle race and ethnic identity spaces—lessons learned from their parents and when interacting with their Caribbean and African American peers. But as they got older, they also became increasingly aware of the ways social class complicated how they would use these lessons to assert their own identities across various situations.

The MSGCI discussed their attempts to dispel negative stereotypes about Caribbean people, emphasizing, for example, that not all black people from the Caribbean with natural hair and locs are like the reggae singer Bob Marley who was Rastafarian and smoked marijuana, or are a loud, unedu-cated, happy people who love to party and have a good time, but are quick to anger and react in violent ways. Dispelling such stereotypes, according to some MSGCIs, became more intentional as they entered into situations where there were whites or people they perceived to be middle class or upwards. Having a command of Standard American English (SAE) in the United States is considered an important aspect of one's social power and his or her ability to impose it onto others. As such, it is commonly perceived among the MSGCIs that a person's ability to communicate well (verbally and in writing) using SAE is considered a cultural signifier and marker of educational, linguistic, and middle class or upwardly mobile distinctions. Therefore, the MSGCIs see being a great communicator in English as necessary to doing well in school and professionally. However, those who spoke other languages besides English, found it equally important to be seen as culturally proficient in their ability to have a mastery of American Standard English and in another language as well. For Claudette, being multilingual says something important about a person's identity and how others perceive her and her abilities. She elaborates:

CLAUDETTE

I consider myself bicultural. I don't think I ever really thought about it too much when I was younger. Now I see it as an advantage. Take language, for instance. With Haitians, language is everything. Language and identity is seen and perceived by others as important. My mom would get on us and point out that my father speaks several languages fluently too, English, French, Creole, and Spanish, and so she was constantly on us to learn other languages, "just one more other than English that you all should be fluent. It's better for you and in life." So, I learned English in school and did very well and I can speak Spanish fluently too. I can go anywhere and travel and speak. They encouraged us to leave the country, to travel and experience the world and be able to talk about these experiences; to be able to speak the language and interact with the people. When I was older, like an older teen and my younger sister, the one who grew up with my father in Miami, they [parents] made sure she made trips to Latin America and to the Spanish-speaking Caribbean. Now, she speaks fluent Spanish.

With the exception of two individuals, all of the MSGCIs are fluent in at least one other world language besides English, either having chosen the language through a course of study and travel, or through learning formal ways of speaking their parents' lingua franca. Mastering SAE and being able to speak other languages fluently is seen as a type of cultural currency for MSGCI mobility that they can "cash in" whether it is helpful to their being competitive in the workplace or culturally aware and conversant in social settings—among white colleagues who seem to value SAE, and family members and peers who value ethno-racial cultural signifiers of the habitus of blackness. The MSGCIs' ability to demonstrate, with ease, their faculty with these cultural codes, language, and behaviors, "to talk the talk and walk the walk" renders them culturally fluent; individuals who are able to use their knowledge and experiences to move through and across social spaces.

TRAPPINGS OF A MIDDLE CLASS LIFESTYLE: MSGCI ADULT PERFORMANCES OF CARIBBEAN VERSUS US CULTURAL CAPITAL AND CULTURAL STRADDLING

Race, ethnic, and gender identities can be performed through symbolic practices and customs, which the MSGCIs demonstrated through various cultural signifiers associated with being black, US-born, and of Caribbean immigrant descent. Along the same vein, one's class identity also can be performed in these same ways. As the MSGCIs continued to share their stories with me from their childhoods and adolescence and through the present, their narratives provide a picture of working class and lower-middle class people striving to "make it" and even to "make it out" of environments where opportunities are limited for racial-ethnics and immigrants. At the same time, these stories also reveal something quite real about the nature of class differences, particularly when they go off to college, are in the workplace, or when traveling domestically and internationally, and are able to witness the different treatments those who have little, live modestly and who live in opulence experience according to their race, ethnicity, and gender.

As such, MSGCIs described the discursive strategies they have developed in order to: combat the stereotype of "acting white" as the singular black in predominately white spaces while also rejecting anti-black stereotypes; and find the balance between taking responsibility for their parents' immigrant generation and setting up a "better and brighter" future for their own children. In doing so, they talked about their frustration with the popular media misconception the black middle class does not exist—only poor or working class blacks do. Granted, MSGCIs' frustration is not far-fetched since there is plenty empirical and rhetorical evidence that suggests there is a stark mismatch in perceptions between what most people (read: white) think about black socioeconomic life in America[3] and the reality that there indeed exist black people who are also middle class (see Gilens 2003). And while the MSGCIs recognize there are clear indicators that show disproportionate black poverty remains a persisting social problem that should be remediated, MSGCIs' frustration speaks to their feeling invisible in the social milieu and the race-class bind they experience, as part of the black middle class in America.

In his book *The New Black Middle Class*, Bart Landry (1987) engages the reader in examining the living standards of the new black middle class. While the backdrop of post-1965 Civil Rights legislation and the increasing War on Poverty rhetoric from the late 1960s through the 1970s are the contextualizing factors in his analysis, Landry poses similar questions to the ones I raise with this MSGCI population. I ask the MSGCIs, how do you perform "making it?" and "what does being black middle class look like?" Of course, if I were to quote Brooklyn's rapper the Notorious B.I.G./Biggie Smalls (a child of Caribbean immigrants) when he says, "mo' money, mo' problems," then consumption and especially conspicuous consumption, is less about purchasing goods based on need and better quality, but more about luxury, responsibility, and ultimately demonstrating one's status as they become upwardly mobile.

Middle Class Conspicuous Consumption: Suburban Living, Vacations, Collecting Black Art, and Shopping

When prompted, the MSGCIs described their own consumption patterns to be more in-line with specific conceptions of a middle class position, such as homeownership, car ownership, having the ability to go on vacation and disposable income to participate in recreational activities. Several MSGCIs attributed their exposure to aspects of middle class cultural capital once they were in college, where they came into contact and developed friendships with other Caribbean and African Americans, middle class and affluent whites, and other ethnic groups. They began to acquire this cultural knowledge through visiting their peers' family homes and hearing about their peers' spring break and summer vacations. Their knowledge seemed to expand and were cultivated through additional opportunities to demonstrate this knowledge, such as hosting and attending work-related formal dinner parties, and learning the customs and etiquette of client engagement. They found having these skills are necessary to functioning in certain employment sectors as law, business, and medicine where the frequency for attending events that require this knowledge is high.

For the MSGCIs, their assertion of a middle class position included moving out of the neighborhoods they grew up in search of significantly better quality housing options, top tier public schools or closer proximity to elite private schools for their children, conveniences to recreational activities (e.g., restaurants, movies, and sporting games), and better shopping options for food and clothing. Even for those who may have attended undergraduate and/or graduate schools out-of-state, there is intentionality behind their choices to move to suburban-like areas, such as sections of cities where whites have previously gentrified, and areas considered "up and coming" because of involved neighborhood associations, or, at the very least, living in newly established middle class black enclaves.

Being able to take annual vacations, particularly to exotic or recreational locations, as opposed to visiting extended family, is another marker of middle class position. The distinction among the MSGCIs is that there is an interest in visiting the home countries of their immigrant parents in addition to visiting other popular destinations, such as Disney World, Lake Tahoe in Nevada, Atlantis in the Bahamas, Aspen for skiing, and Pebble Beach for golfing. A few of the MSGCI felt their US-born peers perceive traveling to Latin America and the Caribbean as pure vacation experiences, whereas they view such trips often as non-recreational and more family-oriented as Erica pointed out, *you'll need a vacation from the "vacation" if you go down there to visit family,* with the exception of traveling to the Caribbean annually for carnival celebrations. Several MSGCIs have ventured to other international destinations for pleasure, including parts of Europe, South Africa, the Middle East, and South Asia, but found the cost associated with some vacation destinations too high for the long-term for their families.

An emerging trend among the MSGCIs was an interest in renting or purchasing vacation properties (including time shares) in these exclusive vacation areas. With the exception of places like La Jolla, where Natalie and her family spend their vacation time visiting her in-laws who live in greater San Diego California, these exclusive vacation spots include islands of St. Johns and St. Thomas and eastern coastal areas such as Martha's Vineyard on the cape of Massachusetts, Sag Harbor near the Hamptons, in Long Island New York and Highland Beach in Maryland, which are known to be ideal for black middle class vacationers. Because these locales are some of the most diverse places historically known to welcome African Americans and Native Americans, MSGCIs have said they feel most comfortable vacationing and are seriously considering purchasing a second home for their families. Erica shares these sentiments:

ERICA

I'd always heard about people going to the Hamptons, being from New York, that's where the rich hang out for the summer. Going to Sag Harbor—it's really nice to learn about its history. Black people creating their own places of relaxation and refuge when they were often denied access to where the whites vacationed. That's an empowering thing. And when I think about it, it's like you are always around white people every day, and it can be really nice and refreshing to be around other blacks on your downtime. Like you have your own space, can feel at home and let your hair down. My friend who invites me to Sag Harbor also alternates her summers and visits Martha's Vineyard since her cousins have a rental property there. She tells me these are the hot spots. These places, sanctuaries, really, are a celebration of black culture and society. It can be bougie, little Jack and Jilly[4] too. There are some older uppity black folks that are just as bad as white folks. It's like they want you to prove your pedigree or your credentials. Yeah, you still get the "what do you do?" but I think the ones that are more secure in themselves are more inclusive and embrace you because it's about the next generation and the legacy and making sure we [middle class] can stay at this status or help one another climb higher and not fall.

MSGCIs' connection to these physical locales of belonging reinforces their belief that blacks throughout the Americas have a rich cultural heritage that is worth preserving and participating in. Not surprisingly, this connection is found to persist among the black middle class, and in this case MSGCIs, and serves to affirm their authenticity and membership as both blacks and as Caribbean ethnics and habitus of blackness (Lacy and Harris 2008; see also Banks 2012; Lamont and Molnar 2001). It can be found in their consumption and patronizing of black cultural content, such as the arts, which historically persisted and that several MSGCIs, for example, feel ancestrally connected to.

Before proceeding, it would be remiss of me if I did not to mention Herbert Gans' (1974) book *Popular Culture and High Culture* in my discussion of middle class cultural capital performances for MSGCIs. In his book, Gans grapples with the relationship between high culture and popular culture (also known as mass/taste culture) and how they differ in their aesthetic standards related to art, music, literature, and other symbolic products. He reminds readers that the standards that exist today are interpreted from the, "golden ages of high culture such as Periclean Athens, Elizabethan England, and the Renaissance" and are linked correspondingly to socio-economic and educational classes: the well-educated European elite, lower-middle class, working class and the poor" (1974:61). As such, people make choices in terms of their consumer behavior and leisure activities according to the perceived social value of the aesthetic standard such as in their preference for watching foreign films over television, listening to classical music over chamber music, playing tennis or golf, and eating gourmet foods. Gans claims ethnic immigrants also make these choices when considering their and their second generation's upward mobility, by selecting cultures that are conceived as having greater sophistication and higher status. I contend ethnic immigrants generations, and particularly the MSGCIs' parent generation were very much influenced by the Caribbean colonial legacy that edifies European cultural aesthetics—as we see this legacy in other spaces of social life (e.g., religion, marriage, and gender role segmentation) discussed thus far.

When it comes to examining the types of popular culture in US society, Gans identified black culture as one of several types of subcultures. He points to its vitality, at least from the perspective of whites, at the time of his writing—the 1970s, though black cultural content has always existed and came with blacks when they were stolen from Africa and brought to the Americas. Gans attributes the increased attention to black culture and popularity to the black middle class for its commercial success, though these art forms are often borrowed (or re-appropriated) by high culture composers and culture artists and become commodities with high prestige (think of American Jazz). For this reason, he argues "black culture is partial culture." Gans (1974:101) goes on to add:

> Blacks [in the United States] share the taste culture created by whites, and their aesthetic standards, leisure, and consumption habits…although they listen to black radio stations, read black newspapers and magazines and watch the few genuinely black films and television programs, they also use the media created predominately by and for whites.

While there is data on the socioeconomic and educational backgrounds that support Gans' thesis of individuals' consumption of particular culture or subcultures, and the social pressure for all groups to aspire to specific class and status markers, I argue, there is some intentionality in MSGCIs' choices to partake in and acquire black cultural content. It is the presumption that MSGCIs' consumption of black art of all types speaks to and justifies the legitimacy of their black racial and ethnic identities. Therefore, such patronizing of black culture via the arts also becomes a way to celebrate and improve the social, economic, and political standing of blacks in the United States and throughout the Diaspora.

The MSGCIs viewed consuming arts of all types to be important, and especially being inclusive in collecting art by black artists from the Americas, including Latin America and the Caribbean and those within the Diaspora. Several described collecting sculptures and other artifacts from their travels. Only a few MSGCIs had framed prints by famous African Americans in their homes, citing expense as the reason they are limited in being able to afford the "real thing." In addition, it was also seen as important to the MSGCIs to attend local plays, musicals, and other types of theatric productions (such as the Alvin Ailey Dance Theater), purchasing black art at art fairs, patronizing African American museums or black exhibits at mainstream museums (e.g., MoMA), and/or serving on boards of local art museums and galleries.

CULTURAL DISSEMBLANCE, TRIPLE IDENTITY CONSCIOUSNESS, AND CULTURAL CAPITAL BLENDING: THE COST AND BENEFITS OF MSGCI UPWARD MOBILITY

For several MSGCIs, their consumption of these cultural objects and symbols (which often can be expensive) becomes a strategy of cultural dissemblance. There are some, even a few among the MSGCIs, that criticize this type of performance of black middle class cultural capital—such as going to the theater or vacationing in exclusive locales, for imitating the lifestyle of middle class and upper class whites as a way to signal status. These few MSGCIs feel buying a very large family home, driving around in a luxury car—BMWs, Mercedes, or Audis, wearing designer clothing and purchasing $2000 or more handbags is more about social status as opposed to purchasing goods on the basis of need. Vershawn Ashanti Young, in his book chapter "Performing Citizenship" (2011), revisits this critique, also evident in E. Franklin Frazier's *Black Bourgeoisie: The Rise of the New Black Middle Class in the United States* (1957). According to Young (2011:4–5), Frazier makes this critique most compelling in his statement about blacks aspiring for such status as living in the "world of make-believe:"

...the black bourgeoisie have an intense feeling of inferiority, constantly seeking various forms of recognition and place great value upon status symbols in order to compensate for their inferiority complex [...] yet must constantly [live] under the domination and contempt of the white man. (quoted in E. Franklin Frazier, *Black Bourgeoisie*, 1957:111–112)

If you recall in the previous chapter, Derrick discussed his own attempts to consume or acquire status symbols. He described feeling stressed every time he met the proverbial benchmark showing he achieved professional and economic success, only for it to seem the mark moved further away and leaving him to feel that he will never measure up. Shana also briefly talks about the pressure to perform being middle class but from the perspective of being an artist:

SHANA

I cannot be a hypocrite; I am an artist, which means I live a lifestyle of leisure. I have to hustle to eat and pay my bills but I do make choices to go the museum and travel because I see it as a necessary part of what I do for my work. But this kind of capitalism we participate in has us spinning our wheels like lab rats. To get the jobs we get the education at the right schools to get this fellowship or that award or publish with this press or show our art in that gallery. And when you "make it," do you really need that large house with the 5 bedrooms and 5 baths to be happy and show you overcame adversity? You could use the same money you spent to support a small village somewhere and help little brown and black children get an education to improve themselves and their families. We run this rat race and forget we should not try to measure up to them [whites] because they are not inherently better than us. We're killing ourselves with worry, depression and anxiety, we're drinking ourselves, getting high to keep the stress at bay, even putting ourselves into a lot of debt—student loan debt, credit card debt, and mortgage debt. There's depression and anxiety. I am not saying you can't get nice things but we need to change our framework and think more holistically about success and the future of our community in more productive, emotionally healthy ways than material ways.

Feeling like an impostor (referring to the impostor syndrome) and "never measuring up" or that making these conspicuous consumption choices is an effort to try to "measure up to them" arguably exemplifies Frazier's point, that blacks are fearful of being, "rejected by the white world" (1957:111). The impostor syndrome impacts people of color and women of color, particularly black people, at a higher rate because of persisting stereotypes that argue they are unworthy and unintelligent. Young (2011:5) asserts, however, "the black middle class must live with racism, [so] they focus their attention on what they can change (their class status) rather than on what they cannot (their race), believing economic equality with whites is attainable." Young raises an interesting assertion: that today's post-1965 civil rights era black middle class, including MSGCIs, recognize achieving middle class status may have certain economic benefits that have helped them more than other working class or poor blacks. I believe, however, Young's assertion is missing an important part of the race-class analysis for people of color; allow me to elaborate more here.

From their stories, many of the MSGCIs do recognize that their middle class status does not compensate for the persisting inequality they experience and must still contend with social and political struggles, including racism. It is the process of balancing societal expectations of acquiring material assets and performing in racially acceptable ways while embracing one's ethnic heritage and engaging in discursive strategies such as cultural dissemblance, which I assert is, essentially, the cost of achieving the perceived stereotype of the American Dream for the MSGCIs. Shana's response to my question about her conception of the middle class and the American Dream pointed to the economic, racial, and psychosocial "price" this cohort has to pay in order to demonstrate their "success." In many ways, the process of balancing all of these is the reason many of the MSGCIs feel like they experience three worlds or levels of consciousness: the ideal world they hoped it to be (free of judgment and full of opportunity for all), the world as it is (filled with struggle and inequality), and the world that could be, in spite of its dysfunction. As such, several MSGCIs are acutely aware of the inequality because they are cultural blenders. The key to being a cultural capital blender is in the way the MSGCIs use their triple identity consciousness—their awareness of this inequality to influence, present, and interrogate their own middle class performances as a means to inform how their empowerment work in and with communities of color.

To combat conspicuous consumption, several MSGCIs talked about the importance of being responsible and spending responsibly. In particular, being financially literate and having sound financial advice from financial advisors not only helps to manage their consumption but also how they manage their financial responsibilities as it relates to their immigrant parents' generation. Here, Derrick talks about his own acute awareness of his MSGCI status and the challenges of being born in America to immigrant parents.

DERRICK

> I am proud to be doing better than my own parents. [...] I make more money to be comfortable and to do all the right things to support my parents. I try to keep a balance but it's exhausting. I live in two worlds: I have to survive in the world as a black man in America; at the same time I have the obligation of family—both ones that are up here and those in the islands. My white counterparts do not have this same burden of family, so they don't understand why I am expected to give back so much.

Derrick was not alone in this reflection. Other MSGCIs talked about feeling burdened with a sense of responsibility for their immigrant parents' physical, social, and financial wellbeing and sometimes, too, expressed some guilt for feeling burdened.

DANIEL explains:

> I think that's where my ex-wife and I differ. Although her family is from Guyana and she's Caribbean, she has a different orientation to family responsibility. She is more selfish. She wanted to spend a lot of money like she was one of those housewives on TV and I was a baller she married. But I have the extra responsibility of looking after my parents. I had to budget for them too and it caused a lot of arguments. It was frustrating for me when I wanted to spend my own money but think they [parents] worked hard to come to this country and they helped me become successful so this is the least I can do. But, man, it was hard. Sometimes it felt like we were living paycheck to paycheck. Sometimes it was like, "do I have enough of an emergency fund in case one of us gets sick or loses our jobs?" These are real concerns we had. But you wouldn't know it because it looked like we had it all together but she and I would fight a lot about money. There just didn't seem like there was enough to go around.

In terms of being more fiscally responsible and how this relates to his own ability to manage his immigrant parents' affairs, Robert discussed reading up on and teaching himself about the stock market and investment strategies as early as high school though he learned how to be more savvy with money (e.g., savings, investing) from graduate school courses and friends. And while Robert is quick to say that he is not an investment banker, he prides himself on using this acquired knowledge to teach his parents and other relatives how to better plan for their retirement or how to live out their remaining years a little more comfortably.

ROBERT explains:

> It's about budgeting for the everyday and investing for the future. You can't just think, "I'm making 6 figures, I'm good." In today's economy, that is not going to get you far. You have to understand how money works and what it means to develop wealth. That's why I work this hard. It's setting up my children for a better future—private school education, minimal debt from college and grad school, things like that. Because us first generation kids have to help the uncle and aunty that's getting old and needs more help with their care or the little house that's on the island. Or that idiot cousin that got him or herself in a bind. I'm seen as successful and therefore I have to help out. That's why we have to be financially responsible and not live too far above our means.

When it comes to their children—the third generation, I found across the board, the MSGCIs all have plans or are currently paying tuition to exclusive preparatory or parochial schools, especially when the public schools in their neighborhoods are in urban areas that are resource-deprived. This was found to be a similar trend among the African American middle class in Melvin Oliver and Thomas Shapiro's book *Black Wealth, White Wealth*, which examined and compared the economic stability and wellbeing of black and white middle class and their sense of financial priorities and the future.

MSGCI mobility into the middle class is not only about cultural capital displays and the intersectional ways race and gender roles play out in these class performances with regards to human capital (e.g., investment in education, skills, and training) and social capital (e.g., social networks and shared values). It is also about financial literacy and fiscal responsibility that helps to secure and maintain such economic security these working class children of Caribbean immigrants did not have growing up. However, as Derrick, Daniel, and Robert mentioned, finances were often stretched thin with an added pressure or obligation to care for their parents while being able to invest in their own children's education and social and emotional development.

To revisit Bourdieu's conception of cultural capital and habitus, he argued that if a person and/or their group is to experience upward mobility, status, and power, they must be exposed to, and have the proficiency in and familiarity with mainstream cultural codes and practices—linguistic styles and styles of interaction, aesthetics, and preferences, which are often linked to white, European (in Bourdieu's case, French) middle and upper class culture and tradition (see DiMaggio 1982; Lamont and

Lareau 1988). It is based on Bourdieu's thesis that scholars contend that if racial-ethnic groups, who have experienced marginalization, cannot access or activate these cultural codes and behaviors, they are more likely to experience alienation and subordination. It is this type of ethnocentric bias in the use of cultural capital and habitus that other cultural resources used by nonwhite groups, including immigrant groups, are often ignored or denigrated (see Lamont and Fournier 1992).

For the MSGCIs, however, they use cultural resources learned from their parents' generation, what they learned from their childhoods, which were working or lower-middle class, and their observations of the black American experience to negotiate their social worlds. As described by Carmen, for example, the MSGCIs often shared symbolic elements of their racial and ethnic identities of being both black American born and of Caribbean ethnicity in their fluid command of Standard American English (SAE) and urban slang, Creole, Spanglish, and Patois that allowed them to signal their racial and ethnic authenticity as well as their ability to partici-pate in environments where there is social value placed on being non-black middle class. In effect, the MSGCIs become cultural capital blenders.

The MSGCIs' process of cultural capital blending is more than strad-dling two cultures—simply drawn only from their immigrant parents' class dispositions necessarily, or whether they struggle to capture and acquire the mainstream cultural codes of middle class-ness per se. Instead their habitus of blackness is the process by which their cultural capital is acquired through a variety of sources and interactions where they learn how to be cultural blenders—learning black American codes or aesthetics while learn-ing mainstream notions of middle class capital. Because one's pedigree and intelligence is both correlated and highly valued in US society writ large with success, the MSGCIs' cultural blending, in many ways, renders them able to use their knowledge and practice of mainstream codes of dress and vernacular as well as having the ability to move into intra-racial and ethnic social spaces and "do"[5] race and ethnicity. In turn, the action of cultural blending fosters MSGCIs' triple identity consciousness.

As cultural capital blenders, the MSGCIs use all of their cultural resources as a type of cultural currency in which the benefits vary and depend on the situation. As they have already described, many MSGCIs used this "currency" to gain mobility (i.e., in the workplace or school) or to express their in-group affiliation with other middle class people, and as signifiers of their authenticity among co-Caribbean ethnics and other black ethnics. Being able to use this currency appears to be an important aspect of the MSGCIs' racial, ethnic, and class identity assertions. We see this further exemplified in MSGCI adult performances of middle class cultural capital, whether acquired from peer interactions in post-secondary educational and work environments, or while traveling and socializing with other middle class people of color. Notwithstanding the stress of cultural dissemblance, their efforts to balance responsibilities related to their parents' generation and managing the financial and emotional costs of conspicuous consumption is vital to the MSGCIs that they collectively employ their triple identity consciousness to create alternative self-images as a shield from everyday micro-aggressions and discrimination. The next chapter will continue to explore MSGCI cultural capital performance as it relates to relying on their middle class status and other lifestyle distinctions in public spaces such as in the workplace and community contexts. The chapter will examine the importance of black philanthropy and giving back, with some MSGCIs linking their philanthropy to the transnational and ancestral connections, they choose to maintain with their parents' country of origin as an important part of MSGCIs' definition and creation of place and space.

NOTES

1. These same beliefs and views are also observable in several nations in Africa (e.g., Uganda) where there was a strong European colonial power that influenced gender conceptualization and ideals around sexuality too.

2. The celebration of Diwali is the Hindu festival of Lights. Celebrated in October or November of each year, it marks the last harvest before the winter. It is considered one of the most important holidays for Indians across the world. Celebrating by lighting clay lamps, setting off fireworks, flowers, and so on, Hindus seek the divine blessing of Lakshmi, the goddess of wealth, for the light and protection from darkness and for financial prosperity in the new year.

3. In his article "How the Poor Became Black: The Racialization of American Poverty in the Mass Media," Martin Gilens analyzed media trends between the 1950s and the 1990s and found the media's tendency to associate blacks with the cultural model of "undeserving poor," which both reflects and reifies the stereotype that blacks are lazy and therefore should be considered unsympathetic. His research also found that media images and news stories helped shape, especially whites' perceptions about the composition of the poor, their concerns and the plausibility of solutions, particularly if it would be considered futile to help a group that is lazy and makes poor choices.

4. Founded in 1938 during the Depression, Jack and Jill is a prestigious social organization for black middle class children. Back then, Jack and Jill's activities emphasized helping black middle class children better fit into white America. In the last three decades, however, the national organization underwent a rebranding strategy to reflect the isolation felt by many middle class blacks living in predominantly white suburbs. Instead of emphasizing the need for black children assimilate into white culture, Jack and Jill seeks to instill a sense of ethnic pride and racial identity in suburban black children. See Lawrence Otis Graham's *Our Kind of People: Inside America's Black Upper Class* (1999).

5. "Doing Race" is a key conceptual framework from Hazel Rose Markus and Paula Moya's (2010) book *Doing Race: 21 Essays for the 21st Century* where the authors focus on race and ethnicity in everyday life. Authors argue that everyday activities such as going to school and work, renting an apartment or buying a house, attending religious services, and going to the doctor are influenced by assumptions about who counts, whom to trust, whom to care about, whom to include, and why.

BIBLIOGRAPHY

Banks, P. A. (2012). *Represent: Art and Identity Among the Black Upper-Middle Class*. New York: Routledge.

Bérubé, A. (2011). How Gay Stays White and What Kind of White it Says. In A. Bérubé, J. D'Emilio, & E. Freedman (Eds.), *My Desire for History: Essays in Gay, Community and Labor History* (pp. 202–230). Chapel Hill: University of North Carolina Press.

Bettie, J. (2003/2014). *Women Without Class: Girls, Race, and Identity*. Berkeley: University of California Press.

Brereton, B. (1999). The Promise of Emancipation. In B. Brereton & K. Yelvington (Eds.), *The Colonial Caribbean in Transition: Essays on Post-Emancipation Social and Cultural History* (p. Introduction). Kingston: University of West Indies Press.

DiMaggio, P. (1982). Cultural Capital and School Success: The Impact of Status Culture Participation on the Grades of U.S. High School Students. *American Sociological Review, 47*, 180–201.

Fields, E. L., Bogart, L. M., Smith, K. C., Malebranche, D. J., Ellen, J., & Schuster, M. A. (2015). I Always Felt I Had to Prove My Manhood: Homosexuality, Masculinity, Gender Role Strain, and HIV Risk Among Young Black Men Who Have Sex With Men. *American Journal of Public Health, 105*(1), 122–131.

Frazier, E. F. (1957). *The Black Bourgeoisie: The Rise of the New Black Middle Class in the United States*. New York: Free Press.

Freeman, M., & Mathison, S. (2009). *Researching Children's Experiences*. New York: Guilford Press.

Gans, H. J. (1974). *Popular Culture and High Culture: An Analysis and Evaluation of Taste*. New York: Basic Books.

Gilbert, D. (1998/2014). *The American Class Structure in an Age of Growing Inequality*. Sage Publications.

Gilens, M. (2003). How the Poor Became Black: The Racialization of American Poverty in the Mass Media. In S. Schram, J. Soss, & R. C. Fording (Eds.), *Race and the Politics of Welfare Reform* (pp. 101–130). Michigan: University of Michigan Press.

Graham, L. O. (1999). *Our Kind of People: Inside America's Black Upper Class*. New York: Harper Perennial.

hooks, b. (1989/2015). *Talking Back: Thinking Feminist, Thinking Black* (2nd ed.). New York: Routledge.

Hughes, M., & Hertel, B. R. (1990). The Significance of Race Remains: A Study of Life Chances, Mate Selection and Ethnic Consciousness among Black Americans. *Social Forces, 68*, 1105–1120.

Kanter, R. M. (1977/1993). *Men and Women of the Corporation* (2nd ed.). New York: Basic Books.

Kempadoo, K. (2009). Caribbean Sexuality: Mapping the Field. *Caribbean Review of Gender Studies, 3*, 1–24.

Lacy, K., & Harris, A. (2008). Breaking the Class Monolith: Understanding Class Differences in Black Adolescents Attachment to Racial Identity. In A. Lareau & D. Conley (Eds.), *Social Class: How Does That Work?* (pp. 152–178). New York: Russell Sage Foundation Press.

Lamont, M., & Fournier, M. (1992). *Cultivating Differences: Symbolic Boundaries and the Making of Inequality*. Chicago: University of Chicago Press.

Lamont, M., & Lareau, A. (1988). Cultural Capital: Allusions, Gaps and Glissandos in Recent Theoretical Developments. *Sociological Theory, 6*(Fall), 153–168.

Lamont, M., & Molnar, V. (2001). How Blacks Use Consumption to Shape Their Collective Identity. *Journal of Consumer Culture, 1*(1), 31–45.

Landry, B. (1987). *The New Black Middle Class*. Berkeley: University of California Press.

Lorick-Wilmot, Y. (2010). *Creating Black Caribbean Ethnic Identity, Book Series, The New Americans: Recent Immigrant and American Society ed.* El Paso: LFB Scholarly Publishing.

Markus, H. R., & Moyas, P. (2010). *Doing Race: 21 Essays for the 21st Century*. New York: W.W. Norton and Company..

Martin, W. (2015). *Primates of Park Avenue: A Memoir*. New York: Simon and Schuster.

Masi De Casanova, E. (2004). "No Ugly Women": Concepts of Race and Beauty among Adolescent Women in Ecuador. *Gender and Society, 18*, 287–308.

Montalvo, F. F., & Codina, G. E. (2001). Skin Color and Latinos in the United States. *Ethnicities, 1*(3), 321–341.

Montoya, R. M. (2008). I'm Hot, So I'd Say You're Not: The Influence of Objective Physical Attractiveness on Mate Selection. *Personality and Social Psychology Bulletin, 34*, 1315–1331.

Nevadomsky, J. (1982). Changing Conceptions of Family Regulation among the Hindu East Indians in Rural Trinidad. *Anthropological Quarterly, 55*(4), 189–198.

Patterson, O. (1967). *The Sociology of Slavery: An Analysis of Origins, Development, and Structure of Negro Slave Society in Jamaica.* London: MacGibbon and Kee.

Reddock, R. (1994). *Women, Labour and Politics in Trinidad and Tobago: A History.* London: Zed Books.

Reddock, R. (2008, October 22). *Lecture at University of West Indies, St. Augustine.* Retrieved April 10, 2016, from Forever Indebted to Women: The Contribution of Women in the Development of the Caribbean Labour Movement: https://sta.uwi.edu/deputyprincipal/documents/Foreverindebtedtowomen_Oct2008_000.pdf

Stephen, D., & Fernández, P. (2012). The Role of Skin Color on Hispanic Women's Perception of Attractiveness. *Hispanic Journal of Behavioral Sciences, 34*(1), 77–94.

Twine, F. W. (1998). *Racism in a Racial Democracy: The Maintenance of White Supremacy in Brazil.* New Brunswick: Rutgers University Press.

Wade, P. (1997). *Race and Ethnicity in Latin America.* London: Pluto Press.

Wekker, G. (2006). *The Politics of Passion: Women's Sexual Culture in the Afro-Surinamese Diaspora.* New York: Columbia University Press.

West, C., & Zimmerman, D. H. (1987). Doing Gender. *Gender and Society, 1*, 125–151.

Wheat, D. (2010). Nharas and Morenas Horras: A Luso-African Model for the Social History of the Spanish Caribbean. *Journal of Early Modern History, 14*, 119–150.

White, R. C., & Carr, R. (2005). Homosexuality and HIV/AIDS Stigma in Jamaica. *Culture, Health and Sexuality, 7*, 1–13.

Young, V. A. (2011). Introduction: Performing Citizenship. In V. A. Young & B. H. Tsemo (Eds.), *From Bourgeois to Boojie: Black Middle Class Performances* (pp. 1–38). Detriot: Wayne State University Press.

CHAPTER 7

Performing Identity in Public

You were born where you were born and faced the future that you faced
because you were black and for no other reason. The limits of your
ambition were, thus, expected to be set forever. You were born into a
society, which spelled out with brutal clarity, and in as many ways as
possible, that you were a worthless human being. You were not expected
to aspire to excellence: you were expected to make peace with mediocrity.

—*James Baldwin, The Fire Next Time*

Throughout my discussions with the MSGCIs, I observed three core themes consistently present across their narratives. First is the theme of what it means to be "Black," "American," and "a child of Caribbean immigrants" in the United States. This theme had significance in the MSGCIs' negotiation and performance of their multiple identities (by skin color, ethnicity, language, religion, gender, and class) and especially in the context of their relationships when they were children, adolescents, and now as adults. Essentially, this theme points to the important role historical, social, and individual influences play in identity formation—the "who am I?" in relationship to the world. This question begs an individual to self-reflect at various points in their life. For instance: "how am I (not) represented in cultural images in mass media and otherwise?" and "what are the messages I receive from friends, family, neighbors, teachers,

© The Author(s) 2018   197
Y.S. Lorick-Wilmot, *Stories of Identity among Black,*
Middle Class, Second Generation Caribbeans,
DOI 10.1007/978-3-319-62208-8_7

colleagues, and strangers about who I am and/or who I am supposed to be?" The answers to these questions, as well as others, can shape how an individual interprets who the world says he or she is and how they choose to perform in it.

The second theme identified across the narratives revolved around the lessons the MSGCIs learned from their immigrant parents' generation about how to "move through the world" and navigate social spaces sometimes similar to but also different from their immigrant parents. These lessons gave insight into the parental influences on MSGCI identity development, which point to some of the cultural capital resources and strategies they developed and continue to rely on as adults. In other words, the lessons MSGCIs learned are an important part of their "looking glass self." A social psychology concept coined by Charles Horton Cooley in *Human Nature and Social Order* (1902/1983), the "looking glass self" takes into account the various social symbols, actions and behaviors individuals use in their everyday interactions with others to establish a front-stage persona (their public-facing selves) with the intention to influence others' perceptions of them in positive ways. Generally speaking, these personas attend to some aspect of an individual's identity that set him or her apart as a member of the "in" group [read: mainstream] or an "outsider" [read: minority or "other"]. More often than not and especially for people of color, they are commonly defined by their race, gender, sexual orientation, and the forms of oppression associated with these characteristics (e.g., racism, sexism, and heterosexism). From the narratives presented thus far, insight has been gained into the MSGCIs' multidimensional expression and blending of particular social symbols and actions across various contexts, such as in their family life, gender role performances. We also see this "blending" in their conspicuous consumption, which signals their social class position and mobility, religious and cultural practices, gender and sexual identity, and ethnicity. MSGCIs' blending of these symbols or cultural capital resources suggests the complex fluidity of identity and the simultaneous position of being both "in" and "out" the group.

This chapter contends with the third theme: the social and political contexts of MSGCI identity in public spaces. In particular, the MSGCIs often reflected on the public places in which they move through daily and the ways these experiences contribute to their own identification and identity assertions. In my examination of this theme, I consider the following questions in my analysis: what are the places, spaces, and circumstances that led MSGCIs to become acutely aware of their "looking glass selves?" How do these spaces and places continue to inform their race, ethnicity, social class, and gender definitions of self? What are, if any, the specific cultural capital performances and activities MSGCIs engage in that respond to the factors of oppression and liberation they experience daily, namely in managing relationships with whites (as the singular black) and nonwhites at work; advocating for job promotions and other employment opportunities; in social circles; and in the neighborhoods they live? MSGCIs' responses to these questions were often framed within the context of being the singular black in these spaces and places.

BLACK SINGULARITY AND SELF-REPRESENTATIONS IN PUBLIC SPACES

In his article "The White Space," Elijah Anderson (2015) discusses the persistence of *de facto* segregation in the United States despite the country's legislative policies of racial integration and incorporation, and economic progress post-Civil Rights to the present. In the last three decades, the United States has seen the number of blacks employed in semi-professional and professional occupations in medicine, law, and business increase more significantly than ever before (see Pattillo 2000/2013). Thus, scholars have looked to the expansion of employment opportunities for blacks and their increased presence in the middle class as a signal of race-class progress and integration. Yet as Anderson (2015:10–11) observes, there is a host of public spaces in the United States that still remain segregated by class as well as by race; "workplaces and neighborhoods [that] may be conceptualized essentially as a mosaic of white space, black spaces and cosmopolitan spaces" where whites can choose to avoid blacks/people of color spaces while blacks/people of color are required to navigate through and within white spaces in order to survive. Blacks' "requirement" to navigate white spaces can have both an economic and psychological toll on their wellbeing. Particularly, some MSGCIs found that persisting racial stereotypes about blacks as being poor and criminal render them "suspicious" in these white spaces even when they appear to display mainstream middle class signifiers. Anderson argues this "requirement" is not necessarily placed upon whites of similar circumstances. He goes on to add:

> When present in the white space, blacks reflexively note the proportion of whites to blacks, or may look around for other blacks with whom to commune if not bond, and then may adjust their comfort level accordingly; when judging a setting as too white, they can feel uneasy and consider it to be informally "off limits." For whites, however, the same settings are generally regarded as unremarkable, or as normal, taken-for-granted reflections of civil society. (Anderson 2015:10)

Constantly having to assess social environments and adjust their comfort level, the MSGCIs discussed the need to have a heightened emotional intelligence (also known as EQ or emotional intelligence quotient) across social contexts, and especially in non-black spaces. Having a high EQ is the ability to develop and master the skills of social awareness, self-management and relationship management, and the ability to adapt to change and solve problems of a social and personal nature, including those in work place settings (Emmerling and Goleman 2003; see also Bar-On 2000; Goleman 2001). I speculate MSGCIs' triple identity consciousness for having a heightened EQ is informed by socialization, their development of cultural capital strategies, and of course, previous personal experience—an important aspect of their cultural capital blending strategies.

When navigating majority-white spaces as the singular black person (or one of few) just as Anderson describes in his article, the MSGCIs' "looking glass self" requires the remarkable skills of managing emotions and actions in ways that can yield a positive response from those around them. Here, I am not arguing that MSGCIs are manipulative and focused on influencing the responses of people around them. On the contrary, I posit the requirement to constantly self-regulate emotions and assess social situations, as the singular black in these white spaces requires a triple identity consciousness; the MSGCIs' thinking about their blackness as interacting with their front-stage persona in their presentation of self in everyday life (see Goffman 1959). This means the MSGCIs consider issues of conformity by asking themselves the following questions: as an MSGCI, am I seen as a legitimate member of the social group in context? Am I embodying or successfully rejecting negative stereotypes associated with being a person of color, a woman, and/or a child of immigrants in the United States? The following section explores how MSGCIs specifically think and talk about their triple identity consciousness in terms of black singularity as they traverse various social spaces and places.

Black Singularity and Triple Identity Consciousness: MSGCI Awareness of Anti-black Stereotypes as "Par for the Course" in Public Spaces

As symbolic interactionists like Goffman have theorized, stereotypes inform everyday relationships between all people, and learning the rules and expectations of the situation and interaction is considered key not only for survival but also for future success. Yet, anti-black racism still means blacks (middle class, working class, and low income) cannot escape existing negative stereotypes and stigmas associated with being "black in America"—the assumption that being black means you are typically uneducated, experience unemployment or underemployment, and live in neighborhoods, albeit urban areas, with persisting, endemic social problems.[1] In fact, the quote used to open this chapter, which is from James Baldwin's *The Fire Next Time*, illustrates the persistence of negative stereotypes that undergird anti-black sentiments about black mediocrity.

When I pushed the MSGCIs to give me concrete examples of instances where they felt their black singularity most strongly, several described the subtle, but non-confrontational ways they felt judged by others, especially whites, in social settings. During my conversation with Yomaira in particular, she described black singularity as typical or "par for the course" when attending predominately white, professional networking events with her husband or professional friends. Yomaira explained the reception portion of a banquet or event serves as an opportunity for its attendees to either reunite with or meet professionals in their respective fields, and exchange business information with hopes of getting an inside edge for a better job or future business opportunities. She clarified that her frustrations with "working the room" is not due to contemporary labor-market politics that privilege favoritism (the "who you know" gets your foot in the door) over skills and merit. Instead, Yomaira suggested it is in the way race and racial ties affect one's networking opportunities and that being the singular black person and the singular woman of color in these settings serve as reminders that she is an outsider trying to get in.

YOMAIRA

Yomaira was born in Boston, Massachusetts in the mid-1970s and is one of five children born to her Haitian parents who immigrated to the United States in the mid-1960s. She uses terms Caribbean and West Indian interchangeably to describe her ethnic identification. After high school,

Yomaira earned her Bachelor's and Master's degrees in education at large universities in Massachusetts. Currently, she teaches at a prestigious preparatory school in the Boston area and lives in Brookline with her husband, who identified as African American, and two school-aged children.

Yomaira pointed to situations where she had an awareness that conversations seemed or felt strained especially when non-blacks attempted to discern how a person like herself gained entry to the event and whether she is "like them" and deemed worthy to network with.

Here, **YOMAIRA** explains:

> People are always trying to figure out and are surprised that you are in the same room as them. They are quick to ask: "Who do you know here?" like in a sly way but what they really want to ask is *how did you get to be in the same room with me?* Now, they don't ask this of other people. It's assumed these other people earned the right to be here and you didn't. Then the way you speak or carry yourself lets them know, oh, okay, I can see why you are here. You get a pass. But then I look around and often I am the ONLY black face in the room. It's like a quota has been filled and I am it. Yes, it's exhausting but you almost get used to it. I think over time you get numb to this attitude because it really does happen often. But no matter what, just because you have earned your spot and are allowed to be in the room, doesn't mean they will make space for you at "the table."

Part of Yomaira's story here serves to illustrate the ways in which inequality in these social spaces reproduces itself. This is not to say, or at least in the way I understood Yomaira's retelling, that non-black attendees at these events are intentionally biased or racist toward people of color, including MSGCIs. On the contrary, I contend racial ties and connections that people make are often reserved for those that are most like them, such as those with whom they may have worked in the past and may patronize similar associations, or simply with those they identify with.

When it comes to employment opportunities, for instance, we see how these ties and connections inform employers' preferences to hire their "own kind" (see also Deidre Royster's *Race and the Invisible Hand*, 2003). Again, to reference Elijah's Anderson's (2015) article and to point to Bonilla-Silva's (2009) book *Racism without Racists* where he argues whites create a habitus through which they experience tremendous segregation from nonwhites both in childhood and adulthood, racial-ethnic groups still live in, work, and travel within segregated spaces. As a result, the significance of racial ties during networking events means there remains a racial uneasiness and divide. Having an awareness of being the singular black in public spaces has meant that these MSGCIs must become self-aware and employ their triple identity consciousness (and use their EQ) to consider their racial, Caribbean ethnic, gender, and class identities consciously and adapt their assertions with intentionality in order to overcome the racial uneasiness that exists in these non-black spaces. They use multiple sources of cultural capital to navigate their insider-outside social positions, and manage discrimination and expectations of conformity—not only at professional networking events but also at work, school, and other social institutions (also see Feagin 1991).

Some MSGCIs mentioned having some uneasiness (and sometimes frustration) with being one of few high-ranking blacks at their jobs, particularly as they began their initial climb up the professional ladder. To MSGCIs like Marshal, having employment mobility was unchartered territory; being one of the first in their generation to hold high ranking corporate positions, which are often highly stressful management positions, and not having parents and many mentors of color to advise on how to navigate non-black spaces and manage social Darwinism and Darwinian culture[2] in the workplace. When I asked Marshal to elaborate more on being the singular black in "unchartered territory," he reflected on the differences between his generation and his parents' experiences in earning and leveraging employment opportunities. In particular, Marshal believes his generation of US-born blacks has had easier access to opportunities than their immigrant parents' generation.

MARSHAL

Marshal was born in the late 1960s and grew up in the North side of Hartford Connecticut with his younger sister and parents. He is married with two school-aged children and lives in Bloomfield, Connecticut. A former teacher, Marshal currently works as a policy advocate in education and is pursuing a doctorate in education. He self-identifies as Black, Caribbean-American, and African American. His father and paternal grandparents, who are from the cities of Colon and Rio Abajo, Panama, can trace their family lineage to the mixed race Afro Colonials (mixtures between freed blacks and Spanish descent) and a group of black migrants from Jamaica and Grenada that assisted in the building of the Panama Canal (often referred to as Afro-Antillanos). Marshal's mother and maternal grandparents migrated from Dominica to the United States in the early

1960s before Dominica's government imposed immigration restrictions. Once the US Immigration Act of 1965 passed, several other family members were able to migrate to the United States. His mother and maternal grandparents can trace their family lineage to their primarily African roots and racial mixtures between African, Lebanese, and Portuguese. Marshal's parents both left their countries of origin and were granted student visas to attend university in New York City, which is where they met, and later married. His parents moved to the greater Hartford Connecticut area when a few extended family members also moved to the area:

> Coming of age in the post-Civil Rights era, there are many more strides made for women and blacks too. There are a few more doors open for my generation than there was for my parents BUT it's still not easy for us. Depending on the age of the employer, they look to my parents' generation as low-skilled "boat people." So, yes, as an American, I have an advantage over immigrants—if I encounter people who are prejudiced against foreigners. Though I should say "advantage" is based on industry, right? Other immigrant groups have stereotypes about them that, depending on their industry, I think some of them take advantage of. I will say this: the glass ceiling remains a challenge. And, even if you are able to break through that ceiling—you still have to prove that you are worthy to be up there.

As Marshal mentions, there is the context of reception[3] that MSGCIs must contend with as a child of Caribbean immigrants and as a black person: how does this reception inform my mobility including any employment prospects and opportunities? Scholars such as Reynolds Farley and Richard Alba (2002) examined trends of upward mobility—economic, educational attainment, and occupational prestige—among second generation immigrants in the United States. In comparison to their immigrant parent generation, researchers found that a higher proportion of adult children of immigrants attend a four-year college and tend to avoid working in ethnic "niche" occupations and industries (e.g., taxi driver, factory worker, clerical worker, bodega shopkeeper, restaurant worker, nail shop worker, housekeeper, or healthcare aide) in favor of corporate, nonprofit, higher education, and/or research jobs. In the case of the MSGCIs, including Marshal, they have pursued additional educational and employment opportunities in corporate sectors at higher rates than their parents' generation was able to achieve. Different from the assumption that second generation immigrants avoid ethnic niche occupations solely because of its perceived lack of prestige, the MSGCIs cite the prevalence of white collar professional opportunities that were recruiting more people of color in management positions than had once existed during their parents' migration.

To put this into context, this cohort of MSGCIs have parents that migrated to the United States between the late 1960s and mid-1980s, a period in which civil rights legislation on school desegregation (1954), equal pay (1963), discrimination in voting, public accommodations and facilities, and public education (1964), voting rights (1965), interracial marriage (1967), fair housing (1968), and Affirmative Action (1978) was passed and shortly enacted. Because the MSGCIs were either born or came of age during this period, it was really their parents' immigrant generation that served as torchbearers, navigating their way through employment and education sectors, which may have been slow to respond to civil rights legislation and expand upon opportunities, and/or had employers with implicit biases toward immigrants of color. By the time most of this cohort of MSGCIs entered the employment sector themselves, there was a statistical increase for high wage jobs that carried status and prestige readily available in comparison to their parents' generation. Notwithstanding the increase in the number of white-collar professional jobs prospective employees can seek, Marshal's comments still point to the hurdles this MSGCI cohort contends with regard to race and occupational segmentation.

Both Yomaira and Marshal also raise an interesting point when talking about black singularity: the notion of having to prove one's worth. Remarkably, MSGCIs' observations on black singularity did not seem to differ whether they grew up in working class or middle class immigrant households. MSGCI responses, however, consistently suggest they think about the saliency of race as being connected to their social status—the black, middle class professional—in these non-black work places. In his article "Race as Class," Herbert Gans (2005:19–20) argues, "race is both a marker of class and status [sometimes using it] to keep people 'in their place'." For newer immigrants and native-born black (including foreign-born people of African descent), there exist a social expectation in order to access the same resources and opportunities as whites, they must prove their worth by performing in racially acceptable ways or remain segregated. In the case of MSGCIs, whether as a self-identified black person or whose phenotype identifies them as black, they quickly learn the social expectation of "performing whiteness" in public by adopting elements of cultural capital that carry status and prestige (e.g., styles of dress, speech, style, taste, and preferences). And while post-1965 Civil Rights legislation was intended to improve those of African descent's access to opportunity, however, both native and foreign-born blacks are perceived as direct "competitors for valued resources such as highly paid jobs, top schools, housing, and the like, also [rendering them] a threat to whites" and whiteness (Gans 2005:19). In this capitalistic economic structure which values hierarchy and Darwinian competition, being perceived as a competitor writ large renders native and foreign-born blacks susceptible to more pervasive discrimination and segregation than any other nonwhite immigrant and native-born groups of equivalent class position, despite any effort to perform in "racially acceptable ways."

Masquerading in Non-black Spaces and Places

Across all of my discussions with MSGCIs, the topic of "performing whiteness" or, more broadly speaking, being conscious about the persisting expectations of presenting oneself in racially acceptable ways, resonated strongly with all participants. By observation, MSGCI awareness that there exist race, class, and gender-based expectations they must perform (and/or reject) strongly points to the powerful ways their identities in public are constructed through signifying practices. During my conversation with Rosalie, for example, she referred to these "performances" as part of the experience of learning to play a game—emphasizing that people of color are "playing a game" where the rules identified specifically for them are constantly changing, and particularly in circumstances when there are opportunities for upward mobility.

ROSALIE

Rosalie was born and raised in the Bronx, New York, in the late 1970s. She is the younger of two girls born to her US-born Puerto Rican mother and mainland Puerto Rico-born father. Rosalie self-identifies as Hispanic and Puerto Rican. Both Rosalie and her older sister attended Catholic School and eventually resettled in Florida with her parents before leaving for a liberal arts college in Connecticut. After graduating, she went on to attend law school at a large university in Boston. Rosalie is an attorney and lives in Meriden, Connecticut with her husband and two children.

ROSALIE

> … Maybe it's the uncertainty of conditions [within these white spaces] that you feel you have to be on guard. It's like you never know when they [whites] will invade your space or try making you the exemplar—the immigrant, the black woman, or the successful Latina who made it out of the

ghetto. But you still have to signal to the gatekeeper that you are worthy to be engaged with. But you can tell some people believe you are an Affirmative Action hire and you are automatically unqualified and undeserving. Or somehow you must be the exception to the rule. It's like a game of chance—am I showing the "correct" status symbols at the right time? Am I making them [whites] feel comfortable? Am I being assertive or too bossy and not a team player? Am I dressing the part? Is my suit the right color, or my skirt too short, or my outfit too masculine? There are so many unsaid rules to play by and as both women and people of color we have to figure out how to manage these constraints imposed by these complex structural and social interactions that are really designed to limit our access to wealth and power in the long term.

The practice of "playing a game" as Rosalie mentioned can be viewed as a deliberate act of subversion—masquerading—that enables the individual to be reflexive about, "the otherness within and beyond" him or herself (Kaiser 2001:xiv). As part of their triple identity consciousness, the MSGCIs' awareness of the potentialities of masquerading is fundamental to their ability to navigate majority white contexts because it provides a space to, "construct, represent, conceal, reveal, transform, defend, give license to, and empower" their identity constructions and assertions (Tseëlon 2001:12). Thus, masquerading becomes a device for defying or subverting stereotypes or particular cultural models that attempt to marginalize and/or other the MSGCI in such circumstances.

This topic of the subversive practice of masquerading has been explored by theorists in the field of gender/queer studies, philosophy, psychoanalysis, and more broadly, postcolonial studies. The field of postcolonial studies is interdisciplinary in its approach to examine power dynamics between the dominant and subaltern. Hence, the concept of "masquerade" has multiple and strategies, which range across various social contexts and circumstances—because not all people use or experience masquerading equally or monolithically (see Spivak 1988/2008).

Scholars such as bell hooks, Gayatri Spivak, Stuart Hall, Homi Bhabha, and Frantz Fanon have considered the representation and normalization of the subaltern as the "other" and how the marginalized often construct and assert their identity to navigate racialization and cultural hegemony via masquerading. For instance, Frantz Fanon focused on the binary relationship between whites and blacks in majority non-black spaces. In *Black Skin, White Masks,* Fanon's (1967) concept of masquerading is operationalized in terms of, "wearing a mask." He frames "wearing a mask" as a black person's desire to overcome his or her perceived racial inferiority (blackness) by adopting the language, practice, and behaviors of whites while rejecting his or her own African roots and culture. Fanon argues blacks' adoption of whiteness is a performance of mimicry—which is not only pathological but an act of submission to white supremacy and domination by colonial forces.

Others such as Homi Bhabha (1985) in "Signs Taken for Wonders" consider masquerading as an opportunity for the subaltern to adopt the characteristics of the colonizer through the act of mimicry and imitation, in which he or she subverts and undermines the absoluteness and fixity of the colonizer's authority. Vastly different from Fanon, Bhabha contends mimicry does not hide or ignore the existence of (black) identity behind "the mask;" instead, mimicry is an act of resistance. Bhabha (1985:153) goes on to clarify:

> Resistance is not necessarily an oppositional act of political intention, nor is it the simple negation or exclusion of the "content" of an Other culture, as a difference once perceived. It is the effect of an ambivalence produced within the rule of recognition of dominating discourses as they articulate the signs of cultural difference and reimplicate them within the deferential relations of colonial power—hierarchy, normalization, marginalization, and so forth.

Bhabha argues mimicry leads to the performance strategy of disavowal, where the aspect of the identity that is often subjugated and discriminated is not repressed but re-expressed as something different—a mutation, a hybrid as opposed to mimetic.

Similarly, Stuart Hall (1999) and bell hooks (1997) also shift away from the concept of mimicry and imitation in their analysis of masquerading and other subversive practices and consider these solely as patterns of resistance (i.e., as in resistance spectators). They argue that people of color utilize their "special knowledge of whiteness, gleaned from close scrutiny of white people, [to transcend] hegemonic structures perpetuated by white supremacy" (hooks 1997:167). For hooks in particular, the practice of masquerading can be seen as a threat to whites (the colonizer) because it puts on a mirrored display of the dominant culture's norms that they may be unwilling to accept as a disturbing version of their normalized knowledge of whiteness. bell hooks (1997:169) argues that many whites are:

> Socialized to believe the fantasy, that whiteness represents goodness and all that is benign and nonthreatening, [and they] assume this is the way black

people conceptualize whiteness. They do not imagine that the way whiteness makes its presence felt in black life, most often as terrorizing imposition, a power that wounds, hurts, tortures, is a reality that disrupts the fantasy of whiteness as representing goodness...

The "fantasy" bell hooks describes, I contend, is a consequence of white hegemony, which renders whiteness as omnipresent and invisible. Applying a postcolonial perspective, the fantasy of whiteness construct is an important colonial practice of the colonizer; it exonerates the colonizer in its pursuit of dehumanization of the colonized other (Memmi 1965/2003). Despite the colonial mythology of the colonized other as bad (the opposite of the colonizer's goodness), hooks (1997) argues that people of color's representations in majority white spaces emerge as efforts to transcend social situations of oppression to their advantage. In this regard, the colonized other develops resistance strategies that deconstruct, reconstruct, or simply reject the effects of colonization (Hall 1999). The colonized other does this by interrogating, reflecting, and challenging—displaying agency as opposed to a passive subject. For all the MSGCIs in this study, their "resistance spectatorship" requires (1) their reliance on an understanding of the culture's normalized knowledge of whiteness via media and elsewhere and as well as their own representations of whiteness in their black imagination and (2) their ability to evoke their triple identity consciousness that informs the way they both acknowledge the existence of and choose to resist the anguish that is a consequence of white supremacy. Their alertness to the issues of "otherness" lends itself to the development of strategies aimed at resisting both structures of American-ness and the constraints of race, ethnicity, gender, and class particularities in public spaces and workplaces.

Performing Whiteness/Blackness in Racially Acceptable Ways in Public

All MSGCIs shared a litany of performance criteria (masquerading) they believed are required for people of color in the workplace to adhere to as well as to signal their worthiness and respectability. Here are six "top" criteria mentioned across the MSGCI interviews; please note, this summary is not exhaustive but acknowledges the ways MSGCIs "mark out" particular symbols and behaviors that intend to defy conventional expectations and stereotypes about blackness.

Self-conscious About Presentation Style

When talking about a person's presentation style within the context of work and social environments, the MSGCIs focused on a person's ability to fit in with their colleagues and managers. The MSGCIs defined presentation style as having to do with one's ability to: (1) interact with others and display emotions deemed appropriate for the social environment, (2) think consciously about one's individual brand and reputation, and (3) accommodate oneself to the workplace culture or while in pursuit of public rewards. Their definition of presentation style aligns well with Goffman's (1959) theory on presentation of self, particularly a person's front-stage and backstage personas.

The front-stage persona is an individual's public-facing self; presenting oneself the way others must see him or her. The front-stage persona requires aligning one's inner values, passions, and interests in a way that complements the image he or she is focused on performing. In terms of identity, there is also meaning associated with a person's front-stage persona that intends to meet the expectation of interaction in particular contexts. For instance, in mass media and other US cultural representations, there are certain personas associated with specific professions and while performing that persona an individual is expected to embody some aspect of that identity, even if it is a stereotype (negative or positive). Take the professions of physician and attorney: on prime-time television programs such as ER or Grey's Anatomy, physicians are perceived as wearing white coats with a stethoscope around their neck, having messy handwriting, being smart but overworked; and on similar prime-time television programs such as L.A. Law, Ally McBeal, or Law and Order, lawyers are thought of as wearing only black or grey suits, spending too much time in the court room overcharging clients, being overly competitive and serious. While there are, of course, exceptions to the rules of behavior, cultural anthropologists contend most members of the public generally share similarly culturally derived ideas and practices based on first hand experiences and/or by observations as to how to be a person, what is good, what is right, and what is not right in certain professions. These ideas also give direction to their individual experiences, in ways that inform their perception, cognition, emotion, and actions (see Shore 1996). Based on the shared cultural models that exist for these two professions, for example, a person will often develop a front-stage persona that will embody some aspect of the characteristics associated with the perceptions and actions of what it means to be a physician or attorney in his or her culture.

An individual's backstage persona is the part of the self that is not as open and exposed to the public. It is the aspect of one's identity in which an individual relies on his or her core values and passions to help refine their goals and objectives in a social environment, and develop plans that speak to his or her intellectual and personal commitments.

While the MSGCIs acknowledge that finding a healthy balance between one's front-stage and backstage personas is relevant to all people, regardless of their age, gender, background, race, and ethnicity, they also believe being a member of a minority group—a woman, a person of color or both, for example—presents particular challenges and expectations. The expectation for MSGCIs to perform in racially and gendered acceptable ways means that being "your authentic self" is not appreciated in many workplace cultures. The MSGCIs often talked about learning to "wear a mask" that intentionally defies persisting negative stereotypes of blacks (and women of color). They believed that wearing a mask enables them to successfully fulfill the expectation of being the "safe" and "mild mannered" black person so that they may achieve mobility in their work environments.

When I asked the MSGCIs to clarify what being the "safe" or "mild mannered" black person means, they focused on the need to reject the anti-black racism they experience in their everyday micro-interactions. For instance, several MSGCIs discussed the racial and gender double standards that exist when it comes to managing one's emotions in the workplace. They explained that a person can be passionate about a project or idea but any display of emotions was deemed inappropriate. In fact, many cited instances where past colleagues, often colleagues of color, were ostracized and labeled, "hard to get along with" when they displayed such passion. Several MSGCIs recommended that any response that might be deemed "emotional" should be presented in a calm and well thought out way, even in circumstances when non-black and male colleagues are rewarded for being assertive and outspoken. For the MSGCI women of color, this expectation resonated strongly as several mentioned they did not want to be labeled or adopt the "angry/sassy black woman" mythical persona that characterizes black women as overly expressive and assertive, overbearing, a "black *bitch*," loud and ignorant without provocation (Chito Childs 2005; Davis 1981; Harris-Perry 2011).

Along the same vein, MSGCIs also talked about the expectation for them to be the "model" minority; not to deny one's racial status as a black person per se but to make sure they are not hyper-focused on diversity issues in a way that may cause colleagues to feel uncomfortable with white privilege. Isaac explained that some workplaces often promote a culture that supports diverse voices are welcomed but behind the scenes, the climate suggests otherwise. He elaborates:

ISAAC

> We don't want to be accused of playing the race or immigrant card but the white privilege of colleagues contributes to the denial and the denial is about the persistence of negative impacts racial profiling, housing discrimination, educational and health inequality is about. And despite the fact that the work we do is about uplifting diverse communities, colleagues will still look to minimizing these impacts as being about individuals' failings or poor culture.

In these workplace cultures and climates, Isaac and other MSGCIs suggested this expectation forces them to embody the persona of a non-threatening conformist, who is afraid of speaking up or that his or her words will not be heard or welcomed. At the same time, Isaac impressed upon me that "the silence" could be a strategy to navigate these workplace conversations about race and other topics of diversity.

ISAAC goes on:

> Sometimes we have to focus on the outcome as opposed to the process. Yes, discrimination happens but fighting with every racist or prejudiced person is exhausting and impossible. Is this person or their actions going to prevent me from getting what I want, need or desire? If yes, then fight. If not, then keep it moving. Get the support of others, you know, rally the troops so that you can fight another day.

While one's silence in the workplace could be used as a helpful tool for some MSGCIs to mobilize others in support of an idea or initiative, a few MSGCIs still felt that workplace cultures that informally discourage certain groups from speaking up and out about important issues or that fail to prioritize issues related to diversity also ensure that workers of color will be in constant fear for their job, fear being isolated, and fear being labeled too militant. As such, being silent solidifies the persona of the non-threatening conformist.

Dressing Up with Care
At its premise, the popular adage "don't judge a book by its cover" means that a person should not make certain assumptions about another person's intelligence or the content of his or her character based solely on outward

appearance. Still, in most settings of social interaction and especially in professional environments, the way a person dresses influences how employers and colleagues choose to interact with him or her. As with most professions, employees are expected to dress in accordance with their organizations' work culture and appropriate for the work situation. With the exception of those who work in the arts, nonprofits, and academia, most MSGCIs described their workplace environments as conservative, requiring conservative attire and appearance that demonstrates they fit into the workplace culture. Here, Carmen makes the connection between fashion and presentation of self within a workplace culture, suggesting that one's attire signals his or her social identity in the social setting and whether he or she is worthy and can meet the social expectation of interaction in that setting.

CARMEN

People judge you on how you're dressed and what you look like. I guess you can think about clothing as a visual metaphor for identity. Are you loud and flashy but have nothing up here [gesturing toward her head]? Are you wearing Payless shoes or Prada? Wearing grey or a tangerine orange? People place value on your clothes and how you dress because it shows people whether you are a member of the group or not and if you are smart or not.

Not surprisingly, there are contextual cues in the workplace that trigger certain stereotypes and prejudices about a person's race and their social status. For instance, whether a person chooses to wear bold and bright colors as red, orange, and royal purple, bold prints and/or body hugging clothing made with Lycra fabrics, the public holds specific perceptions about his or her race based on social status cues in simple things like the clothes he or she wears (see Freeman et al. 2011). An interdisciplinary team of researchers from Tufts University, Stanford University, and the University of California, Irvine examined concepts of race, income and social status, stereotypes, and physical cues (i.e., skin color, hair texture, and clothing), which drive racialization and race categorization, and found these can have significant interpersonal consequences in public spaces (Freeman and Ambady 2011; Penner and Saperstein 2008). Freeman et al. (2011:7) argue when individuals perceive a person's race (phenotypically);

it provides them with the lens [or a set of cultural models by which they] develop judgments and impressions that trigger both affective and behavioral reactions. As such [individuals] readily makes compromises between how [another person] 'actually' appears and the stereotypes and expectations dictating how [her or she] 'should' appear.

Such malleability in perception is at the heart of Carmen's comments and her knowing the interpersonal consequences of such judgments and impressions that persist due to her racialization (her racial self-identification as black and other people's racialization of her as a black person); her presentation of self is focused on defying negative stereotypes related to the way blacks, and specifically poor blacks, may dress in the professional workplace.

Besides skin color, another important physical attribute often used for racial classification across the Americas, in terms of racial hierarchy, is hair. Different from skin color, hair specifically is "an easily controlled variable that can denote status [and signal belongingness], set fashion or serve as a badge" of honor (Cooper 1971:7). For communities of color, a person's hair matters simply on the basis as to whether his or her hair is considered desirable (straight) versus undesirable (curly or tightly coiled) according to mainstream [read: white] beauty standards. In this regard, hair matters in different ways for women and men but particularly less so for the MSGCI men in this study. I observed the topic of beauty standards for men of color in the workplace did not appear to resonate with the MSGCI men as strongly since a few of them expressed they were not personally affected by this double bind of racism and sexism in the workplace in comparison to their female counterparts.

For the MSGCI women, they talked about the significance of wearing straightened hairstyles as the preferred professional and businesslike image of a successful woman. This image in corporate cultures is measured against Eurocentric standards of beauty, which include long and straight hair (usually blonde). More often than not, black women's hair generally fits outside of what is considered desirable in mainstream society. MSGCI women also believed to some extent that a woman's professional success could be affected in negative ways unless she straightens her hair and adheres to this beauty standard.

Several MSGCI women described the social pressures that exist to mimic white beauty standards, both within the black community and from mass media, for black women to alter their hair textures and hair color in order to be considered acceptable and presentable while in professional settings. They suggested the beauty standard and image of the successful professional woman is also embedded within industry-wide trends that help to establish both formal and informal company-grooming policies. These grooming policies, the MSGCI women argue, ultimately serve to discriminate against women of color for not engaging in hair alterations in order to fit the image of professionalism. Ironically, as Ingrid

Banks (2000:46) argues in *Hair Matters*, "hair alteration is effective in transforming the black woman that is simply adequate or sufficient rather than beautiful." Indeed beauty culture across the Americas has socialized and convinced black women to adopt mainstream ideologies of race and beauty—in this case, straight hair—as a prevailing marker of optimal beauty by the rejection of curly or tightly coiled hair as beautiful. Again, as the MSGCI women interpret these ideologies and trends, they argue the messaging they receive about women of color and/or African descended women is that being "black and beautiful" does not automatically equal a successful, professional woman. Framed in this way, I contend Frantz Fanon would argue the pathology of such ideals on the black psyche serves to breed black inferiority and personhood!

A couple of the MSGCIs, however, did make the point that there exist employers who do not see their company's grooming policies as discriminatory, even if these companies may specifically ban natural hairstyles for curly or tightly coiled hair such as locs, braids, twists, and cropped afros. Indeed there is the assumption that certain natural hairstyles are culturally associated with people of African descent; however, there are employers who maintain their grooming policies are race-neutral and employees who do not adhere to such policies will be terminated. In fact, this was the circumstance in the highly publicized case between litigants Chastity Jones and her employer Catastrophe Management Solutions, in which Jones' employment was rescinded in 2010 when she refused to cut her locs in order to comply with the company's grooming policy that requires its employees to present a "professional and businesslike image." Jones later filed a complaint with the US Equal Employment Opportunity Commission (EEOC) in 2013 on the basis of race discrimination and violation of Title VII,[4] which the 11th circuit of US Court of Appeals later dismissed (see Gershman 2016). Other entities such as the US Pentagon have reconsidered cultural signifiers of race as it relates to hairstyles and have since amended their strict, "recommended" military grooming policies in 2014, which previously forbade women (mostly of color) with natural hair from wearing cornrows, locs, and twists to keep their hair out of their faces—an important grooming requirement for military personnel.

Whether an individual looks to hair as a medium to maintain the status quo of mainstream beauty standards or go against it by displaying a black aesthetic that is linked to radical blackness in the public imagination, the MSGCI women's observations about straightened hair in the workplace point to how they negotiate and perform complex identity politics as it relates to their own hairstyle choices. For some, these include wearing their hair curly, in hair weaves, double ponytails, locs, cropped hairstyles and thin braids that can be easily pulled into a bun or ponytail. For others, they continue to choose to chemically alter, press, or blow dry to straighten their hair.

A few MSGCIs thought of conspicuous consumption as a masquerading device to disarm and signal to others that they "dress with care" and can fit in to the social environment. Here, Millicent talks about how she presents herself when out shopping with work friends in high-end, department stores. She emphasizes how one should act and the confidence they should exude that signals belongingness.

MILLICENT goes on:

> Walk with confidence; like you belong. Confidence but not cockiness if you want to make sure you're not seen as a threat. Have on the right shoes, watch, jewelry, the right bag—designer, okay. Not your Sunday best, because that's too obvious. You're trying too hard. They'll either ignore you or follow you around if you are in a store or something. Again, it's subtle but a planned effort. If you are in a store, you pay with your AMEX Gold or Black Card. They will stand up and take notice.

Connecting Millicent's story to the points discussed in the previous chapter on conspicuous consumption, I contend some MSGCIs' performances or their glamorous representations of being the fashionable black can be perceived as attempts to demonstrate their belongingness in predominately white spaces as the singular black. An unintended consequence of such MSGCIs' conspicuous consumption patterns, including when it comes to their attire and their ability to "dress with care," is that it makes it possible for those who believe in Black American exceptionalism to ignore the persistence of racial inequality. An example of this comes from my conversation with Robert, where he describes his effort to always look professional by wearing conservative suits. Here, Robert talks about an instance when he "dressed down" at work and was not wearing a suit, but recalls being treated differently—like he did not belong:

ROBERT

> Because I am senior management, I always look professional. Tailor-made suits. I made the mistake of dressing down one day and security stopped me! I see this white guy every day; we talk every day for at least 10 minutes about sports, kids, the wives. He claims he didn't recognize me...so frustrating.... Once you look black, it doesn't matter if you're division VP or the guy from the mailroom; we're all the same.

Robert as well as other MSGCIs described instances similar to this as, "working as an African American." Robert reasoned that his blackness automatically subsumed him into the ethnic category of African American with its accompanying negative stereotypes, particularly when he "dressed down" or did not fit the image for the situation. Robert went on to add that once his white colleagues became aware of his Caribbean ancestry, their attitude changed to *oh, you're different from the regular blacks*. Robert admitted he was offended by such comments because it negatively implied to him that African Americans (native-born US blacks) do not really belong in these environments and never really will but only with the exception of being a "non-regular black" person.

Standard Public Speech

If an individual works in an office, he or she is most likely familiar with particular workplace etiquette which all employees are expected to adhere to: such as staying home when sick, speaking in hushed tones so as to not disturb colleagues in the nearby office or cubicle space, silencing cell phones during meetings, and being compassionate and empathetic toward others. In effect, these unwritten codes of conduct are perceived as a necessary part of social interaction in the workplace. Following workplace etiquette also has other social implications; not only does a person's ability to master these unwritten codes promote a certain level of comfort among colleagues but a person who is able to perform them well is also perceived as having the competitive advantage for employment opportunities over other colleagues who may not have mastered such valued etiquette codes.

Several MSGCIs focused on the etiquette of one's business vernacular in the workplace as particularly important to their presentation of self. There was general consensus among the MSGCIs that using proper grammar and vocabulary, avoiding profanity, being an attentive, active listener, and engaged in dialogue are critical to one's workplace communication practices. When I asked them to clarify how such etiquette connects to the persisting expectations of presenting oneself in racially acceptable ways, the MSGCIs put emphasis on their communication style, both orally and written, as intending to repudiate negative stereotypes about black intelligence. Here, Natalie describes how she feels that her patterns of speech, her use of preferred terminology and quality of scholarship are under constant scrutiny of her colleagues:

NATALIE

> Most people think professors are a bit nontraditional and less conservative than most folks but professors have bias too, gender bias, class bias and racial bias. During committee meetings you'd hear which student is genius and which one is rough-around-the-edges. I've noticed the rough-around-the-edges comments are typically reserved for the first generation college student or the student of color. You'd hear similar comments about colleagues and the quality of their scholarship. Questioning a colleague's scholarship depends on, in my opinion, how Eurocentric the topic is or not. When I first started teaching, I picked up on these patterns and how important it was to be conscious of the way I spoke to my colleagues. For me, as a woman of color, I have to defy stereotypes and prove my scholarship is of high quality, that my writing is clear, my speech is impeccable and that I can actually speak intelligently about important issues in my field. In informal settings, too, it's like you're *on*; so you have to study and be prepared for a pop quiz that only you are expected to take and do well. And, for some of my white colleagues, and especially for the white men, it's okay if they look disheveled, are somewhat disconnected socially, and their scholarship or their arguments are antiquated and don't make sense. They get a pass just because… Of course that's unfair but that's a privilege I definitely don't have as a woman of color, and with tenure.

Natalie's story illustrates how she and other MSGCIs must rely on their EQ to assess their work environments and adjust their communication style and particularly their speech patterns to meet ethnic and gendered expectations in the workplace.

Other MSGCIs, particularly those who grew up in Spanish-, French-, and or Creole-speaking households described learning when not to speak with an accent (similar to their parents) in order to signal to others "I'm American" and when it is appropriate to be bilingual. Lisa described her experience of managing her bilingualism and developing the skill of code switching in the workplace:

LISA

> Some patients are taken back when the chief attending introduces me as their doctor handling their case. I had one patient comment that I was surprisingly *articulate*. Another time, a white co-worker heard me in the breakroom say something to two Vincentian NPs in patois, and was surprised. I am free to speak all of these ways. I can turn it on and off when I want to and when I am comfortable.

Lisa's story raises two important points regarding speech and the aesthetics of communication style among the singular black in public. First, Lisa's story points to a common theme also raised by other MSGCIs that some members of the general public have lowered expectations regarding blacks' ability to articulate themselves well. Several MSGCIs expressed their frustration and offense when they were the recipients of such comments. They believe these comments reify the stereotype that people of African descent, specifically African Americans, are typically inarticulate and when the MSGCIs' communication style does not adhere to the stereotype, they become, "the exception to the rule." Connecting aesthetics of communication style to the notion of Black American exceptionalism, I contend, is problematic as it serves to reinforce the negative idea, which underpins anti-black racism, that people of African descent with black immigrant backgrounds, are somehow better than and more respectable than native-born blacks.

Second, Lisa's story points to instances where MSGCIs rely on their cultural capital strategies to navigate social spaces via their code switching. In effect, MSGCIs' ability to code switch allows them to be reflexive and reflective of the various cultural and linguistic spaces relevant to their multiple identities that operate simultaneously and across social situations.

Public Displays of Educational Credentials

It is a widely accepted tenet that education is a critical component to an individual's success in life. As Nicholas Negroponte once stated in a lecture at the 2006 Organization of American States (OAS) conference, "No matter what global problem you are dreading, whether it's the elimination of poverty [or] solving environmental energy problems, the solutions always include education; never is it without an education component [nor] can it be done without education." Hence, there is no disputing that education is critical, however, a common presumption within the American meritocracy is that education is also a great equalizer. Unfortunately, the US education system, including higher education, has struggled to ensure all students have equal access to quality education that will enable them to learn, think critically, and act intelligently and purposefully as integral and contributing members of society in the twenty-first century and beyond. The social problem of educational disparities, which is often created by broad patterns of residential segregation, residues of de jure and de facto racism, and ongoing socioeconomic disadvantage, has made it such that there are students attending poor quality schools in communities across the country that are in need of powerful educational and life opportunities. Yet, what happens in instances when some of these students attend both selective and highly selective colleges and university: are these students able to overcome some of these obstacles and gain opportunity and mobility?

If you recall, the MSGCIs in this study, regardless of their working or middle class upbringings, all attended highly selective colleges and universities, for their undergraduate and graduate/professional degrees. In actuality, these MSGCIs are not that different from current statistics on students who attend four-year colleges in the United States. According to S. Michael Gaddis (2015), there is a trend among blacks, Latinos, and low-income students to attend highly selective universities, although it is unclear as to whether their prospective employers are able to overcome their implicit and explicit biases and value these students' degrees when they enter the workforce. In fact, Gaddis found equally qualified black and white graduates of highly selective universities are not treated equally by prospective employers: the white candidate receives an employer response for every six resumes he or she submits, whereas the black or Latino candidate receives a response for every eight resumes. Even in instances where the candidate graduates from a less selective university, whites can expect a response every nine resumes while an equally qualified black candidate needs to submit 15 resumes for a response from a prospective employer. Notwithstanding, since education still remains the tool for lifting oneself up the social and economic ladder, students of color and particularly for those who are children of immigrants will continue to strive for such degrees at elite schools.

When we talked about the pressures to perform whiteness in public, however, most MSGCIs focused on the ways they found it important to emphasize their educational backgrounds to employers and colleagues, particularly with their display of their diplomas on their office walls, alma mater memorabilia on their desks and other credentials noted in their email signatures and office voicemail. Several MSGCIs believed that displaying such credentials signals not only they are "more than qualified" for the position they occupy in their workplace but also their expertise was developed while attending a prestigious institution. Erica discusses the importance of displaying educational credentials in the workplace.

Here, **ERICA** adds:

> I think that it depends on the office culture. Not everyone puts up their diplomas but you see little items here and there, like an alumni sticker, a coffee mug or picture frame with the school's seal on it. But I think that when

people see, okay, you went to THAT school and not some rinky-dink college or grad school, then you're telling them that, "hey, I'm smart and can do this job." Respect me because I've earned this title. My degrees say so. Like, are you double Ivy League--Princeton undergrad and Harvard grad? Got your MBA from Wharton? Put it up! It's another informal way of saying, "yeah I'm part of the alumni network too." That way, you can bond over the school song or something silly even if there is a 10+year difference.

As Erica's story points to, there is a clear link between educational status, respect, and cultural capital that is critical to demonstrating how workers can embody symbolic elements of credentials in order to create a sense of collective identity or community with colleagues that says, "we're the same" or "you're just like me." At the same time, it seems that for the MSGCIs, their need to have to display their educational credentials is an explicit response to the implicit performance criteria the MSGCIs feel compelled to adhere to in the workplace, which in many ways serves to reject preconceived notions and misguided racial stereotypes about their skills and abilities.

Race/Ethnicity of Mate Matters for a Promotion

Mate selection by race and ethnicity was a hot topic among the MSGCIs. Whether participants themselves chose to date or marry outside of their race-ethnic group or not, the MSGCIs had a lot to say about interracial relationships: what does it mean to marry outside of one's race/ethnicity? Do interracial relationships discredit or indicate to others how black a person is? Some MSGCIs, including Erica, asked rhetorically,

with the exception of the President [Obama], why do successful black men marry white women? I'm not judging but it's something I've noticed since I'm dating. Maybe it's a trend but I don't know...

While I will not delve deeply into MSGCIs' broader comments about interracial relationships here as those conversations were ancillary to the main conversation on performance criteria, a few participants did talk about exogamy and its impact specifically in workplace environments.

It is critical to put exogamy into context: in the United States, anti-miscegenation laws were deemed unconstitutional in 1967 with the Supreme Court case of Loving v. State of Virginia[5] and since then, the number of interracial marriages has been on the rise (see Census Bureau 2012).[6] According to the Pew Research Center's 2010 report "Marrying Out: One-in-Seven New U.S. Marriages Is Interracial or Interethnic,"[7] "a record of 14.6% of all new marriages in 2008 were between spouses of a different race or ethnicity from one another; among these, 9% of whites, 16% of blacks, 26% of Hispanics, and 31% of Asian Americans married someone whose race or ethnicity was different from their own" (iii). William H. Frey in his book *Diversity Explosion: How New Racial Demographics Are Remaking America* (2014) found the increase in exogamy reflects the significant influx of post-1965 immigrants from Asia, Latin America, and the Caribbean into the United States, who marry individuals of the post-war baby boom generation and their children's generation (Generation X, born between years 1965 and 1980). Frey argues these two generations have increased access to a broader racial and ethnic marriage market than previous ones, thereby increasing exogamy rates seen in the last two decades alone. Despite this type of diversity explosion, which Frey references in his book, marriage markets for whites and people of color remain dramatically different, especially along gender lines.

Frey and researchers at the Brookings Institute reported in their joint article "Multiracial Marriage on the Rise" that three-fourths of black-white heterosexual marriages involve a black man–white woman, both between the ages of 25 and 35 and college educated (see also Pew Research Center 2015). In contrast, heterosexual black and Latino women who earned a bachelor's degrees or higher[8] and are between the ages of 25 and 34 are less likely to marry outside their race-ethnicity unlike heterosexual white women of their same age and educational cohort who marry men, regardless of race, with similar degrees or higher and/or of a higher socioeconomic status.[9] In terms of the race and gender divide within marriage markets, the research on assortive mating (marrying someone of a similar educational status) also points to data that suggest in cases when black and Latino women marry men, they tend to marry men of color less educated than them because of shortage of black men or men of color in their age cohort who earn a bachelor's degree or higher.[10] This finding has important race-based implications for understanding how the level of education spouses attain, as a predictor of earnings, correlates to income inequality effects on children and families, such as job instability and poor working conditions for spouses and less access to high quality schools for children.

Despite these policy and demographic trends on interracial marriages as well as the more positive global attitudes toward interracial relationships that exist today, these still do not translate into high rates of actual interracial cohabitation and/or marriage (Lee and Edmonston 2005; Torngren 2016). In fact, more than "85% or more marriages in the U.S. tend to be racially endogamous" (Rosenfeld 2008:23). Yet, the topic of interracial relationships is still highly politicized within many communities of color, and particularly black communities (Hill Collins 2004).

A few MSGCIs strongly believed non-black employers and colleagues' attitudes toward the singular black in the workplace were more positive in terms of job promotions and opportunities if he or she married a white person or outside of their race-ethnic group. Interestingly, MSGCIs' consideration of interracial marriages in the workplace (regardless of whether they are currently or were previously in interracial relationships themselves), I contend, speaks to the informal relationships that take place at work, where the social goal is in part to signal one's belongingness. Here, Derrick speculates on the possible benefits of black intermarriages in the workplace:

DERRICK

> Not to downplay the challenges couples face but I sometimes think being in an interracial marriage must make it easier to blend in at work than being in an all-black couple. It's like they see your spouse and think you're safe and approachable, not extra militant. Your spouse with a dark complexion with a natural or locs, you are seen as extra-extra black, already not blending in [laughs]. The way you dress and who you marry can also show your personal politics about race and everything else. Maybe if you marry a white person or like an Asian American person then it might signal that you are open, more inclusive in your politics or thinking.

This assumption presumes that one's mate or spouse selection, particularly a marriage between a person of color and a white person, automatically serves as a buffer from discrimination and negative stereotypes against black militancy. When talking about intermarriage, a few MSGCIs believe there are individuals who choose to intermarry non-blacks also want to "escape into white society" or at the very least improve in their social and economic status by marrying someone not black. Indeed, books such as Edward Telles' (2006) *Race in Another America* explored this trend in Brazil as he found when some blacks intermarry with whites they intend to exchange their perceived "inferior" racial status for one that is presumed to be better based on color.

This trend is not a recent phenomenon, as Frantz Fanon in *Black Skin, White Mask* employed his psychoanalytic lens and revealed, in my opinion, his own biases regarding the colonization of the African mind and the desires of the black man to overcome his state of blackness via a relation-ship with a white woman and his "possession" of her white body. To illus-trate this, Fanon wrote in the opening paragraph of Chap. 3, "The Man of Color and the White Woman" in *Black Skin, White Mask*:

> Out of the blackest part of my soul, across the zebra striping of my mind, surges this desire of my mind to be suddenly *white*. I wish to be acknowl-edged not as *black* but as *white*. Now—and this is a form of recognition that Hegel had not envisaged—who but a white woman can do this for me? By loving me she proves that I am worthy of white love. I am loved like a white man. I am a white man. Her loves takes me onto the noble road that leads to total realization.... I marry white culture, white beauty, white whiteness. When my restless hands caress those white breasts, they grasp white civiliza-tion and dignity and make them mine. (emphasis by Fanon)

It should be noted that Fanon was married to a white woman though he emphatically argued his own marriage was an exception to his thesis because the relationship was solely based on love as opposed to hegemonic power relations. While I find it worthwhile to explore elsewhere Fanon's psychoanalytic standpoint regarding his own relationship or even the plight of women of color in these same terms, I contend his passage makes an important point regarding whiteness, black male desire, and inferiority that I believe undergird MSGCIs' reasoning on the potential benefits of exogamous relationships in the workplace. For Fanon, a man of color con-siders himself worthy when whiteness embraces blackness and, "recodes the pathologies ascribed to black masculinity [he is then rendered] safe, desirable, trustworthy, since the white woman is both the producer and purveyor of her peoples and their values" (Sterling 2012:152). According to this line of thinking, it is blacks' inferiority complex or fear for not being accepted that may motivate the singular black to contemplate exog-amy to gain social acceptance among colleagues and employers in the workplace, which may lead to job promotion and advancement. As of this writing, the research to date has not revealed instances where employers have discriminated against individuals on the basis of their exogamous or endogamous relationships or whether professional blacks in majority white spaces have found exogamous relationships advantageous to their careers.

Zip Codes Say a Lot
Several MSGCIs believe in the notion, "your zip codes say a lot about you." Zip codes correspond with particular geographic regions or neigh-borhoods that may be resource rich or poor. According to equal housing

advocates at the National Fair Housing Alliance and researchers at the Equality of Opportunity Project at Harvard University, an individual's residential zip code and the neighborhoods within its area can have a profound impact on his or her socioeconomic mobility, that of his or her children, and their overall quality of life. An individual's zip code signals his or her neighborhood's quality of resources when it comes to having highly ranked public schools; access to green spaces, grocery stores that sell healthy food items and quality health care organizations; a working transit system; low levels of crime and violence; and limited sources of pollution. For MSGCIs, zip codes and its corresponding neighborhoods also signal to colleagues whether they "share" the same values as them outside of work, such as the importance of choosing to live in the "right" neighborhoods. On the one hand, MSGCIs often referred to the "right" neighborhoods as middle class communities with quality resources as mentioned above and are also known for being safe for nonresidents/visitors, including work colleagues. On the other hand, MSGCIs also believed the "right" neighborhoods their colleagues referred to also intimate majority non-black neighborhoods.

How does one's race and class impact their housing choices and his or her ability to live in these "right" neighborhoods? *American Apartheid* authors Douglas Massey and Nancy Denton (1993) found middle class blacks have not had the same opportunity to live wherever they choose regardless of their income levels, education, and resources and despite the passing of civil rights legislation rendering redlining, discriminatory mortgage lending practices, and other forms of discrimination illegal. Even in more recent research by Robert Sampson (2012) and Patrick Sharkey (2014), for example, scholars have found spatial segmentation of middle class blacks in neighborhoods still continues especially in large metropolitan areas such as Chicago, New York, and Los Angeles. For instance, middle class Blacks with incomes of $100,000 or more often do not live in middle class neighborhoods. Instead, these blacks tend to live in neighborhoods either inhabited by whites making less than $30,000 or in poor and working class neighborhoods with median incomes of $10,000 to $12,000 less than white households making $30,000 (Reardon et al. 2015; Sharkey 2014). Not surprisingly, these are also neighborhoods with less access to quality resources and a long history of residential segregation. The reasons for this pervasive racial segregation are three-fold, which include disparity in accumulated wealth between whites and blacks, discrimination and bias—the most obvious—and racial preference to live with others of the same race or ethnicity.

The MSGCIs themselves see the linkages between the cumulative effects of racism and exclusionary housing policies of the past and the expectation for them to live in the "right" zip code when they talk about their own experiences dealing with discrimination and bias when shopping for apartments or buying a home. Several noted their experiences are different from—perhaps subtler in comparison to—the experiences of their parents' generation who were thought to encounter more blatant forms of housing discrimination when searching for residences outside of their black ethnic enclaves and immigrant networks. When I asked about their zip code decisions or searches for more desirable, resource rich areas, MSGCIs such as Monica, described incidences of realtor bias—instances when the realtor shows the buyer properties in neighborhoods or zip codes that were not areas the buyer wants to be in but more where the realtor needs or thinks the buyer should be in—as is the case for rapid gentrification occurring in certain US urban epicenters such as Harlem, New York City.

MONICA

Monica was born in the late 1970s and grew up in Brooklyn, New York with her parents. At various times throughout the interviews, she self-identifies herself using the following terms interchangeably: black, Caribbean, and West Indian. Her parents both immigrated to the United States in the mid-1960s from Barbados around the same time her maternal and paternal grandparents did. During middle school, Monica gained entry into a nationally recognized scholarship program that provides children of color access and opportunity to independent schools and was accepted into a boarding school in the Baltimore Maryland area. Her parents purchased their own home in Queens, New York, and served the neighborhood community, her mom as an educator and her dad as a reverend, until their retirement. After graduating from high school, Monica attended a prestigious college in Connecticut and earned her Bachelor's degree in computer science. Monica works in the information services and data industry and lives in New Britain, Connecticut, with her husband and two adolescent sons.

Here, **MONICA** reflects on her experiences with realtors, highlighting incidences of their implicit bias:

> I have seen realtors be surprised when they realize my voice over the telephone does not match what they envision my exterior to be. Their eyes get a little wider as I approach or their voices get a bit higher when they say

hello. By that point, I've discussed my price point and may have casually mentioned what I do for work and so on. So, there isn't a need for the realtor to try to figure out whether I can afford the property—although I have been asked in the past. But realtors will try to steer you in a certain direction. Like in Brooklyn and uptown [Harlem], the whites who can't afford the upper East side, go into Brooklyn or go uptown and buy up the Brownstones and old Victorians. And realtors get their cut when they sell more condos or high-end apartments in these areas. If they assume you can't afford the place then they'll tell you, *let me show you this other neighborhood. It's not your preferred neighborhood, which has become really expensive, but you will like this one. It's diverse and I am sure you will feel comfortable.* Oh, please! And where do they show you? Like something out of [the movie] New Jack City or something. I'm trying *not* to get shot, okay. I am civic-minded, I care about and want to live amongst my people, and I also want good schools, a safe community, and parks and museums...

For Monica and other MSGCIs, being "civic-minded" has its limitations when it comes to real estate choices that have been circumscribed. The availability of choices for the black middle class to move into the "right" zip codes and neighborhoods are finite, therefore lessening the numbers of MSGCIs able to buy quality housing and pass down any wealth accumulated in such assets that can allow future generations to move into more stable neighborhoods. For those MSGCIs who moved into the "right" neighborhoods, they describe not always being met with open arms. An overarching sentiment expressed among these MSGCIs is feeling the stress of having to navigate through this complicated race-class landscape not only at work but also on the home front.

The MSGCIs' acknowledgement that these performance criteria exist for the purpose of ensuring they can better "fit in" as the singular black in workspaces makes visible the existence of a white social identity ("whiteness) that is embedded in US culture that reifies systems of dominance for its workers, regardless of their race, ethnicity, gender, religious affiliation, and sexual orientation. I contend the MSGCIs often perform their variable racial-ethnic identities within a context which a habitus of whiteness and race-based cultural narratives represent whiteness as something positive and to aspire to whereas as blackness is something negative and the "inferior other." When I reference the notion of whiteness or the habitus of whiteness, I draw on the definition used by Elena Featherston and Jean Ishibashi (2004) in their chapter, "Oreos and Bananas: Conversations on Whiteness," which they write:

> Whiteness is an interlocking pattern of belief, values, feelings and assumptions; policies, procedures, and laws; behaviors, unwritten rules used to define and underpin a worldview. It is embedded in historic systems of oppression that sustain wealth, power and privilege.

Considering this definition and the existence of race-based cultural narratives, the question begs to be answered: do the MSGCIs think they have to reinvent themselves to perform in the context of a white workplace? In my opinion, I argue, no. Instead, their stories reveal their triple identity consciousness, an awareness of their subjugation that places them—as the singular black—at the margins. MSGCIs often inhabit the tensions that exist between the persisting dual narratives—never fully embodying the positive presentation of self that is expected while never fully free of the negative representations. Based on our conversations, I contend the MSGCIs are not passively following along like sheep within this system of dominance. Via their triple identity consciousness, they are painfully aware of their racialization and the insidiousness of cultural hegemony but also realize they are judged on how best they can "adopt" [read: imitate] whites in order to gain acceptance, respect, and opportunity in the workplace—as **ISAAC** put it,

> ...but you have to play the game and know when to bend the rules to suit you.

As part of their practice and employment of cultural capital strategies, the MSGCIs draw on the knowledge and experience of knowing when and how to "play the game" or "wear the mask" and seek opportunities that demonstrate their agency via masquerading (as opposed to acts of submission, as Frantz Fanon argues in *Black Skin, White Masks*) as they adjust to each social setting.

For the MSGCIs, the performance of masquerading or performing in racially acceptable ways is not about mimicry as Homi Bhabha argues or imitating whiteness as Frantz Fanon asserts; instead, their triple identity consciousness aids in their awareness of the "mask" that opens up possibilities of agency that empowers them to realign and transcode their own meanings of blackness, which are often at odds with mainstream society's typifications of "inferior others," and reimagine their performances (front-stage personas) as being different from their self (backstage personas) across these various spaces (see Hall 1997). They discussed their need to develop and participate in networks of support, both formally and informally, to mitigate the day-to-day stress and isolation they experience when faced with the requirement to constantly self-regulate emotions and assess social situations as the singular black in predominately white spaces. Sadly, the mainstay of white dominance in society as the norm makes it challenging for members of the majority society to fully acknowledge that racial inequality exists and that such inequality has dire consequences for those who do not fully adhere to the ideals set forth in the habitus. For the MSGCIs, these strategies and networks of support are seen as helpful; however, they also elucidate the costs—particularly the emotional costs of such performances and the internalizing effects these costs have on their individual psyches.

Psychological Costs of Black Singularity and the Nuances of Triple Identity Consciousness

Whether referring to these performances metaphorically as "playing a game," "playing a role," or engaging in strategies of subversion such as in masquerading/"wearing a mask," a theme arises from the narratives: the MSGCIs often question the relevance of their own authenticity in social situations that they feel do not fully accept them for being their authentic selves, for being black and of Caribbean descent—as diverse as that identity means to each individual participant. I consider what it means to be aware of one's identity performances in these non-black spaces and look to W.E.B. Du Bois' (1903:122) concept of double consciousness when he says, "from the double life every American Negro must live, as a Negro and as an American...from this must arise a painful self-consciousness an almost morbid sense of personality and a moral hesitancy which is fatal to self-confidence... and this must produce a particular wrenching of the soul, a peculiar sense of doubt and bewilderment." Having "a peculiar sense of doubt and bewilderment" is the emotional tax that is paid daily as a psychological burden many MSGCIs expressed they feel as a result of feeling different in majority white privileged spaces because of their race/ethnicity and gender. In effect, the emotional tax is one of several in the "knapsack of costs"[11] that is the residual impact of managing their working identity—the stresses or burdens from the effects of micro-aggressions and discrimination (perceived and actual) on a person of color's physical and mental wellbeing in majority white workplaces (see Carbadi and Gulati 2000).

In a recent Catalyst's study, *Emotional Tax: How Black Women and Men Pay More at Work and How Leaders Can Take Action* (2016), authors Travis, Thorpe-Moscon, and McCluney present both qualitative and quantitative data from a survey and a series of interviews conducted with approximately 650 Black men and women working in employment industries of retail, healthcare, financial services, education, construction, and information services/IT. Travis et al. (2016) spoke with first-level and middle managers, senior executives, and CEOs/business owners who point to the emotional tax they must bear when aiming high at work but also how such a tax can get in the way of their success, inside and outside of the workplace. The report also proposes strategies for leaders in workplaces to adopt that could minimize the impact of the emotional tax experienced by their employees of color.

Citing specific ways emotional tax are linked to black men's and women's heightened anxiety levels and sleep problems and feeling alienated and isolated, Travis et al.'s (2016) findings strongly correlate with the MSGCIs' own reflections on the impact of this tax, including self-reporting their dealings with depression or "feeling off," feeling increased pressure to perform well all of the time, and being strong (as in fulfilling "the strong black woman" myth).[12] In fact, there are a growing number of research studies examining the "knapsack of costs" and the relationship between micro-aggressions and discrimination for people of color in majority white spaces to underscore the significance and consequence of racism on the mental health of historically disenfranchised communities in white spaces (see Akbari 1991; Balsam et al. 2011; Brown et al. 2000; Carter 1993; Wing Sue 2010; Wing Sue et al. 2008; Thompson 1996; Torres et al. 2010; Utsey et al. 2008).

The MSGCIs, and particularly the women, in more senior management positions admitted to struggling with egoism and feeling like a fraud because perfection (or striving for perfection) is strongly related to demonstrating worthiness for success. Several others described feeling lonely when handling the pressures of perfectionism because they find it necessary to keep a safe distance from colleagues they have yet to trust but realize this behavior can be negatively perceived as antisocial or as embodying the "uppity negro syndrome"[13]—a detriment to team leadership and workplace mobility in white workplaces.

MSGCI women also talked about how the pressures to perform twice as well in these non-black spaces often hinder their ability to properly take care of themselves. Many are unable to exercise, set aside personal time for a self-care routine or go to the doctor regularly to manage stress and chronic health conditions they have developed in recent years (e.g., diabetes, hypertension and high blood pressure, being overweight, ulcers, uterine fibroids, and large cysts). When I asked them to be more specific as to why these pressures to perform well minimize their opportunities for self-care, the women often expressed a strong desire to take better care of themselves but struggle with feeling overwhelmed with the knowledge that being twice as good means they cannot do it all and that "something has to give" even if that means their personal care takes a "back seat" to everything and everyone else.

While the Catalyst report does not provide specific positive strategies professionals of color can employ in these majority white workspaces, several MSGCIs discussed some of their own strategies to help mitigate the effects of the emotional tax in their lives, which include forging relationships with mentors and colleagues of color via professional organizations, and creating social spaces such as predominately nonwhite book clubs, exercise/fit groups, and men's/women's social groups.

In my opinion, the MSGCIs' discussions also revealed a nuance to their identity consciousness and cultural capital strategies they develop, evoked and employ in these social places and spaces. W.E.B. Du Bois (1903:122) was adept when he described the toll experienced by striving African descendants in the United States that results in "a double life, with double thoughts, double duties, and double social classes, must give rise to double works and double ideals and tempt the mind to preference or to revolt, to hypocrisy or to radicalism." I contend, however, the MSGCIs are not resigned to their double bind; their third eye of awareness is evoked. Indeed, the MSGCIs' triple identity consciousness helps them see clearly the realities of their position in the United States—both their privilege of being middle class, American-born, college educated professionals and their racial, ethnic, and gender subjugation that relegates them to the bottom of the social hierarchy.

When describing strategies to help mitigate the emotional tax, almost all MSGCIs were explicit in their limits to performing in racially acceptable ways and, if and when possible, intend to leave workplaces (and job sectors) they feel force them to have to accept being uncomfortable for being the only one or one of few people of color who are, "stressed, unappreciated, undervalued, underpaid and overworked" as Yomaira mentioned or, "make the effort to make white colleagues more comfortable" with their race and ethnicity as Rosalie spoke about. I extend Du

Bois' concept of double consciousness, in which MSGCIs fully acknowledge the contradictions of their position, and argue their triple identity consciousness draws attention to a third level of awareness that sees the importance of transcending these dualities of subversions which are used as strategies to help African descendants in the United States survive subjugation and its miserable consequences that is—as Cornel West (1985) has argued—not of their choosing.[14] In fact, the third level of MSGCI triple identity consciousness is an awareness that surviving subjugation is not enough; it is a third ideal of actionable efforts that seek to forge and maintain transnational connections with others of African descent both locally and globally that embodies and honors ancestral connections vis-à-vis community with tools for wellbeing and mobility. Not to be conflated with elements of Pan Africanism, which is often criticized for homogenizing concepts of African culture and values, I argue that it is the postcolonial lens of triple identity consciousness in which the diverse experiences and narratives of people of African descent—including the MSGCIs who self-identity as Afro-Asian American, Afro-Latino, and/or multiracial—reflect an awareness for the need to have multi-prong approaches that connects people across these contexts and geographies in ways that respect their interests while supporting and uplifting them and the communities they are entrenched.

In the next chapter, I consider the philosophy and practice of "giving back" and black philanthropy and the conditions in which several MSGCIs link their philanthropy to the transnational connections they choose to maintain with their parents' country of origin. My focus on the concept of black philanthropy, and MSGCIs' engagement with it generally speaking, is critical to understanding the impetus for the various practices people of African descent develop when creating a habitus of blackness and the space and physical place of community—both local and symbolic.

NOTES

1. Here, I am considering Michael Dawson's (1995) concept of "linked fate" from his book *Behind the Mule: Race and Class in African American Politics*. According to Dawson, linked fate is a sentiment among blacks that one's prospects are ultimately tied to one's race. Thus, the experiences of the black middle class are linked to their ties, both voluntary and involuntary to working class and low-income blacks on the basis of race—whether it is because of residential segregation that causes blacks to live in the same

urban areas or neighborhoods or by virtue of the persisting gaps in employment, income, wealth, education, and health that exist between blacks and whites in the United States.

2. The reference to the concept of social Darwinism in the workplace derives from Charles Darwin's work and Herbert Spencer's structural functional analysis of Darwin's notion of biological determinism—the idea of "survival of the fittest." Conceptually, the capitalist workplace is observed to privilege a "dog-eat-dog" culture that thrives on competition and hierarchy that place different values on workers' capabilities according their race, ethnicity, and gender. At its worst, the workplace culture is criticized for using tools like evolution and genetics to legitimize discrimination against women and racial-ethnic minorities (e.g., women are blamed for their lack of leadership roles and their inability to negotiate higher salaries).

3. The "context of reception," a concept elaborated by Alejandro Portes and Ruben Rumbaut, calls attention to the complexity of the situation that immigrants enter and the disadvantages that they and their children confront: Success in the new society depends not only on what immigrants bring, such as skills of use in the new labor market, but also on how they are received. See http://www.migrationpolicy.org/article/second-generation-last-great-wave-immigration-setting-record-straight

4. Title VII of the Civil Rights Act of 1964 is a federal law that prohibits employers from discriminating against employees on the basis of sex, race, color, national origin, and religion.

5. Loving v. State of Virginia (1967) is a landmark court decision of the United States Supreme Court, which deemed laws of interracial marriages illegal and unconstitutional. The case was brought by Mildred Loving and Richard Loving, whose marriage violated the state of Virginia's anti-miscegenation statute, the Racial Integrity Act of 1924, which prohibited marriage between people classified as "white" and people classified as "colored." The Supreme Court's unanimous decision ended all race-based legal restrictions on marriage in the United States.

6. In 2012, the US Census Bureau released a brief, "Households and Families 2010," showed interracial or interethnic opposite-sex married couple households grew by 28% over the decade from 7% in 2000 to 10% in 2010. States with higher percentages of couples of a different race or Hispanic origin in 2010 were primarily located in the western and southwestern parts of the United States, along with Hawaii and Alaska.

7. This report is based primarily on two data sources: the Pew Research Center's analysis of demographic data about new marriages in 2008 from the US Census Bureau's American Community Survey (ACS) and the Pew Research Center's analysis of its own data from a nationwide telephone survey conducted from October 28 to November 30, 2009, among a nationally representative sample of 2,884 adults (pp. iii).

8. Data from the National Center for Educational Statistics show that in 2015, 24.6% of black women and 18.5% of Latino women earned bachelor's degrees or higher in comparison to 46.6% of white women earning bachelor's degrees or higher.

9. See National Center for Educational Statistics' table 104.20 "Percentage of Persons 25 to 29 years old with Selected levels of Educational Attainment by Race/Ethnicity and Sex: Selected Years, 1920 through 2015." https://nces.ed.gov/programs/digest/d15/tables/dt15_104.20.asp#; accessed: July 24, 2016.

10. Data from the National Center for Educational Statistics show that in 2015, 17.6% of black men and 14.5% of Latino men earned bachelor's degrees or higher in comparison to 39.5% of white men earning bachelor's degrees or higher.

11. "Knapsack of costs" derives from Peggy McIntosh's (1988) article excerpt "White Privilege: Unpacking the Invisible Knapsack," where she likens white privilege to an invisible knapsack of benefits which whites automatically accrue because of the mere color of their skin and costs which those unable to take advantage of the benefits experience micro-aggressions and the residual impacts of implicit bias.

12. The strong black woman myth stems from post-slavery stereotype that depicts black women as aggressive, indefatigable work mules, able to "plow" through hard situations without any help from others, especially men. They are also depicted as sassy and apathetic, being without vulnerabilities and unable to get hurt (both physically and emotionally). See Tamara Winfrey Harris' (2015) The Sisters are Alright: Changing the Broken Narrative of Black Women in America.

13. At first glance, it would seem that the "Uppity Negro" syndrome is a myth or stereotype that challenges the racist belief of black inferiority. On the contrary, the uppity Negro is the well-dressed black who "puts on airs" and aspires to whiteness (i.e., confident and outspoken and against the ill-treatment of whites) but does not know his or her "true" place, which is to be docile and subservient to whites. See David Pilgrim's (2015) Understanding Jim Crow: Using Racist Memorabilia to Teach Tolerance and Promote Social Justice.

14. Here, I refer to Cornel West's analysis of W.E.B. Du Bois' concept of double consciousness from his essay, "The Dilemma of the Black Intellectual" (1985:124) where he says "caught between an insolent American society and insouciant black community, the Afro-American who takes seriously the life of the mind inhabits an isolated and insulated world. This condition has little to do with the motive and intentions of black intellectuals; rather it is an objective situation created by circumstances not of their choosing."

BIBLIOGRAPHY

Akbar, N. (1991). Mental Disorder Among African Americans. In R. Jones (Ed.), *Black Psychology* (pp. 339–352). Berkeley: Cobb and Henry Publishers.

Anderson, E. (2015). The White Space. *Sociology of Race and Ethnicity, 1*(1), 10–21.

Balsam, K. F., Molina, Y., Beadnell, B., Simoni, J., & Walters, K. (2011). Measuring Multiple Minority Stress: The LGBT People of Color Microaggressions Scale. *Cultural Diversity and Ethnic Minority Psychology, 17*(2), 163–174.

Banks, I. (2000). *Hair Matters: Beauty, Power and Black Woman's Consciousness.* New York: New York University Press.

Bar-On, R. (2000). Emotional and Social Intelligence: Insights from the Emotional Quotient Inventory (EQ-i). In R. Bar-On & J. D. Parker (Eds.), *Handbook of Emotional Intelligence* (pp. 363–388). San Francisco: Jossey-Bass.

Bhabha, H. (1985). Signs Taken for Wonders: Questions of Ambivalence and Authority Under a Tree Outside Delhi, May 1817. *Critical Inquiry, 12*(1), 144–165.

Bonilla-Silva, E. (2009). *Racism without Racists: Color-blind Racism and the Persistence of Racial Inequality.* Lanham: Rowan Littlefield.

Brown, T., Williams, D., Jackson, J., Neighbors, H., Torres, M., Sellers, S., et al. (2000). Being Black and Feeling Blue: The Mental Health Consequences of Racial Discrimination. *Race and Society, 2*(2), 117–131.

Carbadi, D. W., & Gulati, M. (2000). Working Identity. *Cornell Law Review, 85*, 1259–1308.

Carter, J. (1993). Racism's Impact on Mental Health. *Journal of the National Medical Association, 86*, 543–547.

Chito Childs, E. (2005). Looking Behind the Stereotypes of the 'Angry Black Woman': An Exploration of Black Women's Responses to Interracial Relationships. *Gender and Society, 19*(4), 544–561.

Collins, P. H. (2004). *Black Sexual Politics: African Americans, Gender, and the New Racism.* New York: Routledge.

Cooley, C. H. (1902/1983). *Human Nature and the Social Order.* Piscataway: Transaction Publishers.

Cooper, W. (1971). *Hair: Sex. Society and Symbolism.* New York: Stein and Day.

Davis, A. Y. (1981). *Women, Race and Class.* New York: Random House.

Dawson, M. C. (1995). *Behind the Mule: Race and Class in African American Politics.* Princeton: Princeton University Press.

Du Bois, W. (1903/1990). *Souls of Black Folk.* New York: Vintage Books.

Emmerling, R., & Goleman, D. (2003, October 1). *Reprints of Articles.* Retrieved August 2, 2016, from Consortium for Research on Emotional Intelligence in Organizations: http://www.eiconsorium.org

Fanon, F. (1967). *Black Skin, White Masks* (C. L. Markmann, Trans.). New York: Grove Weidenfeld Press.

Farley, R., & Alba, R. (2002). The New Second Generation in the United States. *International Migration Review, 36*(3), 669–701.

Feagin, J. R. (1991, February). The Continuing Significance of Race: Antiblack Discrimination in Public Places. *American Sociological Review, 56*(1), 101–116.

Featherston, E., & Ishibashi, J. (2004). Oreos and Bananas: Conversations on Whiteness. In V. Lea & J. Helfand (Eds.), *Identifying Race and Transforming Whiteness in the Classroom*. New York: Peter Lang.

Freeman, J. B., & Ambady, N. (2011). A Dynamic Interactive Theory of Person Construal. *Psychological Review, 118*, 247–279.

Freeman, J. B., Penner, A. M., Saperstein, A., Scheutz, M., & Ambady, N. (2011). Looking the Part: Social Status Cues Shape Race Perception. *PLoS ONE, 6*(9), 1–10.

Frey, W. H. (2014). *Diversity Explosion: How New Racial Demographics are Remaking America*. Washington, DC: Brookings Institution Press.

Gaddis, S. M. (2015). Discrimination in the Credentialed Society: An Audit Study of Race and College Selectivity in the Labor Market. *Social Forces, 93*(4), 1451–1479.

Gans, H. J. (2005). Race as Class. *Context, 4*(November), 17–21.

Gershman, J. (2016, September 16). *Appeals Court: Employees Don't Have a Right to Wear Dreadlocks*. Retrieved September 20, 2016, from *Wall Street Journal*: http://blogs.wsj.com/law/2016/09/16/appeals-court-employees-dont-have-a-right-to-wear-dreadlocks

Goffman, E. (1959). *Presentation of Self in Everyday Life*. New York: Anchor books.

Goleman, D. (2001). Emotional Intelligence: Issues in Paradigm Building. In C. Cherniss & D. Goleman (Eds.), *The Emotionally Intelligent Workplace* (pp. 13–26). San Francisco: Jossey-Bass.

Hall, S. (1997). *Representation: Cultural Representations and Signifying Practices*. London: Sage Publications.

Hall, S. (1999). Encoding, Decoding. In S. During (Ed.), *The Cultural Studies Reader* (pp. 90–103). London: Routledge.

Harris-Perry, M. (2011). *Sister Citizen: Shame, Stereotypes and Black Women in America*. New Haven: Yale University Press.

hooks, b. (1997). Representing Whiteness in Black Imagination. In R. Frankenberg (Ed.), *Displaying Whiteness: Essays in Social and Cultural Criticism* (pp. 165–179). Durham: Duke University Press.

Kaiser, S. B. (2001). Foreword. In E. Tseëlon (Ed.), *Masquerade and Identities: Essays on Gender, Sexuality and Marginality* (pp. xiii–xixv). London: Routledge.

Lee, S., & Edmonston, B. (2005). New Marriages, New Families: U.S. Racial and Hispanic Intermarriage. *Population Bulletin, 60*(2), 3–36.

Massey, D., & Denton, N. (1993). *American Apartheid: Segregation and the Making of the Underclass*. Cambridge, MA: Harvard University Press.

Pattillo, M. (2000/2013). *Black Picket Fences: Privilege and Peril Among the Black Middle Class.* Chicago: University of Chicago Press.

Penner, A. M., & Saperstein, A. (2008). How Social Status Shapes Race. *Proceedings of the National Academy of Sciences of the United States of America. 105*, pp. 19628–19630. National Academy of Science.

Pew Research Center. (2015, June 12). *Interracial Marriage: Who is 'Marrying Out'?* (Wang, & Wendy, Eds.). Retrieved June 29, 2016, from Fact Tank: http://www.pewresearch.org/fact-tank/2015/06/12/interracial-marriage-who-is-marrying-out/

Pilgrim, D. (2015). *Understanding Jim Crow: Using Racist Memorabilia to Teach Tolerance and Social Justice.* Oakland: PM Press.

Reardon, S., Fox, L., & Townsend, J. (2015). Neighborhood Income Composition by Household Race and Income, 1990–2009. *Annals of the American Academy of Political and Social Science, 660*(1), 78–97.

Rosenfeld, M. J. (2008). Racial, Educational, and Religious Endogamy in the United States: A Comparative Historical Perspective. *Social Forces, 87*(1), 1–32.

Royster, D. (2003). *Race and the Invisible Hand: How White Networks Exclude Black Men from Blue Collar Jobs.* Oakland: University of California Press.

Sampson, R. J. (2012). *Great American City: Chicago and the Enduring Neighborhood Effect.* Chicago: University of Chicago Press.

Sharkey, P. (2014). Spatial Segmentation and the Black Middle Class. *American Journal of Sociology, 4*(January), 903–954.

Shore, B. (1996). *Culture in Mind: Cognition, Culture and the Problem of Meaning.* New York: Oxford University Press.

Spivak, G. C. (1988/2008). Can the Subaltern Speak? In J. Sharp, *Geographies on PostColonialism.* Thousand Oaks: Sage Publications.

Sterling, C. (2012). *African Roots, Brazilian Rites: Cultural and National Identity in Brazil.* New York: Palgrave Macmillan.

Telles, E. E. (2006). *Race in Another America: The Significance of Skin Color in Brazil.* Princeton: Princeton University Press.

The United States Census Bureau. (2012, September 1). *The Two or More Races Population: 2010.* Retrieved February 10, 2013, from U.S. Census Brief 2012: http://www.census.gov/prod/cen2010/briefs/c2010br-13.pdf

Thompson, S. V. (1996). Perceived Experiences of Racism as Stressful Life Events. *Community Mental Health Journal, 32*, 233–248.

Torngren, S. O. (2016). Attitudes Toward Interracial Marriages and the Role of Interracial Contacts in Sweden. *Ethnicities, 16*(4), 568–588.

Torres, L., Driscoll, M., & Burrow, A. (2010). Racial Microaggressions and Psychological Functioning Among Highly Achieving African Americans: A Mixed Methods Approach. *Journal of Social and Clinical Psychology, 29*(10), 1074–1099.

Travis, D., Thorpe-Moscon, J., & McCluney, C. (2016). *Emotional Tax: How Black Women and Men Pay More at Work and How Leaders Can Take Action*. New York: Catalyst.

Tseëlon, E. (2001). *Masquerade and Identities: Essays on Gender, Sexuality and Marginality*. London: Routledge.

Utsey, S. O., Giesbrecht, N., Hook, J., & Stanard, P. M. (2008). Cultural, Sociofamilial and Psychological Resources that Inhibit Psychological Distress in African Americans Exposed to Stressful Life Events and Race-related Stress. *Journal of Counseling Psychology, 55*(1), 49–62.

West, C. (1985). The Dilemma of the Black Intellectual. *Journal of Cultural Critique, 1*, 109–124.

Winfrey Harris, T. (2015). *The Sisters are Alright: Changing the Broken Narrative About Black Women in America*. Oakland: Berrett-Koehler Publishers.

Wing Sue, D. (2010). *Microaggressions in Everyday Life: Race, Gender and Sexual Orientation*. New York: Wiley & Sons.

Wing Sue, D., Nadal, K. L., Capdilupo, C. M., Lin, A. I., Rivera, D. P., & Torino, G. C. (2008). Racial Microaggressions Against Black Americans: Implications for Counseling. *Journal of Counseling and Development, 86*(3), 330–338.

CHAPTER 8

Transnational Community Ties, Black Philanthropy, and Triple Identity Consciousness

Given the rich and complex history of the relationship between African Americans and generations of Caribbean immigrants (as contextualized in Chap. 2), I asked the MSGCIs to discuss their understanding and conception of community, as it exists today and whether they see the dominance of white hegemony fueling the tension between black intragroups. The MSGCIs elaborated on the Caribbean immigrants' (and their children's) problematic use of social distancing strategies as well as African Americans' concern that black immigrants maintain an exit option to return to their home countries to avoid racism as the two major factors for this intragroup divide. To overcome these challenges, the MSGCIs see value in promoting a common racial identity that unites people of African descent—African roots, shared aspects of history, experiences with European colonialism and postcolonialism and slavery. At the same time they also see the importance and value of celebrating the beauty and diversity of black ethnicity that exists in the United States and beyond.

For the MSGCIs, the diversity of blackness is integral to their conceptualization of what the black community means to them: the Pan African, diasporic experience of African descended people in the Americas. In fact, several MSGCIs felt that the diversity of blackness brings about a particular critical consciousness and the ability to perceive oppression within social, political, and economic realms needed to encourage others to take action against oppressive systems—a triple identity consciousness (also see the

© The Author(s) 2018
Y.S. Lorick-Wilmot, *Stories of Identity among Black,
Middle Class, Second Generation Caribbeans,*
DOI 10.1007/978-3-319-62208-8_8

work of Freire 1970). Therefore, carrying shared racial experiences helps the MSGCIs to shift singularity of ethnic difference into unity or a saliency of blackness. This is not to negate or ignore the "ambiguities and contradictions that exist when people inhabit a space of multiplicity" (see de la Rey et al. 1997:22). In effect, triple identity consciousness reconciles the strong need for the MSGCIs to avoid choosing to inhabit only one context or identity when it comes to their race and ethnicity. An awareness of this option rejects mutual exclusivity of race and ethnic identities and instead embraces all aspects of identity including class, gender, and sexuality as mutually enforcing a person's position and interests.

DEFINING COMMUNITY, BLACK PHILANTHROPY, AND TRANSNATIONAL TIES

Defining Community and the Collective Consciousness of a Black Community

The concept of community is multivariable. For some, its conceptualization is based on a specific geographic space or locale in which people live. For others and particularly those in sociology and other social sciences, the concept of community is based on the notion of place—where geographic spaces carry social meaning and value through which individuals develop an understanding regarding its functionality in their lives. Of the two broad conceptualizations, I contend, the notion of community as place is also a lens through which all people, including the MSGCIs, are able to: evaluate their own identity, social position, politics, and practices as well as those of others; develop a psychological and/or emotional attachment to the meanings and values of a "community" and the people/groups associated with it; and make the determination regarding their process of membership into a "community." In this regard, community as place is both a symbol of affinity and a point for unification and collective action.

When I consider MSGCI triple identity consciousness and their conceptualization of community and black habitus, I look to Joseph Gusfield who examined the notion of community as place. According to Gusfield (1975), the concept was initially constructed as a "consciousness of kind," a theoretical framework coined by Franklin Henry Giddings. Both Gusfield and Giddings argued that the evaluations people are engaged in when considering their identification and membership with a group reveals a self-consciousness that is "the explicit recognition of common and exclusive interests that rest on communal foundations...which takes the form of a distinguishing group label... a 'symbol of community' is an 'essential part of the development of communal affinity'" (Gusfield 1975:34; see also Giddings 1922). In this regard, the notion of community as place can also become a signifier of identity that situates both an individual and a group not only within the specific context of a physical space or land but also ideologically—socially, historically, and politically.

These definitions of "community" warranted discussion because much of the discourse on black identity revolves around the cultural collectiveness of blackness and the black community. Although Maureen Mahon (2000:286) makes an important point, which I also assert early on in this book, "there is no single black identity shared by all black [people], that black people are not a monolithic group and that multiple versions of blackness coexists," the notion of community as place as a signifier of identity does point to the existence of a collective black identity that is (to a certain degree) engendered by a history of racialization, racial stigma, and oppression for the African descended across the Americas.

Indeed, I think it is essential to examine the lingering vestiges of the trauma of slavery and subjugation and its impacts on the ways individuals within the African diaspora perceive themselves and relate to one another regardless of their different social classes and life experiences—an exigency I must contend with. It is also important, however, that I emphasize the trauma of slavery and the cultural memory of oppression should not be considered the sole defining characteristic in the narrative on black collectivity and what it means to be black in the black community. Unfortunately, the racialized state of being "black" in the Americas, in my opinion, focuses primarily on embodying a common origin and a past identity of former slave. At the same time, society also refuses to fully acknowledge and make amends for its complicity in committing crimes against humanity of the African descendant. Generations of continued racialization, racial stigma, and systemic oppression for the African descended across the Americas today—often because of genealogy and/or phenotype—is difficult to overcome and forget.

In fact, Ron Eyerman (2001:15) argues in *Cultural Trauma: Slavery and the Formation of the African American Identity*, the commonality of slavery and its trauma for the African descended strongly articulates:

a membership group as it identifies an event or an experience, a primal scene that solidifies individual/collective identity. This event, now identified with the formation of the group, must be recollected by later generations who have had no experience of the "original" event, yet continue to be identified by it [by others] and to identify themselves through it. Because of its distance from the event and because its social circumstances have altered with time, each succeeding generation reinterprets and represents the collective memory around that event according to its needs and means.

The hegemony of racialization as well as the shared cultural memory and trauma that often frames the lives of blacks in the Americas forges a collective consciousness[1] (see Durkheim 1893/1997) or a "consciousness of kind" that defines "the black community" for both blacks and non-blacks alike. Notwithstanding this, collective consciousness helps to establish recollections of a shared and historically rooted past through a set of beliefs, attitudes, ideologies, and rituals as a temporal map—which serves to unify (and create solidarity among) groups of people. Within this temporal map, processes of racial formation are constructed in tandem; "individual identities are shaped as experiential frameworks formed out of, as they are embedded within, narratives of past, present and future" (Eyerman 2001:6). In this regard, the black collective consciousness and the social construction of a black community can have a profound impact on a person's identity formation and assertion, his or her awareness of the spatial landscape in which he or she lives, and his or her role in constituting a group identity when it comes to public representation as both an individual and as part of a collective. To understand MSGCI black collective identity, we must also consider community as place as it relates to their perspective on diasporic blackness and what it means for intragroup diversity and intragroup relations.

MSGCIs' Conception of a Black Community and Black Philanthropy: Connecting Triple Identity Consciousness

Conceptions of a black community, as defined by the MSGCIs, reject anti-black beliefs and practices that relegate African descendants as a monolith but embrace and celebrate the variety of different historical and cultural experiences, structures of behaviors, values, customs, and rituals that are particular to African descendants in various parts of the Americas and abroad. For the MSGCI, the black community is the place and space where these elements—characteristics and practices—reinforce the cultural retentions of ideas and activities that shape the consciousness and behavior of African descended people.

In my own interpretations of their triple identity consciousness, I also observed many MSGCIs describing themselves as having adopted a transnational racial consciousness (see Quintana and Segura-Henera 2003; Quintana 2007) that links to the multiplicity of different experiences and perspectives blacks have with race across time and space—which they believe is necessary for the survival of a multifaceted black community. Indeed, transnationalism as experienced through the "every day activities shaped by multiple connections and linkages to several nations and cultures via travel, technology, and media" inform MSGCIs' conceptions of a black community as transnational and their role in it (Basch et al. 1994:48).

If you recall, almost all the MSGCIs in this study have lived outside of the United States and/or have traveled extensively to different parts of the world, including returning to their parents' countries of origin. To some extent as well, the MSGCIs describe participating in various aspects of black life in these locales through the dense networks they maintain with people and organizations that span across geographic borders. In thinking about their triple identity consciousness as embodying themes of transnationalism, I infer the MSGCIs' value in the diverse experiences of blacks and the ways in which African descendants are connected in order to build and participate in a black community is based on some of the features and qualities in the concept "diaspora." For example, Safran (1991) describes members of a diasporic community as (1) having and maintaining a sense of collective consciousness and solidarity with members of a community who share a history of being dispersed from a common point of origin or a homeland; (2) often experiencing discrimination and marginality; and (3) constructing memories of the common point of origin (i.e., the Motherland, Africa) and expressing a deep longing for the eventual return (or long visit) to their homeland. Here, a participant, Michelle discusses her conceptualization of black community and ethnicity as it relates to her awareness of the diasporic conditions of the African descended:

MICHELLE

The black community is everything I am and represent. It's not the "melting pot" or "fruit salad" that I learned about growing up. I am not interested in talking about race in that way. It is about impacting local communities here and also being concerned about what is happening outside of the community—across the country and around the world. Whether we were brought to America as slaves or came as immigrants, there are generations of folks that are responsible for ensuring the uplifting of our collective circumstance economically, socially, and culturally. Whether we are Muslim, speak Spanish, are dark-skinned or not, that's the beauty of the diversity of our people in the community. The divide and conquer that exists within our community is what is tearing us all apart.

Michelle went on to describe how she has benefited from living in communities with both first- and second generation immigrants like herself and African Americans and the ways her community helps to shape her understanding about the fluidity of transnational spaces and places.

At the same time, however, I also believe MSGCIs' triple identity consciousness is more complicated and nuanced than simply adopting a transnational race consciousness. The MSGCIs' awareness of the ways various African descended groups are socially positioned within black intragroup contexts and in the larger US society are more than a diasporic condition. I contend the MSGCIs' awareness is based on their acknowledgement of the cultural shifts that have occurred in the world and what that means for the future of society (Anthias 1998). Therefore, we can see MSGCIs' awareness and performance of their cultural capital strategies give rise to an identity that incorporates notions of race, ethnicity, immigrant generation, class, and gender in multiple ways which help to guide their philanthropic activities and participation in black community spaces and places, both in the United States and abroad. Hence, I consider the philosophy and practice of "giving back" and black philanthropy, and the conditions in which several MSGCIs link their philanthropy to the communities they live in, the transnational connections they choose to maintain with their parents' country of origin and other geographic boundaries. My focus on the concept of black philanthropy and MSGCIs' engagement with it generally speaking is critical to understanding the impetus for the various practices people of African descent develop when creating a habitus of blackness and the space and place of community—both local and symbolic.

The MSGCIs framed the philosophy and practice of "giving back" to the black community in two intersecting ways: (1) their linked fates with other African descendants in the Americas and (2) their family's experiences with black emigrant mobility. According to the MSGCIs, giving back involved providing financial, time, and social support, sometimes on a regular basis (e.g., monthly), to both family members and co-ethnics. When I asked the MSGCIs to speak a bit more about the specific activities they engaged in while "giving back," 95% (19 out of 20) cited to helping family members pay bills and navigate social service systems; 75% (15 out of 20) tithe to local churches, 90% (18 out of 20) mentor young people, donate their "time, talent and treasure" to US based, local, and national community organizations including fraternal and/or affinity organizations; and 85% (17 out of 20) establish programs and organizations, donate medical services and/or supplies, make contributions toward technology, equipment and educational materials, and conduct trainings to enhance communities outside of the United States. Their reasons for engaging in these various forms of giving were often couched in terms of their connections to other blacks and/or people of color. Here, Claudette applies her definition of community to the concept of linked fates, in her own words. She says:

CLAUDETTE

Community is really the sense of how we build a shared space and place with other people. When I look at my physical community, there are people with different incomes in living in the same area. There are many diverse people representing a range of cultural backgrounds but it is largely of black folks from different parts of the world. I'd say very international and an important part of the community. And that is the reality of the world I would like to pass on to my children. When I think about my community—my black community, I also think of it as sharing a certain sense or value around black people overcoming racism and discrimination, and wanting to get to the next place in life together, like I am my brother's/my sister's keeper? Where globally we are really focused on bolstering other black people and giving back to the community. I think about it in terms of advancing opportunities not just for families and us but also for others in the community. There's a real responsibility we have to one another.

Like Claudette who expressed linked fates as having "real responsibility" for other blacks, many of the MSGCIs achieved middle class mobility within one generation, and often expressed a sense of obligation to assist other blacks, especially those in strained economic circumstances *because who else would do it?* as Eddy posited (see also the works of Billingsley 1992; Dawson 1995). In fact, the MSGCIs' educational and employment experiences within the United States afforded them more contact with diverse blacks (e.g., African Americans, Afro-Latinos) and other racial-ethnics as classmates and colleagues, thereby increasing the likelihood for them to positively associate with and have more psychological attachments toward these intragroup members. This concept rang true for the MSGCIs, especially in situations where members of these groups have shared racial heritage within racialized contexts. Therefore, the notion of linked fate for persons of African descent in the United States makes people of color acutely aware of the power of race and inequality and its impact on life outcomes, and also incentivizes them to want to make a difference (Thorton et al. 2013). Community becomes the space and place where the MSGCIs manage the intractable and enduring features of race and class on their daily experiences and the practice of giving back helps the MSGCIs manage the stress of racialization.

MSGCIs' desire and, perhaps at times, obligation to make a difference in their community also stems from their own economic and social experiences of growing up in working or lower middle class immigrant households. As the children of racial-ethnic immigrants, they also described the philosophy of giving back as important to the mobility and sustainability of black emigrants—whether from different parts of the United States or globally. Talking about their knowledge of black migration but also of their immigrant parents and members of their Caribbean families, the MSGCIs discussed struggle and sacrifice migrants often make for their family to have a better life and how this understanding informs their philanthropy and black collectivist orientation.

Eddy describes how this notion of philanthropy has influenced his role in making a difference in his local community. He talks about his involvement in mentoring youth of color and how this small act affirms for him the need to support other blacks. Interestingly, Eddy thinks of giving back as being engaged in black history.

EDDY explains:

> These young men need positive examples of black men doing something positive. I stay engaged; I tutor, serve on the boards of local organizations. I've also made the effort to learn about black American history and Civil Rights. Caribbean people and their descendants have always been involved in the movement. I can appreciate the struggle; it's in my blood. Today, these young men don't have a clue. I am here to be their friend, a role model, to show them there are other ways to get to drive a nice car, and own your own place. Now, I feel I am making black history too.

His discussion of philanthropy and the black community could be viewed as a contradictory space of ethnic identification. Participants like Eddy described the black community as a place of common marginality signified by a solidarity of a shared history and ancestry. For other MSGCIs, the notion of philanthropy and community could also be seen as a new and re-constructed socio-cultural environment in which he would have an identifiable part to play—as a mentor and role model to youth in his community (see Hall, "Cultural Identity and Diaspora" 392–403; Hall, "Subjects in History: Making Diasporic Identities" 289–300).

In the same way the MSGCIs navigate between their black identification and racialization and their ethnic immigrant origins and sensibilities, I assert, they also do so when it comes to their middle class status. Whether it is in circumstances where the MSGCIs are the singular blacks in white spaces or living in and/or participating in communities with working class blacks (native and foreign-born), navigating different class contexts shaped their ideas about blackness and black ethnicity, black authenticity and habitus (Pattillo 2007). In large part, the MSGCIs connect these ideas to their efforts around "striving" as discussed in previous chapters. The MSGCIs look to their own class mobility or efforts for striving as an important factor to building racial and ethnic solidarity. Interestingly, their perspective is in stark contrast to the points traditional assimilation theorists argue—that economically assimilated immigrants and their children will eventually cut ties to ethnic communities and enclaves as part of their assimilation into American life (Gordon 1964). In fact, the MSGCIs' presence in their local and global communities intends to bridge human and social capital gaps as they provide information about employment, education, and access to networks and structures that support schools and local "minority owned" business, and contribute financial capital to fund scholarships and various programs. The MSGCIs adamantly argue they understand, first hand, the stress and the structural and attitudinal barriers to black upward mobility.

Several MSGCIs mentioned a prevailing assumption they believed other blacks hold toward them—that, despite their black and Caribbean migrant roots, they are disconnected from "real" black people because of their middle class status. I contend the questioning of MSGCI "blackness" and whether they are black (enough) to participate within the habitus of blackness is, of course, constructed in relationship to whiteness for transgressing racial and class boundaries. Yet, this stereotype—regardless of immigrant generation or not—appears to consistently create social distance between black social classes. Here, Robert expresses his frustration with the assumption that because of his material success and upward mobility into white structures, he has lost "touch" with the black community he grew up in and gives back to. He elaborates:

ROBERT

> It is a difficult and delicate line. How are you perceived? Are you still down enough even as you dress in your fancy clothes and drive a nice car? I get it that I represent the "establishment." But at the same time, I am not there to be used as an example for you to feel bad about yourself because you think that I think you couldn't get your shit together. It's not all perfect when you get to this level. It's not like white people let you in and it's good and that you're all set. They still treat you like shit and try to play you. Now what that does say in all of this post-racial rhetoric is that race still matters.

Recognizing the persistence of this stereotype Robert described, scholars such as Hwang et al. (1998) argue that the social distance between working and middle class blacks may be attributed to the greater inclination among the middle class to explain black-white inequality using structural (e.g., government and institutional-sanctioned racism, profiling and redlining) rather than individualistic (e.g., personal responsibility) terms. Despite significant class differences in views about what is responsible for black–white inequality, Hwang et al. (1998:377) found that both groups of blacks "joined in a united front with their attitudes serving as grim reminders of the racial inequalities created and maintained by the current stratification system." Ensuring the hegemonic forces that support anti-black racism and serve to incite intragroup divisions do not continue to strain relationships between the African descended in the Americas, the MSGCIs talk extensively on ways transnational community ties can transcend and resist subjugation and build a stronger black community globally.

Transnational Ties and Triple Identity Consciousness

Overall, the topic of race and its negative effects on people of color in the United States weighed heavily on the hearts and minds of the MSGCIs. While I found MSGCIs' discussions of community as place and the importance of global connections of solidarity between blacks as important to their articulations of a triple identity consciousness, their narratives also revealed the importance of maintaining transnational ties to their parents' homeland and other countries in the world. Considering the role the institution of family has in identity construction, the MSGCIs' maintenance of transnational ties to their parents' countries of origin is an important component of their psychological relationship to the community as place and their interpersonal relationships with the individuals in these communities.

In this regard, MSGCIs' connections to the Caribbean and its specific cultures solidify their social identity and group belonging as "the children of Caribbean immigrants."

MSGCIs' transnational ties and connections to the Caribbean were established by their parents' generation, who determined the MSGCIs' depth of relationship with the country and culture, the frequency of visits and extent of communication with the people in the country when they were children. All the MSGCIs visited and spent various periods of time in their parents' country of origin. In some circumstances, these were short visits or annual pilgrimages. For others, it required an extended stay when their parents engaged in a parenting strategy or "transnational solutions" and sent them to stay with relatives (see Kasinitz et al. 2008:155). Decisions for month-long stays were often dependent on the MSGCI parents' financial situation or out of a concern that their son or daughter needed additional social-emotional support. For the MSGCIs, their parents' choice to visit their country of origin and bring the MSGCIs along with them serves as a significant influence in inculcating the importance of maintaining connections to transnational social spaces and networks.

As the MSGCIs got older, their focus on re-establishing these transnational connections and ties became critical to their psychological wellbeing, in two distinct ways. First, the MSGCIs' transnational activity shifted at various points in their lives (late adolescence and through college) and was often dependent upon the demands of school then later, work and family obligations (Levitt 2002; Vickerman 2002). As they came of age and became re-immersed into their parents' world of consistently traveling back and forth to the Caribbean and/or sending remittances to relatives in their country of origin, the MSGCIs described learning to appreciate and understand their parents' and their own childhood from an adult perspective. Having the opportunity to gain insight and develop a growing appreciation for their parents' transnational activities gave the MSGCIs the confidence of knowing they have the emotional support of their family—both near and far. Second, renewing their connection or ties to the people and circumstances of their parents' country of origin served as a tangible resource for the development of the MSGCIs' triple identity consciousness. These connections enabled the MSGCIs to create community as both a place and space that transcends their US circumstance and makes the stress of anti-black racism and other modes of oppression survivable. Here, Joachim explains why being middle class is important to him, both professionally and personally, and how his class status is connected to his conceptions of black philanthropy and transnational connections.

JOACHIM

Being middle class and having the opportunities—economic and otherwise, that is important to me doing my part here and outside of the U.S. I stood on the shoulders of giants who lifted me up. Now I am lifting up others, black brothers and sisters, to stand on my shoulders so they can do the same for others one day. Everyday I work with families and young people. I go into organizations and work with community funders who sometimes don't get the issues the poor, the immigrant, and the youth deal with. It's not easy. The racism and xenophobia that is expressed here [the United States] is unbelievable. It is also discouraging. It's stressful. But because of the work I do, I am a voice. It's like what I tell the young men I mentor: be the change they want to see in the world. Knowing that keeps pushing me in a society that wants to see me fail and shrivel up into a worthless piece of nothing. For me, I feel we must rise above all of that negativity and use the resources we have access to—the education, the knowledge around financial literacy, you know, to be stronger as a people. I do this work because it is bigger than me, than you and any one person.

Looking at their own access to economic resources, MSGCIs like Joachim are aware of the presumed privilege that comes along with their middle class status and material success. It is this awareness, however, that encourages the MSGCIs to persevere through the psychological costs of their black singularity to do more for members of the black communities they participate in and are connected to—both in the United States and abroad. In particular, the MSGCIs' efforts around social justice and community-building—as Joachim put it, *is bigger than me, than you, and any one person*—reject ideologies of individualism and meritocracy established in the American ethos, which would prefer to have the MSGCIs focus solely on their own long-term financial mobility. Reflecting on my conversation with Joachim and others, it appears that MSGCIs' concern for the black communities they align themselves with and their experiences with racialization and subjugation, despite their individual material success, continues to affirm the fact that this second generation black immigrant group will not have a similar assimilation trajectory as twentieth century European immigrants have had. Hence, their philanthropy goes beyond the enduring assimilation paradox of immigrant connection or rejection of parents' country of origin.

Several MSGCIs also thought of their parents' countries of origin and other majority black countries in the Caribbean and Africa as locales for their "giving back" and other philanthropic activities, while there were some who considered these locales as possible exit options from the stresses of US racism. For some MSGCIs, the stresses of racialization led to feelings of dislocation and even nostalgia for their parents' homeland. They hope life would be easier if they lived in a country that did not discriminate against them just because of how others perceived them and their blackness. At the time these conversations took place, a few of the MSGCIs were already in the process of applying for citizenship in their parents' home countries and/or looking for employment opportunities to leave the United States for other countries in Latin America and the Caribbean, Eurasia and Southern Europe, and parts of western and southern Africa.

For others, the feelings of a nostalgic bond with their parents' home country and Caribbean culture were not as strong as they were with their immigrant parents' generation but recognized their need to maintain a connection to and relationship with these communities and to have their own children continue the tradition. These MSGCIs were not inclined to return to their parents' home countries on a permanent basis, such as Lisa, who sometimes found conditions in some Caribbean countries to be less than ideal:

LISA

I couldn't live there forever, especially in some remote [rural] part where the electricity goes off at eight o'clock or there's no consistent Internet [laughs].

Instead, some of these MSGCIs were focused on building ties with local Caribbean and African communities and institutions through various remittance activities and philanthropic efforts. To be clear, monetary remittances is an important aspect of MSGCIs' participation in their parents' home country—a fact which scholars Kasintiz et al. (2008) and Basch et al. (1994) have focused on among second generation immigrants in the United States, when it comes to sending money to relatives and supporting community projects. Different from their parents' generation, however, the MSGCIs do not engage with their parents' country of origin with the same intensity, frequency, or activity. For instance, several MSGCI parents' still own property (i.e., land and houses) that they maintain in addition to caring for elderly relatives. Here, Isaac describes how his parents remain transnationally connected to Haiti:

ISAAC

> They have varying degrees of engagement in Haiti. For instance my parents, they both still have houses there. We still have relatives in Haiti. My father goes there and spends time in his house pretty frequently. My mom may not go back as often as my father but she still stays engaged in the politics and social happenings. It's important to them to remain connected, especially because they own property there.

In circumstances where there are no properties or relatives to send monetary remittances to for the care and management, the MSGCIs are still engaged in their philanthropic activities, which often means sustaining small communities via social, economic, and political activities such as fundraising for schools or medical clinics, and facilitating workshops and educational trainings for women and children. The MSGCIs see these activities to be equally important to the ones they engage in while in the United States. The consistent sentiment across my conversations with these MSGCIs was that their nativity of being "an American" and "black in America" was very much a part of their identity as a child of Caribbean immigrants so much so that any idea to give up or not support any ongoing efforts toward racial justice, gender equality, and overall freedom for all black people in the United States would jeopardize the wellbeing of all black ethnics throughout the diaspora. Here, Isaac makes this point, yet frames this sentiment within the context of being a "citizen of the world" which he discussed earlier. He says:

ISAAC

> One of the important lessons I learned from my parents but also as I have gotten older and have traveled to Haiti and other black nations is to see legacy of the people before you and the potential of who will come after you. I also take a lesson from my mother; she's conscious. So, she retired but has been a translator for decades and continues to do it part-time. She works with and helps translate for new immigrant patients in different organizations. She is still very much actively engaged in the Haitian community here in Boston just as she is down in Haiti and that is important. Again, that goes back to being a citizen of the world.

Isaac's notion of "citizen of the world" exemplified the MSGCIs' triple identity consciousness—of seeing the connections and the importance of uplifting blacks of the diaspora—which anchors them into believing they are reflected in the hearts and minds of the people in these geographically spaces. Further, by connecting to these individuals in these geographic spaces, the MSGCIs feel they are able to affirm their purpose for the greater good. Below, Isaac continues to link "citizen of the world" to the role of the community and his opinion as to how MSGCIs and other African descendants should be engaged with the global black community. He explains:

ISAAC

> I like Haitian community organizations that are focused on both Haitian and Haitian-American issues and are engaged in service activities and work collaboratively with other organizations on economic and business development in Haiti and across the Caribbean region. That's taking a diaspora approach; a Black Nationalist approach, which means you are a part of the continuum. When I think about slavery and the Middle Passage, and despite where we landed, we are part of the larger black community in the world and we need to make sure that we are all advancing together as a community. Yes, I have Africa tattooed on my shoulder because I have long since realized the connection between my Haitian identity, my blackness, and Africa. I make the connections to history. I feel it and know we need to stand up on our own two feet, together. And when I was at [HBCU] this was further inculcated for me. [...] For me, it's not just our job to excel at what we do in these big institutions and just be happy or complacent to be in the room. As black people, as middle class people, as Caribbean people, as bona fide members of the African diaspora, it is our job to give back resources to our black community. Yes, get the skills and know how to access and manage the resources. I'm speaking liberation and theology.

While some MSGCIs may view their "giving back" to relatives abroad as stressful to manage at times because of their busy family and work schedules, I contend the MSGCIs like Isaac support these transnational ties not out of "joy" but because they support these ties out of the emotional and psychological need to buffer the damaging effects of white supremacy and *making sure we are all advancing together as a community*—as Isaac mentioned above. This is not to say the MSGCIs do not experience a positive, immediate emotion when engaged in an activity that benefits another human being. According to the MSGCIs, however, the effects of white supremacy become amplified so much so that because of their middle class status, race, gender, and so on, they pay a high psychological price daily. Their everyday experiences in the United States, as the MSGCIs described themselves, do not indicate they have the protective social networks to insulate them from racism; therefore, they look to transnational connections as a potential source of power, information, and support. In this regard, establishing and maintaining these connections becomes a clear motivator for the MSGCIs' middle class "striving." Here, Rosalie reflects on the American Dream ethos and describes how her material success is more about leveraging it to better improve those in the diaspora:

ROSALIE

> I think about the American Dream and then I think I am living it. Being middle class, especially when I compare our lives to family still in the Bronx, there is privilege that you sometimes forget you have if you are not aware of how you are supposed to use it. I became a lawyer to make a difference. I am not saying that it is the middle class's job to solve all of the problems because we may have more money or influence but we have an important part in making things better. I am not sure if the American Dream is really attainable for all of us. People are still racist, they say or do ignorant things. The communities I work in cannot wait for those people to change their minds. I use my skills to help write a grant for the community center or help parents advocate for their kids when we all go into the school board meeting. Or use some of my money to purchase or donate books for the kids down in P.R [Puerto Rico]. It's everywhere we have to touch.

Similar to Rosalie, all the MSGCIs realize the immense privilege they have—relative to the individuals of their parents' country of origin in terms of material resources and opportunities (a previously discussed). At the same time, the MSGCIs' giving back is intended to contribute to the social fabric in positive ways and should not be considered a form of cultural imperialism, particularly in their parents' home country. Through these philanthropic activities and "giving back," they enrich their collective consciousness about the issues that persist for the people in these countries because they recognize there is a shared reality that connects them all in spite of the intragroup diversity and are determined to ensure that the individuals across these communities have their voices heard.

CONCLUSION

In this chapter, the MSGCIs' discussion of their community, philanthropy, and transnational connections and ties is critical to understanding how their triple identity consciousness is encouraged and accessed as a source of hope and survival, despite society's structures that (directly and indirectly) contribute to the perpetual exclusion, disadvantage, and exploitation of African descended. The stories shared here challenge dominantly entrenched preconceptions, beliefs, or tropes that conceal the MSGCIs' humanity in ways that justify their invisibility because of the privileges associated with a middle class status.

In particular, the MSGCIs' operationalization of community via black philanthropy, and its implications for their children's generation, reveals a duality of optimism and pessimism for the future. On the one hand, the MSGCIs' indoctrination within the US middle class social structure reveals the omnipresence of the American Creed, the belief that hard work can still reap public rewards to those who have earned it—again, the American middle class dream. On the other hand, MSGCIs' stories reveal a type of pessimism that develops, in part, as a result of the constant racialization and anti-black racism. They are pessimistic regarding the merits of true racial progress and equality for all. The historically disenfranchised and subjugated still have a long way to go when it comes to government-sanctioned policies and programs that continue to privilege whites (and particularly middle class whites). At its core, MSGCIs' narratives speak to their continued racialization as well as their realization of their ethnicized blackness.

When reflecting on the MSGCIs' middle class mobility and philanthropy in relationship to their second generation immigrant status, we must revisit the work of Milton Gordon (1964) and Philip Kasinitz et al. (2008) in order to challenge the enduring paradigms of immigrant assimilation that do not sufficiently explain the experiences of the MSGCIs. As I discussed previously, proponents of straight-line assimilation consider it a process of integration that determine the life outcomes for immigrants and their children. Scholars Alejandro Portes, Ruben Rumbaut, Min Zhou, Michael Omi, and Howard Winant emphasize segmented assimilation trajectories of upward mobility (linking to ethnic enclaves) or downward mobility (rapid Americanization and having an adversarial stance/oppositional identity) for the second generation immigrant. Others such as Philip Kasintiz et al. (2008) in *Inheriting the City* argue the second generation's trajectory reflect both a native advantage (language and cultural acquisition that their parents do not have; access to affirmative action programming and institutions) and an immigrant advantage (ethnic networks and supports) that strategically positions them between two different social systems—a type of biculturalism—which aids in their upward mobility.

Because the MSGCIs discuss their transnational ties as important to their conceptions of black community and philanthropy and not about being bicultural, I am wary to agree with Kasintiz et al. (2008:352–353) when they emphasize immigrant advantage and specifically immigrant parents' immeasurable characteristics as one of three contributing factors to second generation success. On the one hand they argue,

> The second generation are the children of exceptional parents. Although parents may have measurable characteristics that put their children at risk—low education, low incomes, poor language skills, and so on—they have unmeasured characteristics that make them different kinds of parents, mostly in ways that are advantageous for their children.

Indeed, voluntary immigrants are a highly selective group and are presumed to carry a certain level of ambition, drive, and economic means (sometimes limited) to migrate from one nation to another. For immigrant parents in particular, their own measurable qualities to overcome obstacles in their new country and the lessons they learn in the process are ones that are transmitted onto the second generation—a factor the MSGCIs spoke to in Chaps. 5 and 6. The problem with emphasizing immigrant parents' exceptionalism, I contend, is it suggests that immigrant parents are different from or better at advocating for their children than native-born and/or other racial-ethnic parents because of their immigrant ambitions for their children in terms of education, and so forth. In this regard, "immigrant parent exceptionalism" reifies the trappings of the model-minority trope, which this research rejects.

On the other hand, Kasinitz et al. (2008) make an important observation that aligns well with the research presented in this book: that while there may be (native and immigrant) advantages tied to their second generation immigrant position of which the MSGCIs are aware, they develop strategies that impact their mobility. I, however, posit that we still need to push the analysis further. For instance, straight-line assimilation theorists would argue MSGCIs' mobility into the American middle class is a significant marker of assimilation. Throughout this chapter, however, I have demonstrated that it is the MSGCIs' triple identity consciousness that helps them to maintain ties to a black diaspora—not just to their parents' country of origin. In effect, it is this level of consciousness that informs the strategies for their mobility while also fulfilling their sense of community. This does not mean a duality of identity—the traditional binary of national home (United States) versus affinity home (e.g., parents' country of origin)—but one where their racial and ethnic identity, and diasporic ties and connections exist simultaneously.

Also, as I reflect on the MSGCIs' stories in their totality, I am reminded of Susan Bordo's book *Unbearable Weight* (1993:16) where she looks to the works of theorists Karl Marx and Michel Foucault on the roles anatomy and biology play as always interacting with culture. She says:

> What Marx and, later Foucault had in mind in focusing on the "direct grip" that culture has on our bodies, through the practices and the bodily habits of everyday life. Through routine, habitual activity, our bodies learn what is "inner" and what is "outer," which gestures are forbidden and which required, how violable or inviolable are the boundaries of our bodies, how much space around the body may be claimed, and so on. These are often far more powerful lessons than those we learn consciously, through explicit instruction concerning the appropriate behavior for our gender, race, and social class.

The MSGCIs' conceptualization of a racial identity—blackness—is based on their daily experiences through which they live through and internalize. The MSGCIs' definition and perceptions of blackness and their experiences within a black habitus, however, are also embedded in and constituted of history (see Merleau-Ponty 2004). Didier Fassin (2011:429) put it best by saying, "the historical experiences of race corresponds to the way people both individually and collectively, make sense of and give shape to events and situations through which they are racialized and racialize others." It is their shared understanding of these events that undergird MSGCIs' notions of community and the rationale for their philanthropic activities.

In thinking about the significance of racialization and postcolonial theory in identity construction, aspects of the MSGCI singular identity—being "black" for example—are often conferred upon them by an "other" in the articulation of who they are. In these moments it would appear that other people's drawing attention to their black identity (whether their phenotype matches the stereotype of being black or not) negates aspects of their identity and determining blackness as the singular and most dominant marker of identity. Yet, MSGCI experiences within these less salient identities are what shapes their actions, reactions, thoughts, and feelings for the future. It is because of these moments, I contend, we must refuse the fallacy that we live in a post-racial society; singularity of blackness is always pronounced as difference, a difference US society cannot overcome—including diversity of class and class mobility, ethnicity, gender, sexuality, and religion, for the children of immigrants. In the interim, the MSGCIs will rely on their triple identity consciousness to steadily guide their footsteps along a road that is defiantly oppressive, singing "We, Too, Sing America."

NOTES

1. Introduced by social theorist Emile Durkheim (1893) in *Division of Labour in Society*, collective consciousness is the set of shared beliefs, ideas, and moral attitudes, which operate as a unifying force within society.

BIBLIOGRAPHY

Anthias, F. (1998). Evaluating Diaspora: Beyond Ethnicity. *Sociology, 32*(3), 557–581.

Basch, L., Glick-Schiller, N., & Szanton-Blanc, C. (1994). Transnational Projects: A New Perspective. In L. Basch, N. Glick-Schiller, & C. Szanton-Blanc (Eds.), *Nations Unbound: Transnational Projects, Postcolonial Predicaments and Deterriotorialized Nation States* (pp. 1–48). New York: Routledge.

Billingsley, A. (1992). *Climbing Jacob's Ladder: The Enduring Legacy of African American Families.* New York: Simon and Schuster.

Bordo, S. (1993). *Unbearable Weight: Feminism, Western Culture, and the Body.* Los Angeles: University of California Press.

Dawson, M. C. (1995). *Behind the Mule: Race and Class in African American Politics.* Princeton: Princeton University Press.

de la Rey, C., Mama, A., & Magubane, Z. (1997). Beyond the Mask. *Agenda: Empowering Women for Gender Equity, 13*(32), 17–23.

Durkheim, E. (1893/1997). *Division of Labour in Society* (L. Coser, Ed.). New York, New York: Free Press.

Eyerman, R. (2001). *Cultural Trauma: Slavery and the Formation of African American Identity.* Cambridge: Cambridge University Press.

Fassin, D. (2011). How to Do Races with Bodies. In F. Mascia-Lees (Ed.), *A Companion to the Anthropology of the Body and Embodiment.* Hoboken: Blackwell Publishing.

Giddings, F. H. (1922). *Studies in the Theory of Human Society.* New York: Macmillan Company.

Gordon, M. (1964). *Assimilation in American Life: The Role of Race, Religion and National Origins.* New York: Oxford University Press.

Gusfield, J. R. (1975). *Community: A Critical Response.* New York: Harper Colophon.

Hwang, S.-S., Fitzpatrick, K., & Helms, D. (1998). Class Differences in Racial Attitudes: A Divided Black America? *Sociological Perspectives, 41*(2), 367–380.

Kasinitz, P., Mollenkopf, J., Waters, M. C., & Holdaway, J. (2008). *Inheriting the City: The Children of Immigrants Come of Age*. New York: Harvard University Press.

Levitt, P. (2002). The Ties that Change: Relations to the Ancestral Home Over the Life Cycle. In P. Levitt & M. C. Waters (Eds.), *The Changing Face of Home: The Transnational Lives of the Second Generation* (pp. 123–144). New York: Russell Sage Foundation.

Mahon, M. (2000). Black Like This: Race, Generation and Rock in the Post-Civil Rights Era. *American Ethnologist, 27*(2), 286–311.

Merleau-Ponty, M. (2004). *Basic Writings* (T. Baldwin, Ed.). London, England: Routledge.

Pattillo, M. (2007). *Black On the Block: Politics of Race and Class in the City*. Chicago: University of Chicago Press.

Quintana, S. M. (2007). Racial and Ethnic Identity: Developmental Perspectives and Research. *Journal of Counseling Psychology, 54*, 259–270.

Quintana, S. M., & Segura-Herrera, T. (2003). Developmental Transformations of Self and Identity in the Context of Oppression. *Self and Identity, 2*, 269–285.

Safran, W. (1991). Diasporas in Modern Societies: Myths of Homeland and Return. *Diaspora: A Journal of Transnational Studies, 1*(1), 83–99.

Thorton, M., Taylor, R. J., & Chatters, L. (2013). African American and Black Caribbean Immigrant Mutual Feelings of Closeness: Findings from a National Probability Survey. *Journal of Black Studies, 44*(8), 798–828.

Vickerman, M. (2002). Second Generation West Indian Transnationalism. In P. Levitt & M. C. Waters (Eds.), *The Changing Face of Home: The Transnational Lives of the Second Generation* (pp. 341–366). New York: Russell Sage Foundation.

CHAPTER 9

We, Too, Sing America:
Where Do We Go from Here?

Our stories are the glue of what we are. They stitch together what we become. Our ability to tell them is fundamental to how we celebrate and examine our lives. After we have satisfied the need for water, food, a roof, companionship, storytelling is where we turn for encouragement on how to live. Through it we look to affirm our joy and, at times, our despair. Sharing our stories reminds us what we believe in, and helps us make sense of a fickle world. They are common, yet we tell them because our experiences are so uncommon. No two stories are ever the same, even when told by the same person using the same words. They are our fingerprints.

—*Colum McCann, Step into My Shoes, and I'll Step into Yours*

No one can tell you 'you are wrong' because it is your truth.

—*Nasir Jones, Hamilton's America: A PBS Documentary*

This book began with my personal narrative about how I came to examine the experiences of self-identified black, middle class, second generation Caribbean immigrants in the United States (the MSGCIs). Because narratives are connected to what Adrienne Rich (1984) calls "politics of location," I thought it useful as an introduction to this project to share how my own experience influences how I too think, feel, and engage with the social world and all of the social categories and constructs that exist.

© The Author(s) 2018

Y.S. Lorick-Wilmot, *Stories of Identity among Black,
Middle Class, Second Generation Caribbeans,*
DOI 10.1007/978-3-319-62208-8_9

To that end—as Nasir Jones' and Colum McCann's quotes assert—to tell one's story (and in my case, a brief personal narrative) is to tell his or her "truth" or social location. One's social location is an embodiment of a particular space in history—or as scholar Ananya Roy (2009) refers to as—geographies of location.

My own process of storytelling also served as a way to reflect on and make observations about how others—strangers as well as friends, colleagues, and co-workers of similar background—approach the social world. In fact, qualitative researchers, and particularly those who also employ a feminist and postcolonial theoretical lens, are often encouraged to reflect on how their backgrounds impact the way they see the world and how their viewpoint impacts their research. In effect, sociologists engaged in ethnography like myself are expected to provide meaningful linkages between personal experiences and intellectual curiosity. To consider these linkages is not autobiography. According to John Lofland et al. (2006:11–12), "the best work in sociology and other social sciences—within the fieldwork tradition—is grounded in the past and/or current biographies of its creators." In this regard, Lofland et al. argue that "starting where you are" provides important context for fieldwork scholarship.

The format I chose for this book was intentional and reflective of such linkages; the *Introduction* and this last chapter not only serve to bookend the developing collective story of MSGCIs in the project; I see it as a necessary part of doing scholarly qualitative research: make clear my researcher positionality. In effect, how does my racial, ethnic, gender, social class, and religious statuses influence my interactions within the research setting, how do these statuses influence my participants' interactions, and consequently, how do these statuses impact my interpretation of the data collected? Discussing my own positionality at the outset of the book allows me to be forthcoming about my own insider–outsider role in the research, and the lens through which I operate from that inevitably informs my analysis.

As a point of self-reflection, I must recognize my positionality aided in the level of comfort the MSGCIs felt with me during these conversations. I noticed the MSGCIs were, for the most part, at ease when sharing their stories. To some, it may seem odd that two strangers meeting for the first time and under the premise of a research activity would lead to situations where one stranger as the subject of the research would display his or her comfort with the researcher through candor and use of language. To others, it may be obvious that the research topic and population under study have some familiarity to the researcher in that it creates a symbolic meeting space to engage in discourse with the research subject. Indeed, my lived experiences and my previous scholarship on the pervasiveness of race for the Caribbean American community in the United States are well documented and readily found in a simple Google search of my name. Therefore it is no surprise to me that prior to my meeting them, my MSGCI participants may have perceived and easily identified me as an insider to the MSGCI status. In fact, I strongly believe participants used their own perceptions about my interest in the experiences of blacks and Caribbean immigrant generations in the United States to personally vouch for me and to the validity of this book project when they recommended additional participants for my study.

A common concern throughout the ethnographic process is to avoid deceiving participants. As such, I kept my intentions as overt as possible by volunteering information about my work in the Greater Boston area and answered questions about the research and their role in it (especially when it came to honoring their stipulation of participation around anonymity). Doing so, I contend, worked to gain their trust and allowed my MSGCI participants to reveal more of themselves, their family and life histories and their political stance on issues that, in my opinion, would otherwise be hidden if the researcher were perceived as a complete outsider to the MSGCI condition. There is, of course, the issue of balancing this dual position of insider–outsider, particularly when it comes to data analysis and presenting findings.

For this research, my use of internarrative analysis empowers me to help share stories as they are told to me within a specific time and place that exists within the social and historical contexts of the environment. The MSGCI stories, as they were told to me, are reflective in the way the MSGCIs refer to and embrace their own identity. Because I feel empowered by them to recount their narratives, I enter these diverse MSGCI spaces as the researcher (outsider) with the understanding that my dual insider–outsider position is not a disadvantage to contend with but, rather a place of strength and learning about the subtleties of race, ethnicity, gender, and religion from the vantage point of Others than myself. Therefore my discussion in this final chapter intends to contextualize the lessons I learned from this research—as both an insider and an outsider. I examine what it means to be in the position of the postcolonial "other" as I explain the issues I see as problematic within sociological inquiry as it relates to this book project: why *We, Too, Sing America* matters and how, we as a society, can move forward.

REFLECTIONS ON THE SIGNIFICANCE OF "WE, TOO, SING AMERICA"

MSGCIs' Reflections on We, Too, Sing America

Toward the end of my conversations with the MSGCIs, I would share with them my tentative thoughts for the title of this book project, *Stories of Identity among Black Middle Class Second Generation Caribbeans: We, Too, Sing America*. Almost immediately, the majority of the MSGCIs drew reference to either a quote, passage, or other material that referenced Langston Hughes' poem, *I, Too, Sing America*, and thought my play on words was timely for the title and theme of this project. I asked each of them their own thoughts on the meaning of "We, Too, Sing America" given all of the topics we had discussed together and the stories they each shared with me.

Indeed, the MSGCIs' interpretation of "We, Too, Sing America" varied; these ranged from a focus on building a strong and empowered black global community through coalitions between black ethnic groups (e.g., African American, Afro-Latino, Afro-Asian) to demonstrating and performing their own interpretations of success by defying racial and ethnic stereotypes as a means of continuing the "good fight" against oppression and anti-black racism. Yet, their interpretation of "We, Too, Sing America" also signaled their pessimism toward the current state of US race relations and the ways they feel the United States is still "unwilling" to fully contend with the legacies of systematized oppression that persist today.

The MSGCIs' pessimism was often framed within the context of future race relations and what that would entail for their children—the third generation of Caribbean immigrants. Almost all the MSGCIs had children or were expecting their first child. For those with school-aged children and older, many found it imperative to impart specific life lessons and cultural capital strategies to help them better navigate public spaces and places. The MSGCIs focused their lessons primarily on the continued impact of racialization. Isaac, for example, encapsulated this sentiment best when he said:

ISAAC

Being made black starts with your first police stop, interrogation and harassment. And that no matter how much you study, work hard and elevate one's self, you will be seen as an outsider and treated as such.

The MSGCIs discussed their continued concerns about the emotional cost of black singularity for their children, especially when their sons and daughters have/had their early inoculation of racism and prejudice, including micro-aggressions, on their self-esteem and mental health.

Despite the growing social inequality in society, the MSGCIs continue to place great value in education as a tool for knowledge and power that would help advance their children as well as the entire racial-ethnic group. In comparison to their parents' generation, the MSGCIs described being more involved in their children's education because, "they know what is at stake and know the 'game' better" due to their first-hand experience in US educational systems. Whether it is finding ways to be an active class parent or speaking to teachers and administrators in a way that signals their educational level and credentials, the MSGCIs view their public performances as intended to help show their own children how to also navigate a system which does not fully consider the African descended as equal.

Interestingly, few MSGCIs expressed some concern as to whether these explicit lessons and conversations with their children about racism would do more harm than good. They discussed teaching their children the importance of fostering positive relationships with all non-blacks, while acknowledging the fact that not all whites are racist but may hold unconscious biases.

NATALIE elaborates,

> Sometimes I wonder if I am making my children cynical of the world. Nothing seems to change racism, no matter the hurdles we jumped over. No matter how much we achieved, these perspectives will never change. Racism will never die and that people will hold on to it. The system will hold on to it and make it seem as if we [blacks] are the ones preoccupied with racism. Of course racism affects whites as much as it does people of color but in different ways. It's all about how we choose to move forward with the knowledge of knowing how the system works.

This "knowledge" or awareness of how the system works, as Natalie described, is an important aspect of the MSGCIs' triple identity consciousness they hope to impart onto their children. The MSGCIs expressed some optimism in their desire to have their children exposed to the positive aspects of a middle class lifestyle, such as having opportunities to accumulate wealth, and at a minimum, be able to maintain the lifestyle or reproduce it for themselves when they get older. This lesson was particularly important to the MSGCIs because they did not intend for their children to feel entitled to material luxuries and be unappreciative of their access to these items but, instead, wanted them to be in a financial situation that allowed them to carry forth the "torch" of black philanthropy in their local and global communities in the United States, the Caribbean, and beyond. The "torch" of philanthropy includes developing mutually rewarding relationships and economic exchanges with the people and communities of the first generation Caribbean immigrants' countries of origin.

Also, the MSGCIs intend to ensure their children do not internalize and perpetuate racist ideas and narratives. They are cognizant of the individualistic implications of black exceptionalism for the black middle class in the United States, which scholars like Michelle Alexander (2010:175) argue that the problem of looking to people like President Obama and Oprah Winfrey as examples of blacks who have defied the odds and risen to power, fame, and fortune, is that it ignores the existence of oppression. The MSGCIs do not want their children to take the racial bribe of honorary whiteness (though they cannot achieve honorary whiteness due to their blackness) because of their possible middle class mobility. The MSGCIs reject exceptionalism because they believe it is a distraction to the endemic social issues that continue to divide the black community: the working class and affluent African Americans and Caribbean immigrants.

In this regard, their triple identity consciousness is the awareness Dr. Martin Luther King, Jr. spoke of in his 1968 speech, *The Role of the Behavioral Scientist in the Civil Rights Movement*:

> Negroes today are experiencing an inner transformation that is liberating them from ideological dependency on the white majority. What has penetrated substantially all strata of Negro life is the revolutionary idea that the philosophy and morals of the dominant white society are not holy or sacred but in all too many respects are degenerate and profane.

The MSGCIs are constantly seeking inner transformation and ways to declare "We, Too, Sing America," as a means to reject the narratives of white hegemony—which is the chief carrier that denigrates non-white peoples and their cultures and histories. Through their lived experiences, the MSGCIs are excited to point out, "the emperor has no clothes!" when it comes to this fallacy of post-racialism. The MSGCIs' stories are valid and serve as reliable evidence that goes beyond the binary of white = good, black = bad; they represent their diverse blackness, multi-ethnic history, their immigrant background, and middle class achievements in order to highlight the nuance of black existence the United States is ill-equipped to deal with.

My Reflections on MSGCIs' We, Too, Sing America and Triple Identity Consciousness

As I outlined in earlier chapters of this book, I set out on an intellectual journey to explore, examine, and understand the nuances, negotiations, and navigations of identity among the MSGCIs through the stories they tell about their race, ethnicity, gender, and social class experiences as the children of post-1965 Caribbean immigrants in the United States. I presented the reflections and observations MSGCIs made about the white and nonwhite public spaces and places in which they move through daily and the ways these experiences contribute to their own identification and identity assertions.

What I have attempted to do in this book is share stories that reveal frameworks and perspectives for understanding the nuances, joys, pains, and sacrifices of being "Black in America" for the children of post-1965 Caribbean immigrants to the United States. I used various theories to guide my interpretation and analysis about the stories I heard from my participants and reflect on postcoloniality of this project and how it is rooted in the question: why does it matter to hear and understand the stories the MSGCIs tell about themselves? In particular, I employed Bourdieu's concept of habitus in a similar way Eduardo Bonilla-Silva (2009) considered habitus to the field of race in his book, *Racism Without Racists*, in order to examine how the MSGCIs evoked their triple identity consciousness (or awareness) and developed cultural capital strategies to combat persisting anti-black and negative perceptions about nonwhites (regardless of social class and gender) in public spaces, including performance criteria and masquerading. I also explored the ways in which the MSGCIs considered the concept of community and their transnational connections to other African descendants in the United States and within the African diaspora and what lies ahead for future generations. In effect, employing theories on postcolonialism, internarrative identity, and racialization, I present the narratives on the experiences of MSGCIs living in the United States.

W.E.B. Du Bois (1968:198) said in the *Autobiography of W.E.B. Du Bois: A Soliloquy on Viewing My Life from the Last Decade of its First Century*, "being merely born into a group does not necessarily make one possessed of complete knowledge concerning it." In many of the stories shared by the MSGCIs, I did not readily identify with, and in other circumstances, I felt as if these were my own stories being told. The experiences of MSGCIs are multi-faceted and complex, with each person interpreting and expressing their own understanding and connections to their place and position in society, as US citizens, as middle class, as Latinx, as mixed ethnic, as both gay and heterosexual, as men and women, and so on—all juxtaposed with a racialized black identity. While it is encouraging to hear about the ways this group of first generation US-born individuals are able to achieve some semblance of a "dream" of economic and educational success their parents had for them, what price is paid on their bodies and those of their children when black and brown people in the United States (and across the world) continue to be deprived of basic human rights and dignity?

As of this writing, I reflect on the topics MSGCIs raised during my conversations with them and how they relate to ways black men and women in the United States, regardless of income, age, ability, gender identity, and immigrant generation, continue to be criminalized, incarcerated, hyper-sexualized, and oppressed in various ways. I often consider the very real but subtle psychological impact high profiled murders of Treyvon Martin, Michael Brown, Eric Gardner, Freddie Gray, Sandra Bland, and others, and the subsequent #BlackLivesMatter movement has had on the MSGCIs. I wonder what the MSGCIs would say, or how they would reflect on these events using their triple identity consciousness since these murders and the rise of the #BlackLivesMatter movement took place after our interviews were completed. How would they approach the notion of what it means to be "black in America," especially since the public discourse surrounding #BlackLivesMatter is highly charged? In what ways would the MSGCIs consider community as space and place and their role in it? What lessons would they teach their children as strategies to better manage their understandings and responses to these events? Further, in the era of a post-Obama presidency, what will the state of black America be for the children of black Caribbean immigrants?

As I demonstrated throughout this book, the MSGCIs themselves come from a variety of racial-ethnic backgrounds and their concerns and positions regarding specific social issues are equally as diverse. But on the whole, I view my conversations with each of them and the stories they shared with me as linked by a common thread (to which I will speculate on): that they live in a hegemonic society and are frustrated with the inequity and injustice people of color experience. So, I consider the aforementioned questions, particularly those related to #BlackLivesMatter, and to the current and future state of black America as I assume they would see it.

The current state of race relations in the United States and abroad, despite the United Nations' pronouncement for the Decade for People of African Descent, is such that those racialized as black continue to experience terror, subjugation, and brutality. The simple three word phrase and ubiquitous messaging of #BlackLivesMatter would strongly resonate with MSGCIs and further fuel their current engagement in the black community spaces and places they traverse. In its simplest form, the #BlackLivesMatter would not be considered controversial to MSGCIs' notion of "being black in America" since they contend "black issues" are Caribbean people issues, African and African American people issues—all are one and the same when it comes to racism, oppression, and imperialist policies. In addition to their current "give back" activities, I speculate the MSGCIs would also be engaged in some form of social protest in support of the mass mobilization efforts and solidarity that has erupted around the globe—protests in Ireland, Canada, and Germany to South Africa, Brazil, and London. The MSGCIs' activities would take the form of locally organized "die-ins" that shut down major city highways and streets or involve community organizing and other philanthropic activities both in the United States and in the Caribbean and creating works of art and literature that speak "truth to power" to issues of oppression and brutality. The MSGCIs' triple identity consciousness would continue to incite them to create and uplift the consciousness of others and to assist the change in the history of the world. I speculate the MSGCIs will remain torn between reality and hope—since their shared pessimism regarding society's ability to overcome its racism casts a long shadow on the future of race relations; but it is their hope and dreams for their children and for future generations of young people of color (once very much like them) that will inspire them to achieve what seems to be the impossible: a collective black liberation.

Like the MSGCIs, I strongly believe "We, Too, Sing America" is an important rallying cry that draws attention to the diverse experiences and contributions of MSGCIs in US society. In this regard, it is the first important step to offering tangible solidarity to the African descended voice in the United States. Because white hegemonic forces insidiously work to categorize whiteness as normal and all else as an "other," it reinforces its normalcy as invisible. Hegemony easily creates a culture of exclusion and obfuscation that denies the existence and undervalues the experiences of those who do not embody "whiteness" (white, cis male, heterosexual, and middle class). As such, white hegemony creates the black monolith because it does not need or want to interrogate blackness or nonwhiteness; the impact of systematized forms of oppression; or consider nonwhite articulations and interpretations of a broad black nationalism that is not only global but one that is aware of the oppression and privilege of black personhood across various societies. Challenging and interrogating hegemony would mean recognizing and removing the deeply embedded racist, homophobic, classist, sexist, and non-Christian consciousness of society that serves to privilege some at the expense of subjugating others.

Stories of Identity among Black Middle Class Second Generation Caribbeans: We, Too, Sing America intends to make clear—to the deniers who shy away from conversations on racism and systemic failures and prefer to emphasize individual pathologies to explain injustices of racial profiling and police abuse and misconduct, housing segregation and discrimination, educational inequality, and health disparity—"that the MSGCIs are here." To be clear, MSGCIs are not seeking "approval" from the hegemonic forces to exist. The supporters of this hegemony render it necessary to see the race of a people as one single personality; a perspective entirely bleak without nuance or distinction (Morrison 1975). In contrast to this, MSGCIs want their stories to highlight that their existence not only empowers but also celebrates the contexts in which they live as part of a larger community of people of color focused on dismantling hegemony with small actions at a time. *Stories of Identity among Black Middle Class Second Generation Caribbeans: We, Too, Sing America* is an opportunity for which narrative storytelling will record all that is lost in the act of hegemony: the MSGCIs describing their black racial identity and their Caribbean ethnic backgrounds as an important social, cultural, spiritual, and economic resource that is valuable and central to who they are as individuals and as members of a larger diasporic community.

I refer to Kimberle Crenshaw's (1991) concept of "intersectionality" and reimagine the MSGCIs' triple identity consciousness to be intersectional in psychological form. The MSGCIs' triple identity consciousness allows them to be aware and reflective of a third realm of consciousness that goes beyond the bind of double consciousness that W.E.B. Du Bois referred. I think of it as an existential awareness of racial, ethnic, gender, and class conditions that deeply impact black peoples of the diaspora. A triple identity consciousness is not unique to MSGCIs only; however, their stories reveal a nuanced awareness and need to transcend the binary of black subjugation in white society by (1) being black and (2) being black and learning to be economically and physically integrated, yet racially excluded in a predominately white society. Instead, I think it is a combination of factors that informs their triple identity awareness: growing up in Caribbean immigrant households; accumulating particular middle class mobility experiences; having to traverse various social, political, and economic environments and develop specific cultural capital strategies; and, their experience in living in various parts of the world, engaged in and transnationally connected to local, global, and immigrant communities, including their parents' country of origin. With all of these factors considered, I wonder: what is all of this striving for? What do the MSGCIs intend to accomplish in terms of ensuring the inclusion and protection of their children? Indeed, the MSGCIs' stories highlighted instances when they felt stressed, compelled to masquerade and wear multiple masks, and as a result, developed performance criteria to navigate white spaces—all while figuring ways to give back to their community as both space and place. I consider the MSGCIs' stories as a type of resistance to race, ethnic, gender, and class stereotypes that exist for the African descended in the United States.

I posit, which hegemonic forces at play imprison us all, particularly through racism, racialization, classism, sexism, and ableism for instance, distract us from truly challenging inequality and justice. Making this point, I am reminded of Toni Morrison's (1975) panel presentation entitled, "Public Dialogue on the American Dream, Part 2" when she asserts a similar argument as it relates to racism:

> The function, the very serious function of racism, is distraction. It keeps you from doing your work. It keeps you explaining, over and over again, your reasons for being. Somebody says you have no language, so you spend twenty years proving that you do. Somebody says your head isn't shaped properly, so you have scientists working on the fact that it is. Someone says you have no art, so you dredge that up. Somebody says you have no kingdoms, so you dredge that up. None of that is necessary. There will always be one more thing.

Indeed fighting against oppression and subjugation is extremely important because of the direct implications these forces have on the lives of people. But I also consider Toni Morrison's cautious words, that members of society should not be mired by the distractions of forces that refuse to understand ethnic groups outside of mainstream conceptions and are ignorant in their appreciation of the interrelationships between co-existing cultures in mutually constructive ways. Morrison's point is, in my opinion, to be vigilant in awareness that, despite the daily efforts to navigate racially problematic or hostile situations, to be black in the Americas is to conceive of blackness, racial, and ethnic identities as something positive and easily transmittable across generations. To do this, of course, is in direct contradiction to what social science research has concluded in the past, with most scholars choosing to only focus on racism and its dysfunctional effects or as casting the monolith of blacks as social deviants without getting to the heart of the problem in the first place: the causation of racism.

WHERE DO WE GO FROM HERE?

A central argument of this book has been that the voices and the racially, ethnically, and class-based nuanced experiences of the MSGCIs are often anonymous and/or peripheral to contemporary discussions of race relations and immigrant generation in the Americas. These stories are important because they point out the fallacy of racism, which white hegemony creates and maintains certain conditions for its own benefit, and convinces deniers of racism that the state of being "Black in America" is one that remains a "negro problem" of his or her own making. Therefore, the claim Du Bois made in *Souls of Black Folk* (1903) over a century ago about race, which he referred to as the color-line and the condition of the black–white binary as a central problem of the twentieth century, is a fact that remains true today.

Over the last several decades we continue to see postcolonial, Western domination, and exploitation of people of color universally, via social, political, and economic projects often brought on by globalization's imposition of hegemonic values and practices around the world. Achieved through the media and technology, we see the effects of these projects in the political and social movement responses from communities of color in the United States (e.g., #BlackLivesMatter) that are, once again, rising up in resistance to wage war against: the profiling, criminalization, and mass incarceration of blacks, Latinos, Arabs, Muslims, and other groups automatically deemed dangerous to the country's way of life; marginalizing the transgender community and persons with disabilities; and subjugating poor and working class and immigrant communities of color (Karenga 2002).

In the midst of these voices of resistance are the voices of the MSGCIs condemning racism and the aforementioned forms of subjugation by strongly advocating for black freedom and justice in the United States and abroad. Attempts to suppress these black middle class and immigrant voices as unnoticeable intend to punish a stratum of people who traverse between segregated white and black Americas and defy the sanctioned racist belief that African descendants (and people of color, generally) are not full human beings. In reality, the MSGCIs represent the "negro problem" which hegemonic forces desperately find ways to "solve" by maintaining opposites in opposition in spite of legal integration. For this reason, this book draws attention to the fact that there continues to be a black critical voice, one that has an expanding consciousness around social responsibility. The MSGCIs are a part of this black community and their triple identity consciousness (because of their immigrant generation, social class mobility, and lived experiences as children of immigrants of color) anchors their perspectives and positively contributes to both micro- and macro-actions focused on empowering their children, their neighborhoods, and the larger community to resist a subordinate, low status condition that society works hard to impose.

Unfortunately, people of color will continue to bear the burden and pay the cost of gross inequities of power, wealth, opportunity, and access wherever there continues to be imperial expansion of white hegemony: in education, law and social policy, economic and political structures. In fact, we see this in the way self-identified and racialized black racial-ethnics (including Afro-Latinos and Afro-Asian Americans) in the United States continue to thwart schemes that attempt to block their vote via claims of voter fraud as they struggle for unfettered political representation in this democratic process. We also see this in the way some recent US immigrants of color engage in an assessment of themselves using Eurocentric views and racial hierarchies. These recent immigrants of color attempt to socially distance themselves from native and foreign-born blacks, with the intention to enhance social status and class mobility, only to find over time race and racism is fundamental to US culture and serves as a barrier to their mobility and self-awareness—their triple identity consciousness. In this book, however, the voices of the black ethnic and the children of black Caribbean immigrants bring to the forefront the ways in which the MSGCIs are unapologetic about being black, Caribbean, immigrant, gay, woman, or for occupying any other social category that comprise their own identity conceptualization. MSGCIs' stories serve as definitive evidence of the diverse black experience—the stories that capture the joys, the pains, and the anxieties of being a child of immigrants, a middle class person of African descent in the United States. Their stories are richly complex, nuanced, and self-conscious in that they indicate the significance of social forces of race in MSGCIs' own identity conceptualization and assertions. With this book, I endeavor to inspire others so that they do not need to endure the estrangement that may accompany being MSGCI in certain social areas, which has been a consistent dynamic of race and representation in the United States. But in its appeal of simplicity, the MSGCIs' narratives reveal the instability of all the categories (especially race) that both define and divide us as a society.

It is for this reason, I argue, the assertion that race is declining in its significance remains an outmoded analytical concept. The United States's first black President Barack H. Obama (2008–2016) makes this point clear in his Farewell Address on January 10, 2017, when he says:

> … After my election, there was talk of a post-racial America. Such a vision, however well-intended, was never realistic. For race remains a potent and often divisive force in our society. I've lived long enough to know that race relations are better than they were 10, or 20, or 30 years ago—you can see it not just in statistics, but in the attitudes of young Americans across the political spectrum. But we're not where we need to be. All of us have more work to do. After all, if every economic issue is framed as a struggle between a hard-working white middle class and undeserving minorities, then workers of all shades will be left fighting for scraps while the wealthy withdraw further into their private enclaves. If we decline to invest in the children of immigrants, just because they don't look like us, we diminish the prospects of our own children—because those brown kids will represent a larger share of America's workforce. And our economy doesn't have to be a zero-sum game. Going forward, we must uphold laws against discrimination—in hiring, in housing, in education and the criminal justice system. That's what our Constitution and highest ideals require. But laws alone won't be enough. Hearts must change. If our democracy is to work in this increasingly diverse nation, each one of us must try to heed the advice of one of the great characters in American fiction, Atticus Finch, who said, "You never really understand a person until you consider things from his point of view… until you climb into his skin and walk around in it.

From the point of view of the MSGCIs and other second generation immigrants of color, society can learn how race-ethnic identity codes everyday life: as an aspect of individual and collective awareness when it comes to ethnicity, social class mobility, and gender; and as a medium of social practice, political action, and philanthropy. This is necessary to understand the intersections of race, ethnicity, class, and gender as modes of division, domination, and resistance on the national and international level. The stories told by the MSGCIs offer an important approach to thinking about and achieving a more unified vision for social justice and true democracy. The MSGCIs' approach is in their awareness of a reality that there is a host of material conditions under which people of color live that intend to marginalize them. It is, however, the MSGCIs' communal approach to life, their mutually beneficial ties and connections to communities of African descendants both locally and abroad that can represent the possibility for positive human excellence for all: dignity of human rights, economic and social justice, meaningful political participation, and mutual respect.

BIBLIOGRAPHY

Alexander, M. (2010). *The New Jim Crow: Mass Incarceration in an Era of Colorblindness*. New York: The New Press.

Bonilla-Silva, E. (2009). *Racism without Racists: Color-blind Racism and the Persistence of Racial Inequality*. Lanham: Rowan Littlefield.

Crenshaw, K. (1991). Mapping the margins: Intersectionality, Identity Politics, and Violence against Women of Color. *Stanford Law Review, 43*(6), 1241–1299.

Du Bois, W. (1903/1990). *Souls of Black Folk*. New York: Vintage Books.

Du Bois, W. (1968). *Autobiography of W.E.B Du Bois: A Soliloquy on Viewing My Life from the Last Decade of its First Century*. New York: International Publisher.

Karenga, M. (2002). 9/11 Liberation Struggles and International Relations: Sharing the Burden and Possibilities of Crisis. In N. Ahmad, J. Catalinotto, S. Flounders, N. Mustapha, & U. Shaikh (Eds.), *Unveiling the Real Terrorist Mind* (pp. 229–235). New York: Students for International Peace and Justice.

Lofland, J., Snow, D., Anderson, L., & Lofland, L. H. (2006). *Analyzing Social Settings: A Guide to Qualitative Observation and Analysis*. Belmont: Wadsworth Cengage.

Morrison, T. (1975, May 30). *Black Studies Center Public Dialogue*. Pt. 2 on the American Dream Theme. Portland, Oregon.

Rich, A. (1984). Notes Toward a Politics of Location. In A. Rich (Ed.), *Blood, Bread and Poetry: Selected Prose, 1979–1985* (pp. 210–231). London: Little, Brown and Co.

Roy, A. (2009). The 21st Century Metropolis: New Geographies of Theory. *Regional Studies, 43*(6), 819–830.

BIBLIOGRAPHY

Achebe, C. (1958/1994). *Things Fall Apart*. Knopf Doubleday Publishing.

American Sociological Association. (2015, September/October). William Julius Wilson Says His Arguments on Race and Class Still Apply. *Footnotes, 43*(6), 3.

Bhatia, S. (2002). Acculturation, Dialogical Voices and the Construction of the Diasporic Self. *Theory and Psychology, 12*, 55–73.

Bhatia, S., & Ram, A. (2001). Rethinking "Acculturation" in Relation to Diasporic Cultures and Postcolonial Identities. *Human Development, 44*, 1–17.

Bishop, B. (2008). *The Big Sort: Why the Clustering of Like-Minded America is Tearing Us Apart*.

Blay, Y. (2013). *(1)ne Drop: Shifting the Lens on Race*. Philadelphia: Blackprint Press.

Bricker, J., Dettling, L. J., Henriques, A., Hsu, J. W., Moore, K. B., Sabelhaus, J., et al. (2014). Changes in U.S. Family Finances from 2010 to 2013: Evidence from the Survey of Consumer Finances. *Federal Reserve Bulletin, 100*(4), 1–41.

Clark, G. (2014, August 26). *Council on Foreign Affairs: The American Dream is an Illusion*. Retrieved January 10, 2015, from http://www.foreignaffairs.com/articles/141932/gregory-clark/the-american-dream-is-an-illusion

Clifford, J., & Marcus, G. E. (1986). *Writing Culture: The Poetics and Politics of Ethnography*. Berkeley: University of California Press.

Du Bois, W. E. (1903). Talented Tenth. In B. T. Washington (Ed.), *The Negro Problem* (pp. 33–75). New York: James Pott and Company.

Dzidzienyo, A., & Oboler, S. (2005). *Neither Enemies nor Friends: Latinos, Blacks, Afro-Latinos*. New York: Palgrave Macmillan.

Ellison, R. (1952/1995). *The Invisible Man* (2nd ed.). New York: Vintage Books.

© The Author(s) 2018
Y.S. Lorick-Wilmot, *Stories of Identity among Black,
Middle Class, Second Generation Caribbeans*,
DOI 10.1007/978-3-319-62208-8

Frey, W. H., & Brookings. (2012, December 14). *Multiracial Marriage on the Rise*. Retrieved June 28, 2016, from Brookings Institute: Blog Series: https://www.brookings.edu/blog/the-avenue/2014/12/18/multiracial-marriage-on-the-rise/

Gallagher, C. A. (2008). *Racism in Post Race America: New Theories, New Directions*. Chapel Hill: Social Forces Press.

Gans, H. J. (2007). Acculturation, Assimilation and Mobility. *Ethnic and Racial Studies, 30*(1), 125–164.

Giguere, B., Lalonde, R., & Lou, E. (2010). Living at the Crossroads of Cultural Worlds: The Experience of Normative Conflicts by Second Generation Immigrant Youth. *Social and Personality Psychology Compass, 4*(1), 14–29.

Gramsci, A. (1971). History of the Subaltern Classes. In Q. Hoare (Ed.), *Selections from the Prison Notebooks*. New York: International Publishers Co.

Hall, S., Held, D., Hubert, D., & Thompson, K. (1996). *Modernity: An Introduction to Modern Societies*. Malden: Wiley-Blackwell.

Hamilton's America: A Documentary on Lin-Manuel Miranda's Broadway show Hamilton (2016). [Motion Picture].

Higginbotham, E. B. (1993). *Righteous Discontent: The Women's Movement in the Black Baptist Church, 1880–1920*. Cambridge, MA: Harvard University Press.

Hine, D. C. (1989). Rape and the Inner Lives of Black Women in the Middle West: Preliminary Thoughts on the Culture of Dissemblance. *Signs, 14*(4), 912–920.

Hine, D. C. (1994/1997). *Hine Sight: Black Women and the Re-Construction of American History*. Indiana: Indiana University Press.

Hughes, L. (1994). I, Too, Sing America. In A. Rampersad (Ed.), *The Collected Poems of Langston Hughes*. New York: Knopf and Vintage Books.

John, M. (2014). A Study of Race, Class and Naturalization: Are Afro Caribbean Immigrants Gaining Higher Degrees of Assimilation than Cuban Immigrants Through Voter Registration? *Ethnic and Racial Studies, 38*(6), 1011–1028.

Jordan, J. (1989). Moving Towards Home. In J. Jordan (Ed.), *Naming Our Destiny: New and Selected Poems* (p. 143). New York: Thunder's Mouth.

Josselson, R. (1995). *The Space Between Us: Exploring Dimensions of Human Relationships*. Thousand Oaks: Sage Publications.

King, J. M. (1968). The Role of the Behavioral Scientist in the Civil Rights Movement. *Journal of Social Issues, 24*(1), 1–12.

Lee, C. D., Spencer, M. B., & Harpalani, V. (2003). Every Eye Shut Ain't Sleeping: Studying How People Live Culturally. *Educational Researcher, 32*(5), 6–13.

Lewis, A. E. (2003). *Race in the Schoolyard: Negotiating the Color Line in Classrooms and Communities*. New Jersey: Rutgers University Press.

Massey, D. (2001). Residential Segregation and Neighborhood Conditions. In N. Smelser (Ed.), *America Becoming: Racial Trends and Their Consequences*. Washington, DC: National Academy Press.

McCann, C. (2015, September 1). Step into My Shoes, and I'll Step into Yours. *O Magazine, 16*(9), 110.

Moss, L. (2003). The Politics of Everyday Hybridity. *Wasafiri, 18*(39), 11–17.

Moynihan, D. P. (1965, March 1). *United States Department of Labor.* Retrieved August 1, 2014, from Office of the Assistant Secretary for Administration and Management: http://www.dol.gov/oasam/programs/history/webid-meynihan. htm

Murray, P. (1987). *Proud Shoes: The Story of an American Family.* New York: Harper Collins.

Negroponte, N. (2006, July 25). One Laptop Per Child. *One Laptop Per Child Lecture Series.* Organization of American States: Democracy for Peace, Security and Development.

Obama, B. H. (Performer). (2017, January 10). *President of the United States Farewell Address.* Chicago: McCormick Place.

Oliver, M., & Shapiro, T. (2006). *Black Wealth/White Wealth: A New Perspective on Racial Inequality* (2nd ed.). New York: Routledge.

Ortner, S. (1998). Identities: The Hidden Life of Class. *Journal of Anthropological Research, 54*(1), 1–17.

Peterson, K. (2015, April 1). *8 Ways to Know if You're Middle Class.* Retrieved June 27, 2015, from CBS News Money Watch: http://www.cbsnews.com/media/8-ways-to-know-if-youre-middle-class/

Pew Research Center. (2010). *Marrying Out: One-in-Seven New U.S. Marriages is Interracial or Interethnic.* Washington, DC: Pew Research Center: Social and Demographic Trends Project.

Pew Research Center. (2013). *Second-Generation Americans: A Portrait of the Adult Children of Immigrants.* Research Report.

Renan, J. E. (1992). What is a Nation? Qu'est-ce qu'une nation? *Sorbonne on March 11 1882.* Paris: Presses-Pocket.

Rich, F. (2012, May 20). Post Racial Farce. *New York Magazine,* pp. 1–3.

Rowling, R. M. (2008). *Slumming in New York: From the Waterfront to Mythic Harlem.* Champaign: University of Illinois Press.

Rusk, D. (2001, October 1). Segregation Tax: The Cost of Racial Segregation to Black Homeowners. *Center on Urban and Metropolitan Policy, Survey Series.*

Rutherford, J., & Hall, S. (1990). A Place Called Home: Identity and the Culture Politics of Difference. In J. Rutherford (Ed.), *Identity: Community, Culture, Difference* (pp. 9–27). London: Lawrence and Wishart.

The United States Census Bureau. (2015, September 1). *Income and Poverty in the United States: 2014.* Retrieved November 1, 2015, from Current Population Report: https://www.census.gov/content/dam/Census/library/publications/2015/demo/p60-252.pdf

The White House. (2014, May 30). *The United States of America, The White House, Press Office*. Retrieved January 22, 2015, from https://www.whitehouse. gov/the-press-office/2014/05/30/presidential-proclamation-national-caribbean-american-heritage-month-201

Waldinger, R., & Feliciano, C. (2004). Will the New Second Generation Experience 'Downward Assimilation'? Segmented Assimilation Re-assessed. *Ethnic and Racial Studies, 27*(3), 376–402.

Waters, M. C. (1994). Ethnic and Racial Identities of Second Generation Black Immigrants in New York City. *International Migration Review, 28*, 795–820.

Waters, M. C. (2002). Twenty-first Century Melting Pot. *Contexts, 1*(2), 62–63.

Wilson, W. J. (1978/1980). *The Declining Significance of Race: Blacks and Changing American Institutions*. Chicago: University of Chicago Press.

Wilson, W. J. (1987). *The Truly Disadvantaged: The Inner City, the Underclass and Public Policy*. Chicago: University of Chicago Press.

Wilson, W. J. (2015, June 5). *Voice of America* (C. Castiel, Interviewer). http://www.voanews.com/audio/2801299.html

Wing Sue, D. (2003). *Overcoming Our Racism: The Journey to Liberation*. Jossey-Bass.

Woldemikael, T. M. (1989). *Becoming Black American: Haitians and American Institutions in Evanston, Illinois*. Brooklyn: AMS Press.

INDEX

© The Author(s) 2018
Y.S. Lorick-Wilmot, *Stories of Identity among Black, Middle Class, Second Generation Caribbeans,*
DOI 10.1007/978-3-319-62208-8

CPSIA information can be obtained
at www.ICGtesting.com
Printed in the USA
LVHW08*2051290818
588399LV00011BA/258/P